Dan Janal's Guide to Marketing on the Internet

Getting People to Visit, Buy,
and Become Customers for Life

Daniel S. Janal

John Wiley & Sons, Inc.

New York • Chichester • Weinheim • Brisbane • Singapore • Toronto

This book is printed on acid-free paper. ⊚

Copyright © 2000 by Daniel S. Janal. All rights reserved.

Published by John Wiley & Sons, Inc.

Published simultaneously in Canada.

Designations used by companies to distinguish their products are often claimed by trademarks. In all instances where the author or publisher is aware of a claim, the product names appear in Initial Capital letters. Readers, however, should contact the appropriate companies for more complete information regarding trademarks and registration.

No part of this publication may be reproduced, stored in a retrieval system or transmitted in any form or by any means, electronic, mechanical, photocopying, recording, scanning or otherwise, except as permitted under Sections 107 or 108 of the 1976 United States Copyright Act, without either the prior written permission of the Publisher, or authorization through payment of the appropriate per-copy fee to the Copyright Clearance Center, 222 Rosewood Drive, Danvers, MA 01923, (978) 750-8400, fax (978) 750-4744. Requests to the Publisher for permission should be addressed to the Permissions Department, John Wiley & Sons, Inc., 605 Third Avenue, New York, NY 10158-0012, (212) 850-6011, fax (212) 850-6008, E-Mail: PERMREQ @ WILEY.COM.

This publication is designed to provide accurate and authoritative information in regard to the subject matter covered. It is sold with the understanding that the publisher is not engaged in rendering legal, accounting, or other professional services. If legal advice or other expert assistance is required, the services of a competent professional person should be sought.

Library of Congress Cataloging-in-Publication Data:

Janal, Daniel S.
    Dan Janal's guide to marketing on the Internet: getting people to visit, buy, and become customers for life/Daniel S. Janal.
        p.   cm.
    Includes index.
    ISBN 0-471-34976-3 (alk. paper)
    1. Internet marketing. I. Title. II. Title: Guide to marketing on the Internet.
HF5415.1265.J358   2000
658.8 '00285' 4678—dc21   99-15787

Printed in the United States of America.

10 9 8 7 6 5 4

Dedicated to my mother, Florence Janal.

Contents

Preface

More than fifteen years ago, I was on the public relations team that introduced America Online to the world. In the early days of online computing, we had to convince the world that cyberspace was a great place to do research, meet and chat with new friends from around the world, and, yes, buy products.

It has been a long and rewarding struggle. Through my books on online marketing and my seminars at Berkeley, Stanford, and at many trade associations' educational conferences, I have helped more than fifty thousand small businesses, entrepreneurs, and wild-eyed dreamers set up shop on the Internet. I've also worked with the likes of the *Reader's Digest,* IBM, and American Express/IDS on refining their online marketing strategy. Through my seminars at trade associations' conventions, I've developed an expertise in the travel, insurance, leasing, and communications industries.

From this perspective, I've been able to see the best practices in many different industries and present information that helps companies in any industry learn how to improve their sales and marketing processes by studying the best practices in their industry and in others.

WHY BUY A BOOK WHEN YOU CAN READ IT ONLINE?

Two frequent comments (complaints) about printed books is that the material could be out of date or available online for free. Certain aspects of these concerns are true. Because the Internet changes so quickly and adopts new marketing methods almost as quickly as it abandons them, one is well served to check the Internet to find the latest thinking in the field. Also, many marketing people write articles that they post on the Internet for free as a way of increasing their business. In fact, I heartily endorse many of the publications. Here is a list of suggested ezines, newsletters, and other sources to keep up-to-date.

First of course, is my web site, which features my latest thinking on this topic:

www.janal.com

Others:

Ralph Wilson, www.wilsonweb.com

Jakob Nielson, www.useit.com

John Audette, www.mmgco.com/isales/

Kim Bayne, www.cybermedia.org

Larry Chase, www.wdfm.com

Efuse, www.efuse.com

So why buy a book? Many reasons:

1. It is portable. You can read it anywhere. The material is all in one easy-to-find place.
2. It is easily searchable. You can make notes, highlight sections, and retrieve desired sections easily.
3. It is impartial. While online consultants write free articles, they are essentially selling their marketing services. I don't make my money that way. I speak at conventions, conferences, and universities. I won't write an article saying sweepstakes are great because I run a company specializing in sweepstakes.
4. It is time tested. I've been involved in online marketing for nearly twenty years. I was on the public relations team that launched America Online and have been involved with online marketing in public relations, promotions, branding, and many other aspects on a day-to-day basis before many of today's online marketers were still in elementary school (and I'm only 44!).
5. You can put it on your bookshelf and decorate your office.

6. You can slam the book on your conference table to prove your points to a committee. This book is guaranteed to give a good solid whack.

WHO WOULD BENEFIT FROM READING THIS BOOK

No one will benefit from this book unless he is committed to actually carry out its strategies and tactics. This isn't a philosophical book; it is an action book. If you are committed to action, you will benefit.

You might be wondering if one book can meet the needs of many diverse audiences. It can. This material is time tested. I've been teaching online marketing courses at Berkeley and Stanford for the past four years. I've also spoken to conventions hosted by professional marketers, public relations professionals, insurance agents, travel industry proprietors, credit union executives, leasing company owners, small business and home office executives, law enforcement officials, lawyers, entrepreneurs, nonprofit associations, government agencies, association executives, and many, many other groups.

There are common concerns among all these groups, and there are important differences. In this book, I have noted how marketers in various industries can make the material their own. So if you work for a company selling consumer products or a business-to-business organization or a nonprofit or government association, you'll find material targeted for your needs. This information will be clearly highlighted in the text so you can find it easily.

WHY YOU NEED THIS BOOK

Dan Janal's Guide to Marketing on the Internet is aimed at marketers and communicators who know that their successes are tied to a well-founded, integrated marketing plan that uses as many corporate resources in the most beneficial ways possible for maximum return on investment. Entrepreneurs and small business owners also will benefit from the tactics and insights and strategies presented. This book tries to separate the hype from the reality of marketing on the Internet.

By following the guidelines, examples, strategies, and case studies in this book, your company will have a much better chance of maximizing its investment in the Internet.

WHAT IS IN THIS BOOK AND WHY SHOULD YOU READ IT?

This book is presented in an easy-to-read format. It is a book that marketers can read without having a background in technology.

The book contains 28 chapters covering online marketing strategy, tools, building traffic for your web site, and making the sale.

Most chapters feature strategies and tactics for succeeding as an online marketer and include step-by-step instructions on how to carry out each task.

Here is a summary of the book:

Part 1—Online Marketing Strategy
- Chapter 1 shows the powerful advantages of going online and highlights the web's success stories. You'll also see why your overall marketing program should include the Internet and how it can support all your other marketing efforts.
- Chapter 2 explains how online marketing differs from current marketing and hits you over the head repeatedly on the need to exercise caution and respect the "netiquette" code of conduct.
- Chapter 3 describes how to build an online marketing plan. We'll discuss the benefits of online marketing and how to overcome some of their shortfalls. This chapter can help you make money and save money! It describes the factors that should be included in writing an online business plan and offers several samples that try to accomplish different objectives.
- Chapter 4 explores the issues corporations need to deal with when deciding to go online.

Part 2—Online Selling
- Chapter 5 explains how to write advertising messages for the Internet.
- Chapter 6 shows how to design a web site to maximize marketing efforts.

- Chapters 7, 8, and 9 explain how to use web sites to sell consumer and business-to-business products and services online.
- Chapter 10 examines the issues in using the Internet to sell to international markets.

Part 3—Promoting Your Web Site

- Chapters 11 and 12 offer the largest source of proven strategies for publicizing and promoting traffic to your web site and encouraging repeat visits. Many are low cost or no cost!
- Chapter 13 examines ways to measure the return on your investment in online marketing activities.

Part 4—Creating Customers for Life with One-to-One Marketing Programs

- Chapter 14 begins a new section on how to create customers for life using one-to-one marketing strategies on the Internet.
- Chapter 15 explains how to build relationships with your communities with e-mail and private mailing lists.
- Chapter 16 discusses how to use newsgroups and public mailing lists to create relationships.
- Chapter 17 breaks new ground by showing how advertisers create online communities of raving fans who bond with the company.
- Chapter 18 provides you with the tools you need to conduct a public relations campaign to influence your communities.
- Chapter 19 shows you how to conduct market research online. You'll also learn about online resources to enhance your marketing program.
- Chapter 20 describes how to use the Internet as a customer support center.

Part 5—Online Marketing Tools

- Chapter 21 explains how to conduct competitive research step by step.
- Chapter 22 lists online resources for networking with peers and finding solid marketing advice. You'll find out about news and reference sources online and learn how to network with marketers residing in forums and mailing lists.
- Chapter 23 shows you how to write effective banner ads.

- Chapter 24 explains the new terms of advertising online, like *banner ads, click-through,* and *visits.* You'll learn how to buy and sell online ads. You'll also discover which measurement techniques are most effective and which ones are outright lies.

Part 6—Online Media Relations

- Chapter 25 provides a framework and tools for creating online publicity.
- Chapter 26 describes how to write and send publicity material.
- Chapter 27 provides you with strategies for building relationships with reporters online.
- Chapter 28 explores how to use the Internet to solve crises.

This book builds on the groundbreaking work and strategies contained in the first edition of the *Online Marketing Handbook* but has been revised to include new marketing strategies, tools, and perceptions on the Internet.

In keeping with the spirit of giving back to the Internet, several chapters have been previewed online and subjected to comments from readers from all types of businesses and industries. Although my publisher can't put the entire book online for free (we do have to make money!), I can put my newest thoughts on my home page, www.janal.com. You'll be able to find new strategies, commentaries on newsmakers, and other marketing information that will make your job more productive. Check it out! And feel free to comment on these chapters, or ask new questions. I'll answer them personally, and if you give permission, print the questions and answers on my web site for all my readers to learn from.

Daniel Janal
dan@janal.com

Acknowledgments

This book is a collaboration of great minds who consented to share their wisdom and experience with me. In addition to the people interviewed for the book, I'd like to thank everyone who has helped me over the years. We learn from our experiences and chance encounters. Sometimes it amazes me how much we really do learn from each other and how the most trivial of information gained one day can play an important role in our lives years later.

I'd also like to thank my friends for life who are always available for good conversation, good advice, and good times: Steven Kessler, Stuart Gruber, Barry Block, Alan Dauber, Lynne Marcus, Pat Meier, George Thibault, and Len Zandrow.

Thanks also go to the excellent staff at John Wiley & Sons, including Jeanne Glasser and Debra Alpern, and to Matt Wagner and Maureen Maloney at Waterside Productions. Special thanks go to Larry Chase, Shel Holtz, and Kim Bayne, my online marketing gurus. Thanks also to my research associate, Darrell Monda.

Special thanks to Susan Tracy. May all your fortune cookies come true.

PART 1

Online
Marketing
Strategy

CHAPTER 1

Integrating the Internet into Your Marketing Mix

While listening to KCBS Newsradio in San Francisco the other day, I heard Martha Stewart talking about the wonders of green beans and how they can be used to help shade trees and plants in the garden. The one-minute report was full of great advice and information. Unfortunately, I was driving my car, so I couldn't take notes. Then she said a full transcript was available on her web site (www.marthastewart.com).

When the United State's leading evangelist of mass-market consumerism—and in my opinion, the world's smartest marketer—tells a general consumer audience to go online and check out her web site, then I knew that the Internet had truly arrived. After spending the past 15 years conducting online marketing campaigns for IBM, Reader's Digest, and American Express and lecturing at the University of California at Berkeley and Stanford University, I realized that the rest of the world was finally getting it! When I was on the publicity team that helped launch America Online (AOL) more than 15 years ago, I wondered if this day would ever happen. Companies, large and small, now know that the Internet is a powerful marketing force that can take their businesses to new heights.

The Internet does not exist in a vacuum. It should be integrated into your marketing program just as you would use public relations, advertising, direct mail, and outbound calls to make more sales. Enlightened companies are realizing that the Internet is but one more tool to use in your marketing program to build brand identity and sell more products and services. Here are several examples and case studies of how companies from all walks of life are using the Internet to build profits.

Southwest Airlines is known for its slogan "I Fly SWA." The company uses this theme in its advertisements as well as its toll-free number (1-800-I-FLY-SWA). When the airline went onto the Internet, it chose www.iflyswa.com as its universal resource locator (URL), or web address.

Roche Laboratories uses a print ad in *USA Weekend* magazine to create interest in acne treatments with a startling picture of a boy with a pockmarked face and then leads readers to find out more at its web site (www.facefacts.com) or to call its toll-free phone number.

Don Johnson promotes himself, the *Nash Bridges* TV show, and an online chat on America Online.

AFLAC Insurance designed its home page (www.aflac.com) to incorporate the images of boys and girls used in its TV ads so that viewers could readily see the connection between the two media.

Nike (www.nike.com) presented an integrated approach to combat claims that it exploited workers in Third World countries. The company issued a press release showing the results of a study conducted by Anthony Young, former U.S. Ambassador to the United Nations; backed it up with full-page ads in major newspapers; and provided a web address with more detailed information.

Even cereal celebrity Tony the Tiger has a web site (www.tonythetiger.com)! The cereal boxes for Frosted Flakes list the web site address and tell kids about the great games and activities they will find there.

The Internet is becoming so pervasive that 14 percent of ads on television now display a web site address so that prospects can find more information online. As time goes on, this number will only grow.

Although these examples might give the impression that only big businesses can benefit from integrated marketing campaigns, that would be a misconception. Companies of all sizes are using the web as part of their marketing efforts. Let's look at several case studies.

Case Study: Sonoma Golf School

When I was learning to play golf, I picked up a newspaper for golfers. I looked in the back and saw little, three-line classified advertisements for golf schools in the area. There isn't a whole lot to be said in three lines, so they all just gave their name, phone number, and a brief line about their specialties. Only one had a web address. Being a web kind of guy, I checked out the web site for the Sonoma Golf School (www.sonomagolfschools .com) and learned that the instructor, Kris Moe, had been on the Professional Golfers' Association (PGA) circuit and had beaten Nick Faldo in a tournament; that his rates were in line with what I could afford to pay; and that the chair of the Bank of America had written a testimonial for him. That all sounded pretty good to me, but I still needed to know what time the class met so I could see if I could commute from home instead of renting a hotel, which would have been too expensive for me. I sent Kris an e-mail, and he wrote back a few hours later. He erased my problem, but I was still hesitating because we were talking in December, which isn't exactly the best time of year to play golf in California. However, he didn't give up. He called me on the phone and left a message on my machine. Just by hearing his voice, I developed confidence in him and decided to take the class.

Let's review the integrated marketing techniques. I read classified ad in a free newspaper that was highly targeted. The inexpensive ad led me to the Internet to check out the web site, which contained far more information than could ever fit in a classified advertisement. I had a question, so I used e-mail to ask it, and he responded by e-mail as well. When I didn't buy, he picked up the phone and made a sales call. That clinched the deal.

Do you see how we used newspaper, the Internet, e-mail, and phone to perform all aspects of the sale—from creating interest to closing? If Kris had not followed through on any one part of that chain, he would have lost the sale. But because he used the Internet in an integrated manner, he was able to make money that weekend.

Case Study: EasiDemographics

One day, I was reading the San Francisco Chronicle about a company, Easy Analytic Software, Inc. (EASI), that offered a free demographic report on the Internet. That sounded like a good marketing idea to me, so I decided to check out its web site, The Right Site (www.easidemographics.com).

The site told EASI's story to build credibility for a product it sells, a CD-ROM with demographic material; basically, the front page did a sales job for the company and the product and made an offer to web buyers. I declined. The site also indicated that I could get a free demographic report online if I clicked a button, which I did. Instead of showing me a report, I saw a screen that contained an application form; if I filled out the form, then I would get the free report. That's common practice on the Internet, so I wasn't offended.

But the form was one of the best I had seen. You see, the more questions you ask, the greater chance you have of turning people off. Many sites ask the dumbest questions in the most irritating manner. The EasiDemographics site asked only six questions, and they were very smart ones. The folks at EASI wanted my name, street address, e-mail address, and phone number; now they can contact me. They wanted to know how I used demographic reports and how much money I spend a year on demographic reports; now they know how qualified I am. With just a few questions, they have everything they need to know to sell me! Notice that they didn't ask irrelevant questions like how many vacations I take or how many years of schooling I had completed. This should be a warning to you to check your forms for relevant information.

I clicked the SUBMIT button and got the report I wanted; now I could see how much money my neighbors made. The report was fine. The site made me another offer to buy the CD-ROM because I now knew that the product was legitimate. But I didn't bite. I left to surf the Net.

Now the fun begins.

A few hours later, I checked my e-mail and saw a message from the president of EASI. I opened the message and read a letter (Figure 1.1) that thanked me for visiting the site. The letter went on to tell me what a great and trustworthy company EASI was, how valuable its CD-ROM of demographics was, and how I could buy it for a special price because I had visited its web site. I declined the generous offer.

A few days later, the phone rang; it was a sales representative from EASI (in fact, it was EASI's sales director, Greg Gergen). He thanked me for visiting the site and reminded me about the company's background and the special offer on the CD-ROM. Because he was reading from my application form, he said, "I see that you spend ten thousand dollars a year buying demographic reports to help you determine where to build your shopping centers." I cut him off politely and told him I had lied. I really didn't buy demographic reports: I was a writer, consultant, and speaker and was using his site as background for my research.

Instead of being upset, he was delighted and began to tell me his life story. It turns out he had been with another company that sold demographic reports and had been making cold calls for his entire professional life. Then he joined this new company, which had integrated public relations and the Internet to find prospects.

"The San Francisco Chronicle ran an article about us, and we got 60 leads in three days," said Gergen. "I don't do any cold calls anymore. Here we are, a new company, and we get thousands of leads from the Internet. I've been in sales most of my career, and I've never had it so easy."

Now he spends his life following up on qualified prospects who willingly gave information about themselves on the company web site!

The story gets even better when you appreciate all the steps involved. He lured me to the site by public relations, one of the least expensive marketing tools around. I read the information on the web site and could have bought

Dear Colleague:

Thanks for visiting our web site, The Right Site®, and for your interest in our ring study and site selection section.

Easy Analytic Software, Inc. (EASI) is a New York–based independent developer and marketer of CD-ROM and Internet demographic data and software solutions that provide simple-to-interpret demographic reports with unique search and analysis tools. EASI provides targeted site analysis and demographic reference software that is easy to use, designed and priced for any value-conscious business.

EASI can offer you several options to help with your site selections needs.

1. Use our free service from our web site.

2. Try The Right Site—Updated Census Tract & Block Group Edition ($1,975), which is designed our with special analysis software and updated to 1/1/97 data (280+ variables). This product is created just for the Site Selection and Ring Study market place. It works well with all desktop mapping (e.g., Maptitude, ArcView, Rand McNally's Streetfinder).

3. You can call us or e-mail us and arrange for EASI to prepare a series of ring studies—3 circles around one point plus a B & W map all for $75.

For those who have purchased ring studies from a competitor, we also would like to offer you a free EASI updated ring study to compare the results against. At our web site we also have a varied collection of unsolicited testimonials.

- E-mail (ggergen@aol.com or howeasi@msn.com) us a request for an updated analysis around a specific site. Please include the complete address, city, state, and zip code of the site.

- Also include your name, company, telephone number, and fax number and, of course, the ring size (in miles) that you'd like.

- We will then send you a printout of the key updated variables at this site FREE. Compare our results to any that you already have!

If you need details or want to try one of our software products (check out our web site) call 800-469-3274 (800-HOW-EASI), or if you have any questions about our data and software you can get answers by calling Greg Gergen, Sales Director, at 302-762-4271 (e-mail ggergen@aol.com). He'll be happy to help you.

Thanks again for your interest.

Bob Katz, President
e-mail howeasi@msn.com

P. S. At our web site (www.easidemographics.com) are complete descriptions of the data elements. Please review the details of The Right Site—Updated Census Tract & Block Group Edition ($1,975); it just may be the perfect and simplest way to analyze all your sites.

Figure 1.1 E-mail sent by EASI to reinforce its sales message.

the product there. If I had done so, the entire transaction would have taken place without human intervention, thus saving EASI a lot of money. Because I didn't buy online, my name fell into a bucket marked "send him an offer by e-mail." The offer took the form of a prewritten letter sent to hundreds of people, so there was no additional work beyond setup. If I had bought via e-mail, again there would have been no human intervention. But I didn't, so my name fell into another bucket that earmarked me for a phone call from the sales director. At that point, the cost of the sale began to increase, but only at that point. The company had presented me with three ways to buy automatically before an expensive human being entered the picture.

The point of this story is that you should consider how to revise your web site so that the Internet can cherry-pick the easy sales that are developed from prospects you attract from other marketing methods. Also, realize that in some cases you will need to follow up with calls from a real, live human being to complete the transaction.

Case Study: Best Software

Best Software, a publisher of accounting software, used a direct-mail campaign that urged recipients to go to the company's web site (www.bestsoftware .com), enter a code number printed on the offer form, and enter it online to get a special price. By using a code number, the company was able to track sales that started with the direct-mail piece. Sales from the web were 220 percent better than the control, and downloads were 50 percent better than the control.

Not only that, the direct-mail/Internet offer collapsed the time sequence. In normal direct-mail campaigns, the first orders come in eight weeks, but the online offers started flowing in just three weeks.

Although some direct-mail experts have said they didn't want to use the web in an integrated manner because they didn't want to place another barrier in the way of the prospect picking up the phone and ordering or simply filling out the order form, this study shows that direct mail and the Internet can work well together.

BUILDING AN INTEGRATED MARKETING PROGRAM WITH THE INTERNET

Online marketing should support the entire marketing program. To conduct a successful marketing campaign, online services should be thought of as another marketing and distribution channel that provides a service to prospects and customers. Your company's key marketing messages should be seen in its online advertising, publicity, and promotion. Companies must use a consistent message, typeface, logo, and other elements of a marketing campaign so that consumers find the same content regardless of the medium used, thus creating a solid, familiar feeling with customers.

Professional speaker Patricia Fripp (www.fripp.com) has done a masterful job of integrating the Internet into her successful marketing program. Her web site incorporates the look and feel of her marketing materials, as you can see in the Figures 1.2 and 1.3. She uses the same

Figure 1.2 Patricia Fripp's hardcopy marketing material. (© 1999, Patricia Fripp)

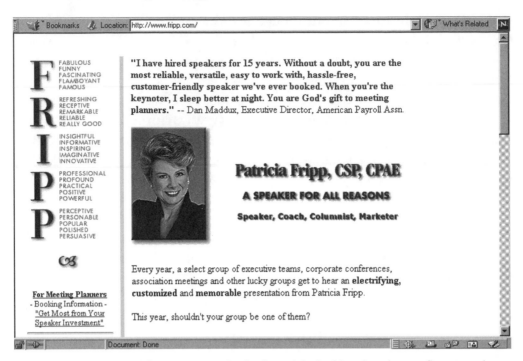

Figure 1.3 Fripp's web site carries the look and feel of her brochures, flyers, and handouts. (© 1999, Patricia Fripp)

typeface, angle, and picture in all her presentations. If a meeting planner received her print materials in the mail and decided to read more about her services on the Internet, he would be greeted by a web site that looks like an extension of the papers he was holding in his hand. This integration creates a sense of continuity that leads to comfort in the minds of buyers. Following Fripp's example is a good idea for any consultant, doctor, or other service provider.

Larger companies with many different products, brands, or international divisions might wonder how to present a unified front to its many publics. Surprisingly, this is not hard to do. Just follow the examples of industry leaders such as 3M and Microsoft. Everyone knows 3M's famous logo: a 3M in red with a black background; the company has adopted this logo on its web site. The words "Innovation Network" appear in the web site's banner, but if you select one of its products or divisions, the 3M stays in the banner, while the division's or product's name appears next to it in its familiar fonts and colors. Keeping a consistent design might seem a problem at first, but you can see that it really isn't.

Although these examples show how easy it can be to standardize your message, look, and feel between different advertising formats and the Internet, perhaps you can really grasp this concept by looking at a web site that *doesn't* integrate its messages well.

One company that seems to totally disregard integrated marketing concepts is Ragu, the manufacturer of fine pasta sauces. They have created a charming site (www.ragu.com) that seems to say "We are everything Italian." You can learn to speak Italian; take a tour of Little Italy in New York; read about Italian art and architecture, and even banter with the company's online mascot, Mama, a white-haired, grandmotherly figure who adorns nearly every page on the site—in fact, the site is called "Mama's Cucina." This would be a great marketing tactic except for one thing: You can barely see the Ragu name or logo on the site! If you go deeper into the site and look at other pages, you might not even see the Ragu label at all, and if you do, then the Mama's Cucina logo is larger. You might wonder who owns the site.

However, the site does a wonderful job of creating brand identity. You can really get wrapped up in it. I was so taken with the site that one day when I was shopping, I got the urge to go Italian and buy Ragu sauce. So I went down the pasta aisle and grabbed the first jar that had a picture of my favorite white-haired sage. Unfortunately, when I looked at the label, I was staring at Paul Newman—not Mama! After looking around the shelves for a few moments, I found the Ragu sauce. The labels featured pictures of gondolas, mushrooms, and tomatoes, all of which says "Italian" but doesn't say "Mama" I wondered why Ragu had spent millions of dollars creating an online character that brought them incredible amounts of publicity and exposure but didn't use her picture in the real world—where it counts! After all, you can't buy sauce online, but you can buy it in the stores. This example illustrates how companies can run afoul of generally accepted principles of integrated marketing and the confusion that it can cause in the marketplace.

SUMMARY

Consumers don't like to be confused. If they have the slightest hesitation about you, your brand, or your identity, they will pass you by. By integrating the web into your marketing program and using the same design, look, feel, and messages as found in your other promotional materials, you will reinforce your image and themes to your customers, who in turn will reward you with sales and loyalty.

The need to integrate online services into the marketing mix is important for companies that need to expand their sales bases by building brand identities and tapping into the online world. The online program must tie into the goals of the traditional marketing program, not go off on its own tangent. Building a brand identity is important for companies as they race to stake out claims in cyberspace because mass-market consumers going online will look for familiar names.

CHAPTER 2

New Paradigms of Online Marketing

Imagine you are the marketing manager of a nice-sized business in the early 1950s. One day your college intern rushes into your office and says, "There's a cool new medium through which we can advertise our products. Everyone on campus is talking about it."

"Really? What's it called?"

"Television," he says.

"Television? What's television?"

"It's radio with pictures," he clucks.

If TV were truly just radio with pictures, then we'd see a camera focused on an announcer reading from a script in his hands. Instead, TV ads today are phenomenal vehicles that use pictures and sounds to create an emotional yearning for products we didn't know that we desperately needed. Some ads don't even show pictures of the products, and we want them anyway!

There's no way the college student of the 1950s could have foreseen this change.

Now let's fast-forward to the 1990s. You are the marketing manager of a good-sized company, and your college intern rushes into your office and says, "Hey, there's a cool new medium we can advertise on. It's called the Internet."

"Internet? What's the Internet?"

"It's like television, with interactivity."

Well, the Internet is no more like TV with interactivity than TV was radio with pictures. As the medium evolves, new ways of using it develop. And it develops in ways we never imagined.

This chapter will explore:

- Key concepts of Internet marketing and advertising.

- How online marketing differs from traditional marketing.
- How to be a success online.
- Netiquette: forbidden marketing activities.

KEY CONCEPTS OF INTERNET MARKETING AND ADVERTISING

When I conducted a seminar for Pacific Bell for their small business owners who were new to the Net, a middle-aged woman asked the first question: "What is the Internet?"

A million ideas flashed through my mind. Do I tell her about the complicated and confusing way in which computers all around the world are linked together to share information so that a consumer in Monterey, California, can read about a concrete company in Monterrey, Mexico, and create a business relationship?

Do I tell her about the arcane history of the Internet that includes its beginnings as a communications vehicle to allow the government to send messages in case of a nuclear war?

No, I thought quickly. Marketers don't need to understand those technical or historical anecdotes to understand the Internet any more than they need to know the history of the fax machine or how telephones send voices around the world. All they need to know is that the Internet is the least expensive marketing tool in their arsenal as well as the most cost-effective. People from around the world can read their message and create a business relationship with them for a fraction of the cost of any other marketing method.

Pure and simple.

Some people are uncomfortable with the Internet because they are afraid of high tech or don't think they can understand the jargon that might go along with it. They needn't worry about the intricacies of the technology because that isn't what is relevant to marketing. What is relevant is that the Internet is not just high tech—it is high touch. With the Internet, you can create one-to-one relationships with prospects and build lasting relationships with consumers in a very personal, individualized manner.

"Why is the Internet more effective?" another seminar participant asked.

Here's the answer to that question according to Carol Wallace, program manager of communications for Prodigy: "You are never going to get more attention from any customer than when they are online. Both their hands are on the keyboard and both their eyes are on the monitor. You are interacting with them. They have preselected you. They want to see you. This is a very intimate selling situation."

If you are writing a business plan, you might consider using this quote. In the next chapter, you will read about more than one hundred benefits to being online that you also might want to insert into your marketing proposal to convince your bosses or investors that online marketing is the way to go.

Just as it is important to know what the Internet is, it is vitally important to understand what it is not. The Internet is not a get-rich-quick scheme. Success on the Internet requires hard work, attention to detail, and constant promotional activity. Online success is not guaranteed.

Online marketers can use several vehicles to reach consumers. We'll go into each topic in greater detail later in the book. Here is an executive overview:

- Web sites are company-sponsored areas that allow the company to interact with its customers and prospects. Web sites can contain information about products and the company itself, including its history. They can also include interactive elements such as conferences, chatrooms, and mailing lists (e-mail newsletters) as well as shopping opportunities and customer support. Companies can create strong bonds with customers, who may become lifelong buyers of their products. Companies can also sell products on some forums.
- The Internet's Usenet newsgroups are discussion boards covering more than one hundred thousand topics. These groups cannot be used for blatant commercial activities. However, company officials can find targeted groups of consumers interested in certain products and join in the discussion by providing information, not sales pitches.
- E-mail is the primary communications vehicle between consumers and companies. Online services offer a tremendous amount of flexibility for online marketers, who can automatically respond to customers' e-mail information requests and product orders 24 hours a day. You won't lose sales, because your e-mail operator is always on duty.
- Automated e-mail, also called infobots or mailbots (as in *robots*), works like an automated fax system that sends prewritten mes-

sages describing your product or service in response to consumers' e-mail requests. You can have any number of mailbots.

- Conferences enable marketers to build relationships with consumers by providing information, speakers, or access to famous
  personalities (such as Mick Jagger and William Shatner).
  Companies can also feature their CEOs or product managers to
  build relationships with employees, consumers, dealers, and investors.

- News and financial services provide consumers with information
  from wire services and more than one thousand newspapers
  worldwide.

HOW ONLINE MARKETING DIFFERS FROM TRADITIONAL MARKETING

The Internet is a marketing medium that requires you to follow specific
rules and regulations for doing business effectively. Online marketing
turns the traditional broadcast methods of advertising on their heads.
Instead of sending a message to a targeted audience that either responds to or dismisses the call to action, online consumers seek out
information and advertising. They, not the advertiser, initiate the communication.

This means that advertisers need to deliver and create messages in
entirely new ways. The key differences involve the following issues:

- Space.
- Time.
- Image creation.
- Communication direction.
- Interactivity.
- Call to action.

Let's explore these concepts to better understand how to create a message that will appeal to Internet consumers.

Space

Old Advertising—Space is a commodity you buy. It is expensive and fi-
nite. No matter which standard size you purchase (a 30-second TV or ra-

dio commercial, a full-page ad in a newspaper or magazine), you have only begun to tell your story. You are forced to leave out information because of the limitations, constraints, and costs of space.

New Advertising—Space is unlimited and cheap. You can post an encyclopedia's worth of information about your company and its products on the Internet for a modest amount of money. Because of this, you can tailor sales messages to different kinds of buyers: information seeking, money conscious, value oriented, and so on. If they are visual, you can post pictures and movies. If they are numbers oriented, you can post reams of statistics. In fact, consumers can create their own sales scripts as they seek out the information that interests them and avoid the other stuff. Interview your salespeople. They know which techniques work for each kind of buyer who walks into the showroom.

Time

Old Advertising—Time is a commodity you buy on TV and radio. It is expensive and limited. You have a short period of time to convey a message. Advertisers tend to try to create an image of a company or product through visual means because of these limitations.

New Advertising—Time is what consumers spend. It is a valuable commodity to them for two reasons: They are spending hard dollars to be on line, and they are spending real time away from other business or personal activities that constantly pull at them. To attract them to your store, hold them at your web site, keep them coming back, and tell their friends to stop by; you must add value to their experience at your online store.

The first step is to have high-quality products and information displayed in an attractive manner. The second step is to add real value to the consumer's experience—and that might have only tangential reference to your product or sales or advertising as we know it today. For example:

- Wells Fargo Bank allows its customers to find their account balances online.
- Visa lets anyone read free information about how to get out of debt.
- Federal Express and UPS let customers find packages for free online.

- Southwest Airlines has free travel information about vacation destinations.

These experiences help create goodwill with consumers by enriching the time they spend online.

Image Creation

Old Advertising—Images are created with static or motion pictures, music, lighting, and action. Images are primary; information is secondary. For example:

- A cigarette manufacturer shows a film of a cowboy on a horse lighting up, thus creating the rugged image of the Marlboro Man.
- A sleek sports car's door opens, a woman's bare leg emerges, and seductive music plays in the background as the announcer says, "The night belongs to Michelob."
- Teenagers are shown having fun playing volleyball at the beach and drinking Pepsi.

In each of these cases, an image is created with words and pictures that trigger emotions. Information is not used at all.

New Advertising—Images are created with information. Because the tools for audio and video on the Internet are still fairly crude, the main way to get information across is through the printed word—and the Internet takes full advantage of it Sales scripts and product information can be written to take advantage of *hypertext,* the feature that allows consumers to go from one piece of information to another at will instead of having to plow through an entire document in a linear format, from top to bottom. For example, let's say you are selling a product that can be understood on several levels, such as food. You could have a picture of a piece of chocolate accompanied by a paragraph of copy extolling the virtues of the dark, seductive candy and its smooth, silky texture. However, a health-conscious person would want to know about the fat and calorie content of the product. You could include that information as well. You could further increase sales opportunities by showing gift box options and describing the flavors available.

For a more technical product, such as phone systems, you could begin by showing the phone and basic information like features, benefits, and price. That would probably be enough for the owner of a small business. However, people buying large phone systems need more detailed information. Will it work with their current system? Will it work with their remote offices? The Internet allows you to create the image needed based on as much information as the consumer needs to make a buying decision.

Communication Direction

Old Advertising—TV broadcasts images and messages to couch potatoes who sit by passively and either hear or ignore your message. If they have questions, answers are not immediately available. For example, if they see a picture of a car and want to know how much it costs, they have to turn off the TV and drive to the dealer. If they see an ad for a bottle of beer and want to know how many calories it contains, they have to turn off the TV and go to the supermarket. Some commercials post a toll-free telephone number to call and begin a relationship in that manner. But that is the exception rather than the rule (except, of course, for infomercials and shopping programs).

New Advertising—Consumers seek out your message. They choose to be at your cyberstore and read the information. Not only that, they expect communication to be interactive; they want to be able to establish a line of communication with the company and find out answers to questions quickly, if not immediately.

Right now, technology allows consumers to find information at your store and send e-mail to your staff. You must respond as quickly as possible to build a relationship. The first step is to create an infobot, which immediately sends a prepared note to the consumer who emailed you that answers most questions she would have. Of course, people always think of a question your staff didn't think of and send another note. At this point, human intervention is required to answer the question. This is good, as the action begins to build a relationship between the company and consumer. From this interchange, good marketers can create a customer for life.

Interactivity

Old Advertising—You are watching TV when you see a commercial for a new car. You like the car and want more information. How much does it cost? How many miles per gallon does it get? Where is the local dealer? The company doesn't tell you. It doesn't have the space to fit it all in. A toll-free number flashes a cross the screen. Maybe you'll call. Maybe you'll forget as the next commercial begins.

New Advertising—You see the ad on TV and get really excited by the image. You read the web address on the TV and sign on to your Internet service to read the home page. You find all the information you need and then switch to a car discussion group and read messages that people have posted about that automobile. You post a question of your own, and a few minutes later it is answered by a car owner, not a company representative. You get a stream of information on which to base a buying decision.

Call to Action

Old Advertising—Requests are based on appeals to emotions and fears. They're going fast! Last one in stock! This offer expires at the end of the week! Requests also are based on incentives. Buy one, get one free!

New Advertising—Requests are based on information. Consumers are looking for answers to specific questions. If you have the right product and describe it correctly, you have a better chance of making the sale than if you appeal to emotion.

The jury is still out on whether traditional off-the-page selling methods work in cyberspace or not. These tools include time-limited offers that hinge on product scarcity. No one has conducted a serious study of the extent to which persuasion works on Internet users before they get turned off. Serious marketers will want to push the envelope.

HOW TO BE A SUCCESS ONLINE

"Being the first online will not only establish initiative but will accelerate the learning curve of conducting business online," says Leslie Laredo, an authority on online advertising. "As the old lottery ad stated, 'You've got to be in it to win it.' participation at almost any level is fast becoming necessary."

Marketers will be most successful when they follow these keys to online marketing success, as defined by Laredo and other experts interviewed for this book:

- Appreciate the new paradigms in online marketing and advertising.
- Customers rule.
- Mass marketing is over—customization is in.
- Build relationships one at a time.
- Appreciate the long-term value of the customer.
- Provide reams of information, not persuasion.
- Create interactive dialogue.
- Contribute to the community.
- Free products will generate interest.
- Adjust to the compression and distortion of time.
- Online is a competitive advantage.

Appreciate the New Paradigms in Marketing and Advertising

Online marketing is a new branch of an old tree—marketing, which can be defined as the process of satisfying human needs and wants with information, services, or products through the exchange of money. To be a successful online marketer, you must know the basics of the marketing process, including needs assessment, market research, product development, pricing, distribution, advertising, public relations, promotions, and sales.

Online marketing has its roots in traditional marketing concepts but branches out in a most important manner to encompass interactivity. Vendors now can deal interactively with consumers in their own homes or office at any hour of the day or night. Conversely, buyers can interact with vendors in a new way.

However, the most striking contrast between online marketing and other forms is the technology itself. Communicating messages via computers replaces paper with on-screen displays of information, text, art, and sound. Principles of layout, design, typography, and art need to be reconsidered in this context. Also, computers allow communication to become an interactive, two-way process, unlike print and television advertisements, which are one-way processes. Simply uploading ads to online services means your company misses the chance to take advantage of technology and its tools to empower your messages.

Online marketing can take advantage of presenting interactive sale materials that meet the needs of every type of buyer. Instead of creating a message for the lowest common denominator, as does broadcast advertising, for example, online marketers can create interactive brochures that allow consumers to choose the information they want to see when they want to see it. Companies can create individual sales presentations to match the needs of each buyer.

"Cyberads must leverage the online medium by providing more and deeper information, more entertainment value, and faster and more personalized fulfillment than what can be jammed into a 30-second TV commercial or a single-page print ad," says Laredo. "What's more, online advertising dictates customized communication, not broad general messages. Target marketing can be exercised in a much finer fashion. Individual message management or one-to-one selling, with ad placement in the context of relevant, sought-after content, is the new rule. Online advertising is more like personal selling than anything else."

Customers Rule

With a single keystroke, customers can decide to buy your product or leave you in the dust. In a split second, customers can find prices from your competitors. In a heartbeat, they can find news, reviews, and comments from other customers about your product. They have access to a mountain of information they can use to make an informed decision. This is not a high-pressure medium; this is an audience filled with the desire to make an educated purchase.

Mass Marketing Is Over—Customization Is In

Online marketing allows companies to target customers in a way that other media cannot.

"For the last 30 years, mass marketing has torn the business away from the customer. We've been advertising mass-produced product to a mass audience. We end up counting the people we reach, not reaching the people who count," says Dan Fine, president of Fine Communications, a database marketing company based in Seattle. "Customers have been bombarded with more advertising messages than they could stand. As a result, they've become increasingly selective as to which messages they give their attention to. We have come to a time when the consumer wants to talk back to the marketing message and a place where individual relationships must be reestablished."

To get an even better perspective of online marketing, perhaps it is best to compare it to mass marketing and direct marketing:

- Mass marketing needs a mass market to survive. It reaches consumers through television and magazines. It does best when it sells food, health and beauty aids, beer, and cars.
- Direct marketing needs a highly targeted audience. It finds consumers through mailing lists. It is a good vehicle to sell credit cards, travel, software, and catalog goods.
- Online marketing targets individuals through online services. It sells travel, stocks, upscale consumer goods, and computer equipment and software.

Think of the Internet as a mass of audiences instead of a mass audience, and you will begin to understand online marketing.

Build Relationships One at a Time

Successful online marketers know that businesses are built one customer at a time.

"You must get personally involved in the virtual community. You must invest the time to start relationships," says Prodigy's Wallace. "Through that process, you will begin to understand how this society operates. Then you will be in a better position to sell to them."

Companies can create warm relationships with prospects by using personalized e-mail, welcome messages on web pages, and keeping track of their interests, previous orders, and passwords. A flower store can track customers' birthdays, holidays, and anniversaries and remind them well in advance so they can order flowers. Stock brokerages can notify customers when their stocks hit buy and sell points or when there is news about the companies in their portfolio.

Appreciate the Long-Term Value of the Customer

For marketers, a major change in thinking must occur regarding the value of the customer. For too long companies have regarded consumers as replaceable commodities. Marketers must look to the long-term value of a customer. This concept will be a stretch for many sales-people.

For example, when was the last time you got a call, card, or note from the person who sold you your car? Probably never. Do you have any sense of loyalty to that salesperson or dealership? Probably not. That's too bad for them, because you will probably buy a new car one day, and it won't be from them!

What does this cost the company? Let's look at the figures. If you are an average consumer, you'll buy a new car every three to five years. You will be influenced by peers, ads, and other factors. One factor that will *not* influence you is a sense of loyalty or commitment to a salesper-son or dealership. If the average car costs $20,000 in today's dollars and is held for five years, that means the lifetime value of a 30-year-old cus-tomer for a car dealership is $160,000, assuming that person buys a new car every five years until he is 70. You'd think it would be worth $1.50 to send a birthday card or personal note once a year to build a relationship worth that much money. Few car salespeople do this—even though they make their living by commission.

For marketers to succeed, they must make additional sales to their established base of customers. Online communication offers relevant tools. Marketers can create individual sales messages that draw on each person's likes and dislikes and buying patterns and what kind of persua-sion works best for her. Savvy promoters can send targeted communica-tions to build relations with customers who approve of that interaction with newsletters describing new products, sales, or productivity tips.

Online marketing didn't invent this process—it just made it easier and less costly.

Case Study: Wally Bock

Wally Bock, an author, speaker, and consultant who trains police depart-ments on human relations and procedural issues, uses online services to reach his target audience: police chiefs. He participates in discussions on online bulletin boards and answers questions such as "How do I deal with sexual harassment?" He replies with a message that provides a few exam-ples from his book.

"The last time I did that, I got an individual order from a police chief in Wisconsin. He posted a message praising the book," says Bock. "This led to more orders. An East Coast police chief asked for a review copy and then ordered 50. He promotes his staff every 18 months, so I expect to sell 50 new orders every 18 months. That's the value of long-term customers."

Bock also publishes two newsletters for businesses going online, *CyberPower Alert™* and *CyberPower for Business™* (www.bockinfo.com), that place the lifelong value of one of his customers at $500 to $5,000.

"That's what the future of this marketing is about," he says. "I am not in the business of one-time sales. That is not smart. If you are a customer of mine, you will be a subscriber for years. You become a prospect for additional businesses and products and consulting. My primary focus is getting quality people who stay a long time. Secondarily, get as many as possible."

For Bock, the key to success is target marketing. "We tailor what we have to specific people," he says of the forums and newsgroups and mailing lists that have tightly defined readers. "What I can do on the Internet I can't do with paper mailing lists. There is no other technology that lets me do this as well."

Provide Reams of Information, Not Persuasion

The stereotype of the overbearing salesperson is the antimodel for on-line marketing. Online consumers are information seekers and are persuaded by facts and logic. The medium itself is mostly text based, which attracts an educated audience used to making decisions based on reading reports. They go online to find information from company databases and peer discussion groups. These are not people who are persuaded by the classic techniques of image advertising, which is based on irrational and emotional appeals that boost the ego and allude to sex. Online consumers are turned off by hype and oversell. The successful online marketer has a better chance to succeed if he offers information and rich content instead of self-serving materials.

This is good news for online marketers because space on the Internet and forums on commercial online services are inexpensive or free. Companies that were forced to condense their messages to fit printed advertisements on half a newspaper page will enjoy the freedom of virtually unlimited space online to post file after file of product information, complete with text, pictures, and sound.

"You are not constrained by pages like print magazines. Advertising becomes more interactive and creative," says Marcos Sanchez, a marketing consultant. "With magazines, you had to match your message to a limited space. On the Net, you can use an inverted pyramid. Start with overview and then go very broad or deep. The ad becomes an amorphous space."

Another advantage is that you can find out what people are really interested in. Let's say you are selling cars and have information stored on separate pages listing options such as air bags, stereos, J.D. Power ratings, safety tests, and colors. By counting the number of times a page is read, you can see that more people are interested in air bags than, say, colors. These data can be used to fine-tune advertising messages online and in other media.

"This changes the model of how we look at advertising," Sanchez says. "It is no longer a 3-by-5-inch ad that goes out to 20,000 people. It is unlimited space going out to the world, limited only by the capacity of your server."

Remember, hard sells don't work.

Create Interactive Dialogue

After the prospect has read your online information, you must create a way for her to continue developing a relationship with the company. E-mail provides a great way to create a new dialogue. Customers should be encouraged to send questions to the company—and the company should be equipped to send a prompt reply.

Technology allows several reply methods. A customer support representative can respond to e-mail as soon as a message is received in the company mailbox. Mailbots can send the desired information immediately to the requester at any time of the day or night.

Companies can also create relationships by having representatives scan online forums for conversations concerning their company, products, or product area. When they find these messages, they quickly provide information, answer questions, and dispel rumors with the goal of finding new prospects and building loyalty to the company and brand.

Contribute to the Community

Online marketing is a two-way, interactive process. You are asking for the consumer's time and money. In return, you must offer valuable free information, releasing surveys, reports, and impartial information packets that contribute to the greater good of the online community. For example, an insurance agency could post files about saving money on insurance, a real estate agency could explain how to choose a house, and a swimming pool installer might post an article about how to select a pool manufacturer.

Companies can also offer free samples of their products, such as online newsletters and reports and demo versions of software. In addition to being useful to the consumer, these products cost nothing to deliver via e-mail and file transfers.

Free Offers Will Generate Interest

If *location, location, location* are the three magic words of real estate, then *free, free, free* are the three magic words of the Internet. If you give people something for free, they will come visit your site, participate in a survey, or try your product. Marketers should think of giving away free information, free software, or free samples, depending on their business. For example, many companies offer free articles on their specialty.

The Seattle Filmworks company gives away two free rolls of film. To get the film, people had only to tell the company where to send it. Voilà! The company got the name and address of a prospect for its database.

Adjust to the Compression and Distortion of Time

Remember the first time you searched your computerized address book for the name of a colleague? You were so amazed that the computer could sort through so many names so quickly. The same act would have taken much longer if you had done it by hand. Then you got used to the speed of the computer and would complain if the operation took longer than two seconds. This example shows how people's perceptions of time have changed thanks to the computer.

Fast is a relative term. In the world of online marketing, speed can be measured in seconds. People get impatient when their questions aren't answered by support staff in minutes. These same people might have been happy to grant a 24-hour call-return policy from a customer service representative. Companies that conduct business online must deliver information quickly because the customer demands it and because the technology can make it possible. For example, automated mail systems can send information-packed files to customers who request specific information. This is the norm, not the exception.

Being Online Is a Competitive Advantage

Having a commercial presence online presents a competitive advantage to companies. It provides them with an alternative, additional distribution channel for their products and services. For computer and software companies, not having an online forum to offer customer support can be seen as a distinct disadvantage. If a prospect wants to buy a modem or flowers or coffee and searches through Yahoo! and finds 50 companies but yours isn't listed, you can't possibly make the sale. If you are one of the 50, you might please a new customer if your marketing materials and prices fit his needs.

Company Size Is Irrelevant Online

When you drive past a shopping center, you can tell the big players from the startups. Online, you can't. In many ways, online services are the great levelers of companies. At this stage in online marketing, small companies can compete effectively with their large counterparts. This will change as more large companies come onto the web and bring the power of their famous brand names. There is a short window of opportunity for new or small companies to establish a brand identity on the web.

"Small companies with a well-designed home page can look every bit as professional and credible as a large, multinational company. Small companies can build instant credibility with a web home page," says Wendie Bernstein Lash, president of WebChat Broadcasting Network, a large chat system on the Internet. "People can't tell if you do business from a 90-story office building or a two-room rented suite. Web home pages level the playing field for small companies." Her company was later sold for several million dollars.

Although online marketing is still in its infancy, quite a few small companies have become big companies by using online marketing to sell flowers, T-shirts, novelties, and computer software. In some cases, online marketing was their only sales method and distribution channel.

In this stage of the Internet's development, people are willing to give business to companies they have never heard of. People buy wine at Virtual Vineyards and books from Amazon.com. What will happen when large companies and well-known catalogers go on the Internet? Will people be loyal to the brand names or try new cybercompanies? Time will tell.

If you follow these steps, you will enhance your chances for success. However, read the next section to make sure you don't mess it all up by violating a cardinal rule of marketing online.

NETIQUETTE: FORBIDDEN MARKETING ACTIVITIES

You are attending a cocktail party. You want to relax and have some fun or meet some future business contacts. From across the room, you see an attractive stranger who smiles at you and gives you good eye contact. You move closer together. You say, "Hi." The stranger says, "Want to buy some life insurance?"

You find out that everyone there is selling life insurance! Sure, there is no law prohibiting them from selling life insurance, but you didn't attend the cocktail party to buy same. If you had known that you would be pitched, you would not have attended the party!

The same is true with online services. People don't go online to receive broadcast advertising. If they want to find commercial information, that's fine. But they don't want to find their e-mailboxes filled with get-rich-quick schemes or ads for products they don't care about. The same is true with the electronic bulletin boards called forums, newsgroups, mailing lists, and clubs. People go to those areas to exchange relevant information, not find improper commercial notices.

Effective marketers observe the unwritten rules of "netiquette," the etiquette of the cyberworld, which hold that unsolicited material is unappreciated.

Companies that violate this simple policy risk being "flamed," that is, bombarded with hate mail filled with four-letter words or threats.

Idiotic marketers say they have thick skin and don't care about offending tens of thousands of people as long as they get a buying response rate that justifies their efforts.

This group is despised. If your company is planning a marketing campaign that violates netiquette, you might find yourself trying to stamp out a crisis of global proportions. If your outside marketing company suggests renting a list of e-mail names, fire the company before the online world throws flames at you!

This whole area of practice is called "spamming." Much debate has been given to this topic in newsgroups, marketing mailing lists, and even daily newspapers. The bottom line is that people hate getting spam in their mailbox. Companies that participate in this odious form of advertising have been flamed, blacklisted, and boycotted by the more radical elements of the Internet community. No big-name marketer or Fortune 500 company has resorted to spamming—that should tell you something. Most companies that spam seem to be in the get-rich-quick or lose-lots-of-weight-fast categories. Don't be fooled into thinking that this technique works. If it did, you wouldn't see so much venom spewed toward the purveyors of this trashy marketing technique.

SUMMARY

Being an online marketer requires you to take a fresh look at the Internet and treat it as a new medium with different benefits and limitations. In some ways, marketing on the Internet is like marketing at the mom-and-pop grocery store, with an emphasis on customer service, interactivity, and an appreciation of each customer's long-term value. At the same time, online tools make marketing more efficient and easier.

CHAPTER 3

Constructing the Online Marketing Business Plan

Sad to say, many companies that have web sites have neither a clue as to why they are online nor a reasonable set of goals to judge whether their site is effective. One research survey actually showed that a good percentage of companies have no idea why they are online or are online only because their competitors are. It is no wonder why these sites fail to show the company in a good light and why their customers have bad experiences there. To put your company ahead of the pack, you need to create a solid business plan for your online marketing plan.

In this chapter you will learn:

- Ten essential steps toward creating an online marketing plan.
- One hundred reasons to go online to promote marketing goals.
- Five business models for online companies.

TEN ESSENTIAL STEPS TOWARD CREATING AN ONLINE MARKETING PLAN

Definition: Online marketing is a system for selling products and services to target audiences who use the Internet and commercial online services by utilizing online tools and services in a strategic manner consistent with the company's overall marketing program.

Every company that intends to go on the Internet needs to have a marketing plan to outline the common goals and objectives that meet its needs. Too many companies (even Fortune 500 companies) have ventured onto the Internet with a home page but without a clear goal and wondered why their efforts were not effective. Here are the 10 essential steps to creating an online marketing plan:

1. Define the marketing mission by setting reasonable goals and objectives, which is the first step in any successful venture. Once you have goals, you can determine if your plan is working and take steps to improve results. Without goals, web sites tend to become a big cash drain with no visible signs of helping the company. This chapter will show you more than one hundred reasons to be online from a marketing point of view.

2. Gain cooperation from different departments in the company. Because a web site can affect sales, advertising, public relations, customer service, and product research and design as well as investor relations, it is important for all departments to work in harmony to create a web site that helps the entire company. Without this type of cooperation, the web site can become a minefield of political agendas that hurt the company. The following chapter will address this issue as well as the following two topics.

3. Assign areas of responsibility. People and departments must know who will be responsible for each step of the plan—from design, implementation, and promotion to revisions.

4. Determine budgets.

5. Create the marketing materials that support the mission. Once you have a goal, you need messages that make the vision a reality. In the following chapters, we'll learn how to create a web site from a marketing point of view (Chapter 6), how to write marketing copy for the web (Chapter 5), how to sell consumer product (Chapter 8), and professional services on the web and how to sell business-to-business products (Chapter 9).

6. Create the web from an artistic view to present the marketing materials in a friendly and efficient manner (See Chapter 6, "Designing Your Web Site to Increase Sales").

7. Connect to the Internet. (This topic is beyond the scope of this book.)

8. Promote the web site. Online promotion can take many forms. We'll discuss search engine tactics in Chapter 11, advertising and publicity, and promotional tactics in Chapter 12, e-mail tactics in Chapter 15, and newsgroup tactics in Chapter 16.

9. Test and revise the effectiveness of the home page (see Chapter 13, "Measuring Return on Investment"). Now that people are coming to your site, you need to see if your messages are working.

10. The web allows you to turn prospects into customers and customers into raving, lifelong fans (see Chapter 17). The Internet also has a variety of tools to help you create one-to-one marketing relationships with customers that increase loyalty and repeat business (see Chapter 14).

DEFINE YOUR MARKETING MISSION—YOUR SUCCESS BLUEPRINT

A very successful Internet marketer called the other day to ask my advice on how to quadruple the size of his very popular mailing list. Mind you, any one of us would kill to have the number of subscribers he does, and he makes a very nice living from the advertising on his list and his web site. But we all want to do better, so we brainstormed on how to achieve his goals. I mentioned all the tried-and-true strategies. Links. Publicity. Search engine strategies. Comarketing alliances with opinion leaders. No matter which strategy I suggested, he had done them all with varying degrees of success. Flustered, I apologized, and we parted as friends.

Then it dawned on me what had gone wrong with our conversation. It could have been one of three things:

1. He had unrealistic goals.
2. He had bad execution.
3. He wasn't doing what he should be doing often enough.

Let's look at these.

First, he might have had unrealistic goals. He wanted to grow his subscriber list from 150,000 to 500,000 overnight. We all know that can't be done so quickly. However, we both failed to appreciate the value of incrementally growing the list over a period of several months so that he could reach that lofty number. We both were guilty of trying to win the lottery or picking the next Internet stock that goes through the roof, metaphorically speaking. Instead, we should have realized that steady and deliberate marketing steps will win the race. That's how compound interest works. That's how the tortoise beat the hare. If he had followed through on the marketing programs that worked in the past and picked up 100 subscribers here and 50 subscribers there, then he would have reached his goals—but it wouldn't have happened overnight.

Second, the execution of the marketing programs might have been awful. He might have had bad slogans on his banner ads or rotten copy-writing on his offers. You can't force someone to subscribe if you don't write copy that hits a nerve. So the tactics might have worked if he had better marketing materials. Don't get me wrong—I'm not saying he had bad execution, but it might have been a reason. I remember him saying "Every slogan I thought of for an ad didn't work. And believe me, I tried them all." That's commendable, but the fire can't get any hotter than the candle. Just because you have the talent to cherry-pick the easiest 150,000 subscribers doesn't mean you have the ability to take it to the next level. You can always get help on the Net, usually by trading services. With 150,000 readers, I'm sure an ad or two could be exchanged for some consulting time with a top-notch copywriter.

Third, he obviously had successful marketing ventures; otherwise, his lists wouldn't be as large. He must be doing something right. So why wasn't he doing that more often? You've probably heard of the 80/20 rule in business that says that most of your income comes from a small number of clients. He probably should concentrate on doing what he does well and forget about the other stuff.

We'll never know what the fault was. But we can learn important lessons from this exchange:

1. Set clear, definable, and obtainable goals. Be realistic. How big is your market? Are they on the Internet? Can you reach them easily and in a cost-efficient way?
2. How much time will it take to achieve the goal? Our friend wanted to double his subscriber base overnight. No one can do that. You need to figure out a time line to make it happen.
3. How much money or energy will it take? On the Net, you can barter and trade to great success with other entrepreneurs. If

you have a great deal of energy, you can do a lot of marketing online for no cost at all. You can trade links with other noncompetitive vendors, list your site on search engines, write press releases, or become an active member in an online community that reaches your targeted audience. If you have money to invest, you can buy advertisements that reach your audience. For example, you can buy a keyword in search engine so that every time someone types "N scale railroad," your hobby store pops up. How much money you can budget will determine how many people you can reach.

4. Don't set yourself up for failure. If you have your sights set on 1 million readers and you get 500,000, you shouldn't consider yourself a failure! My friend pocketed more than $100,000 a year from his online venture—and that goes a long way in Ohio!

5. Use the 80/20 rule to analyze your marketing efforts and see what is working—and then continue doing it. This rule says that 80 percent of your income will come from 20 percent of your clients or activities. This means you don't have to use every strategy in the book—just the ones that work for your company, product, or service. Because each business is just a little bit different, what works for me might not necessarily work for you, or vice versa.

6. Test your marketing materials and improve them. Then test again until you get it right.

If you follow these steps, you'll be well on your way to reaching the goals that will truly take you where you want to go. Still not sure why you should be online or what you can accomplish? Read the next section for ideas.

ONE HUNDRED AND THREE REASONS TO BE ONLINE

Marketing, according to leading U.S. marketing educator and writer Phillip Kotler, is the process of making selling easier. The Internet can help in that process. The first step of going online is to decide what you want to accomplish. From that decision, you can plan your budget and personnel assignments. When I teach my Internet Marketing class at Stanford University and the University of California at Berkeley, my students, all of whom are professionals, generally come up with these

themes: save time, save money, make money, build relationships with reporters and communities, and cut the cost of doing business.

Here's the number-one reason you should be online, and you can
put it in your business plan with my compliments: The Internet is the
world's least expensive and most efficient marketing tool, and it helps
companies of all sizes from all parts of the world disseminate sales and
marketing messages, create one-to-one relationships, educate prospects,
and support existing customers on a worldwide scale.

General Benefits

1. Deal with an audience that wants to hear your message. "You are
   never going to get more attention from any customer than when
   they are online. Both their hands are on the keyboard and both
   their eyes are on the screen. You are interacting with them. They
   have preselected you. They want to see you. This is a very intimate selling situation," says Carol Wallace of Prodigy.
2. Reach a worldwide audience. People everywhere can read the
   information on your site and decide to start a business relationship with you.
3. Be completely accessible. Your site never closes. People can read
   it 24 hours a day, seven days a week.
4. Deal with an affluent market. All reports show that the first wave
   of Internet citizens make more money and have completed
   higher education levels than the average American.
5. Deal with a market that has sought you out to compare products. Unlike television, the Internet is customer driven. Prospects
   read your materials because they need to find out about your
   product. Other media can't pinpoint their messages and audiences.
6. Deal with customers when they are ready to buy. Customers
   come to your site when they begin the buying process. Either
   they are comparing your product to competitors' products, or
   they have the desire to buy directly from you. Alex Perriello, the
   president of real estate giant Coldwell Banker, estimates that 10
   percent of the almost eighteen thousand customer leads developed by its web site have turned into transactions. The Corcoran
   Group in New York sold three Manhattan apartments worth a total of $1.4 million to buyers who saw the units on the Internet
   but never visited the property!

7. Create specialized sales scripts appealing to each type of consumer, using their unique buying buzzwords. With the advantages
of hyperlinking information, pictures, sound, and video, merchants can create customized sales presentations involving several senses, appealing to logic, and listing benefits. Consumers
can pick the sales presentation and information they want.

8. Appeal to customers who hate pushy salespeople and manipula-
tive sales pitches. Consumers can use the Internet to find the
products they need and place orders without fear of manipulation by aggressive sales personnel. American Leasing (www
.americanleasing.com) is closing business on its web site with
minimal employee intervention. "We just received the check and
contract by Federal Express for a $50,000 notebook computer
lease, from an inquiry on our web site, sent to Fisher-Anderson
in Iowa, who approved it within two hours after we sent the application, for a major company with a foreign parent corporation. I never spoke to the person who signed the lease. I did this
all over the Internet and Federal Express," says Kit Menken, president of American Leasing. "And this wasn't the first time we have
gotten business."

9. Enjoy low cost of entry. The World Wide Web is the least expensive printing press ever invented. Merchants have an unlimited
amount of space to describe and demonstrate their entire range
of products. Companies can spend as little as $100 for a software
program to create their site.

10. Enjoy low rent, especially compared with storefront rent.
Internet service providers charge $30 a month to host your site,
and consumers can read it any time of day from anywhere on
the planet. Opening a store in the real world requires thousands
of dollars to fix, paint, carpet, and outfit the property as well as
to obtain insurance. These limitations don't exist on the Internet.

Competitive Advantage

11. Doing business online costs less. As it costs so little to go online
compared with opening a store on Main Street, merchants can
pass the savings along to consumers. MCI said the lower cost of
doing business online will allow the company to offer lower
long-distance telephone rates to new customers who switch service online.

12. Lack of salespeople online means lower overhead costs for merchants. Automation features like autoresponders, e-mail, and frequently asked questions (FAQ) files can reduce the need for salespeople to answer redundant questions, thus enabling them to be more efficient with their time.

13. Without the need to warehouse products, inventory and warehousing costs as well as shipping costs decline. Companies can order products from suppliers when they receive customers' payments.

14. Enjoy access to a large inventory of product. Online merchants don't have to have products on hand, so they can offer a wider range of products to the public. Online bookseller Amazon.com (www.amazon.com) claims to offer the largest number of titles in the world.

15. Cut out distributors. Companies that sell direct make more money because they don't pay intermediary agents.

16. Beat competitors who aren't online. If your competitors are online and you aren't, guess who will make the sale to the Internet shopper.

17 Engage customers' senses (and business) by using audio, video, and multimedia to create relationships.

18. Compete on an equal footing against larger companies. Online, no one knows how big a company you have or how long it has been in business. Consumers only care that you have the product they are looking for at an attractive price.

Competitive Research

19. Find out what is going on with competitors. You can visit their web sites and find out what new products they are offering. By reading messages in specialized newsgroups and mailing lists, you can find out what people think about your competitors' products as well as your own.

20. Find out what is going on in your industry. By using online news services and specialized newsgroups and mailing lists, you can read about breaking news and discern trends.

21. Form alliances with companies. Dealers, vendors, and distributors who read your material might want to represent your company in new channels around the nation and the world. Your research might turn up companies for which you could be a supplier, or you could engage in other relationships.

Customer Research

22. Conduct consumer surveys. With feedback forms, consumers can tell companies what they like and don't like.
23. Conduct market research. Companies can determine customers' preferences for new products and services.
24. Determine which products are most popular. Merchants can look over consumers' shoulders and see which products are most frequently considered and purchased.
25. Find out which features and benefits are requested most.
26. Find out how long it takes to convert a prospect. By capturing keystrokes and counting time spent online learning about and purchasing a product, companies can understand the buying process more accurately.

Prospecting

27. Generate inquiries. People who read the information on your home page can let you know they are interested in learning more.
28. Qualify prospects. Your web site can ask questions of prospects to find out their buying power, interests, and needs.
29. Create lists of qualified prospects. Prospects who visit your home page or request information via e-mail can be added to your e-mail lists and databases.
30. Follow up on leads from ads in other media. Prospects who see your URL or e-mail address in advertisements in print and television ads can read more on your home page or ask for a call.
31. Make appointments via e-mail or phone.
32. Answer questions via e-mail or phone.
33. Fulfill literature requests. Literature can be sent via e-mail, or the customer can be directed to the web site for more information.
34. Invite prospects to seminars and product demonstrations.

Sales

35. Sell new products to new markets.
36. Sell old products to new markets.
37. Sell old products to new international markets.
38. Sell products that have a hard time moving through the distribution channel.
39. Sell products in your catalog with more description than is available in print. Online catalogs have an unlimited amount of space

to create sales messages that answer virtually every question posed by prospects.

40. Sell products that wouldn't normally fit in your store or catalog. Companies with large product lines might not be able to describe all products in a printed catalog because of the price of printing and mailing. These costs are minimal online, so companies can display and describe their entire product line. Wal-Mart (www.walmart.com) sells 500,000 products on its web site but only 80,000 in a retail outlet. Amazon.com claims to have access to more than three million books in its online store. The typical superstore bookstore has less than 1 percent of that number on display in a mall store.

41. Quickly and easily distribute time-sensitive information about price changes, sales, and new products. E-mail is virtually free, so communication with prospects and customers is easy.

42. Test sales prices and products. Information on a site can be updated quickly and inexpensively, so companies can test every variable imaginable.

43. Rotate featured items. Companies can test the product selection and change the display for any kind of audience. For example, a clothier can show one page for teenage girls and others for their mothers, brothers, and fathers. Companies that sell internationally can offer products depending on the seasons.

44. Distribute product information (news, software, reports, financial information, etc.) electronically. This is much less expensive than traditional printing and mailing.

45. Make sales directly on the Internet or through your inbound sales department. You have the option of taking orders in the manner that best meets your needs and your customers'. Dell Computers (www.dell.com) says it takes five phone calls to close a sale, but on the Internet, many sales are finished in one sitting.

46. Lead people into stores locally. Kodak doesn't sell products from its site but rather leads prospects to local dealers.

47. Amass and distribute inbound leads for telemarketers and outbound sales professionals. People who respond to your ads via e-mail leave their e-mail address when they correspond with you.

48. Further the sales process by providing more content and demonstrations. The Internet offers companies the opportunity

to present an unlimited amount of information to close the sale.

49. Make sales directly over the Internet or by phone, mail, or fax.

50. Drive sales by offering coupons that can be redeemed at the store. Sites can include coupons for prospects to print and redeem.

51. Sell to targeted audiences with special interests (i.e., fishing, gardening, or vacationing).

52. Sell to targeted audiences with lifestyle interests (i.e., children, education, or parents).

53. Increase business-to-business sales. Many businesses use the Internet to find products and suppliers.

54. Educate customers. Use your site or e-mail to provide prospects with background information that helps make the sale.

55. Show products in action with video and sound. Prospects can learn more about a product by seeing it in action.

56. Supply maps and directions to your stores or offices.

57. Handle catalog sales more efficiently.

58. Cut the cost per lead. Toyota spent $75,000 on 1.5 million banner ads in Yahoo! over a two-week period. More than twenty thousand qualified buyers were sent to the company's nationwide network of 1,200 dealers. The cost per lead was less than $4.

Publicity

59. Build rapport with reporters by responding to their online queries, sending information quickly via e-mail, and tailoring messages to each reporter's needs.

60. Build relationships with your stakeholders (employees, stockholders, local residents, etc.) by sending them press material, financial statements, and demonstration products.

61. Notify reporters and customers of new policies. E-mail is a quick and efficient method for distributing information.

62. Distribute press materials inexpensively to reporters, employees, stockholders, and vendors. Xerox saves more than $100,000 a year with Internet and fax delivery of annual reports.

63. Warehouse press material for retrieval by reporters and various publics.

64. Spur word-of-mouth campaigns to sell products or create buzz about a company.

65. Manage crises. Communications professionals can manage reports sent to the press and stakeholders with information presented on the site, sent via e-mail, and stored in data libraries.
66. Debunk misinformation. By monitoring and participating in newsgroups and mailing lists, company representatives can set the record straight if people disseminate inaccurate information.
67. Hold press conferences and annual meetings online for reporters or stakeholders. People who cannot travel to attend a meeting can view the proceedings online. If the proceedings are recorded, people can listen at their convenience.

Collateral

68. Distribute materials inexpensively. Sun Microsystems says it saves more than $1,000,000 a year by referring people to their home page instead of sending out literature. Tandem Computers says it saves the same amount of money and reaches five times as many people as before.
69. Create targeted materials. Pages can be created on the fly so that consumers interested in certain products can get clearly targeted information.
70. Create targeted materials more economically. Online brochures are much less expensive to produce than print versions, so companies can create pages clearly labeled for targeted audiences.

Customer Relations

71. Establish one-to-one relationships with customers and prospects using e-mail.
72. Send targeted messages and advertisements to customers who request them.
73. Build long-term relationships by responding to customers' initial requests and then sending newsletters and notes about new products, upgrades, and sales.
74. Answer frequently asked questions via a cost-effective response system. As most questions are asked by large numbers of people, standard answers can be sent via e-mail.
75. Find disgruntled customers and deal with their concerns. By monitoring newsgroups, you can identify customers who are bad-mouthing the company and deal with the situation.
76. Build a base of evangelists. Customers who love your product can be recruited to solve people's problems online, answer tech-

nical questions, and alert the company to loud-mouthed trouble-makers.

Advertising

77. Present ads on the Internet to targeted audiences to increase sales

78. Display ads on the Internet to general audiences to increase awareness.

79. Test ads. Because of the low cost of updating information, companies can test their advertisements and all factors involved in the sales process.

80. Test prices.

81. Test headlines.

82. Test offers.

83. Measure response. Every action on the Internet can be tracked, so companies can review each consumer's decision process.

84. Test to determine why prospects didn't purchase.

85. Integrate ad sales with other media (i.e., direct mail, postcard, TV, and print ads). Many companies print their URLs and e-mail addresses on ads in other media. Sporting goods cataloger REI received as many requests for catalogs through an online promotion with *Outside* magazine on ESPN's web site as it ever had through traditional media.

86. Deliver more information online to prospects who were initially attracted by ads in other media. Once prospects are attracted to a site, companies can present more information than could ever fit into a print ad or run on television.

87. Generate income from selling advertising on your web site.

88. Build mailing lists of purchasers and build long-term relationships with them.

Cut Product Support Costs

89. Cut costs of support. Online support techniques can answer most routine questions without human intervention. Netscape (www.home.netscape.com) saves more than $10 each time a person uses the online support system instead of talking to a human being. Kodak saved $4 million in one year by delivering software drivers for the company's imaging and photography products via the Internet instead of by mail. Cisco (www.cisco.com) will sell $5 billion of products on the Internet

and handle 70 percent of the technical support online—with greater customer satisfaction than when people deal with people.

90. Reduce human cost. As consumers become accustomed to using online support, companies might be able to reduce support staffs or train their human staff to deal with higher-level problems. In banking, for instance, a $1.15 teller transaction costs 38 cents at an automated teller machine and 2 cents online, according to Forrester Research, Inc.

91. Savvy customers want to use online support centers. Hewlett-Packard (www.hewlett-packard.com) gets 1 million customer questions on the web per month compared to 600,000 on the phone.

92. Provide 24-hour support. Online service centers are open 24 hours a day, unlike many in the real world. This increases customer satisfaction, as questions are resolved at the customer's convenience.

93. Educate customers after they've found their answers. By receiving additional information about a product, customers become more knowledgeable and can solve future problems.

94. Lead people to purchase upgrades and new products. Once consumers resolve their problems, they are interested in learning more about your product line.

95. Let customers find solutions to problems without tying up high-priced staffers. Federal Express and UPS let customers trace their own product shipments. Wells Fargo lets customers find their account balances. Stock brokerage firms let customers find account balances and stock quotes, and place trades online.

Branding

96. Brand building. Extend brand image through a new medium. Customers who are loyal to companies and products with trusted brand images will follow them online.

97. Preempt position from virtual competitors. A first wave of online entrepreneurs is selling wine and books and holding online auctions. Companies that sell these products in the real world will need to go online to recapture lost sales. Customers of these new companies will need to be targeted to buy from established companies with deep brand recognition.

International Sales

98. Sell products to an international audience.
99. Build and extend brand identity.

General Business

100. Post job notices online. Companies that have done this report they find better-qualified applicants than they do from advertisements in newspapers.
101. Distribute reports to employees quickly, even if they operate in satellite offices.
102. Revise price lists quickly via e-mail or updates to home pages.
103. Test products. Customers can download new versions of software tools or first drafts of information-based products such as books, newsletters, and reports. They can give the company their opinions via forms sent by e-mail.

BUSINESS MODELS

There are many ways to make money on the web. Operating a mall, renting space on your server, and providing consulting services to companies entering the market have been explored. Here are additional business models to consider.

- *Business Model: Sell Promotional Space on an Information Product.*
  Best for information providers.

  A popular Internet business model is creating frequently updated product information, sending it free to subscribers, and charging sponsors a fee for a special listing. For example, a mailing list on a given topic can be sent to 30,000 people and contain a sponsor's message at the top of the document. One could charge $20 to $40 per 1,000 readers.

- *Business Model: Create and Distribute a Sample Product; Charge for the Full Version.*
  Best for software publishers.

  Software publishers can create their own web sites to offer free downloads of new software programs. These files can contain complete software programs, shareware versions of full programs, or demo programs. To make money, the publisher attaches an unlocking code to the file. This code allows the consumer to try the product for a period of time and then locks the program so it cannot be reused. If the consumer wants to use the product again, he has to call the publisher, pay for the product, and receive the keys to the lock.

Using the Internet and commercial online services has been a boon for many publishers of software distributed as shareware. Examples of products that began as shareware and have become retail products selling hundreds of thousands of copies include Procomm, Virus Scan, Doom, PC Write, and AutoMenu. Now it seems like every piece of software intended for Internet use is released online for a trial period, as publishers hope to convert prospect to buyers with a "try before you buy" policy.

- *Business Model: Create Editorial Content: Sell Advertising Space and Subscriptions.*
  Best for information publishers.

  Publishers of books, magazines, zines, newsletters, and reports can make money using the Internet by creating web sites where readers can read current and historical issues. Although some publications offer only a few key articles, others print the entire issue online. This strategy introduces new readers to the publications. The publishers hope to make money either by selling subscriptions to the print edition or by selling online advertising in the form of ads or paid sponsorships.

  Many information providers are having a difficult time selling subscriptions. *USA Today* and *The New York Times* dropped their plans to charge for subscribers, perhaps because so much news and information is already on the Internet and people felt there was no reason to pay a premium for those articles.

- *Business Model: Create Information Products.*
  Best for consultants, speakers, trainers.

  By writing informative articles and reports, consultants, speakers, and trainers can build their credibility and gain exposure that can lead to revenue from selling their services. Such articles can be posted to mailing lists, newsgroups, and web sites—the author's and others—to create links between complementary sites.

- *Business Model: Sell Products Online.*

  Best for companies that sell products either in the real world or only online.

  This should be painfully obvious. You can sell products on the Internet and build a fortune. Although most of the major categories have been staked out by Amazon.com, CDNOW, Reel.com, and several computer hardware and software companies, there are riches in niches. Sell products that are hard to find in the real world, and you'll build your fortune. If you want to sell books, sell Spanish books for children. If you want to sell music, sell international music.

SO WHAT'S YOUR GOAL?

Okay, you've read 100 reasons to be online and several business models for various types of business. Now you have to decide. Why are you online? Go back through the list and circle the reasons that appeal to you. Cross out the ones that don't apply to you. Select the ones you liked and prioritize them by what needs to happen first to get the most payback; then determine what has to be done first, second or third. For example, you might decide your main goal is to cut the cost of customer support. So you want to build a web site, fill it with customer support files, and build an interactive community that will help other customers answer their questions. You could decide you want to sell more products automatically and cut the costs of sales personnel. There is no end to the kinds of marketing problems that the Net can solve. In a perfect world, your only restrictions should be your imagination. However, in this world, you must add time and budget as well. Once you cross those hurdles, the web will help you reach your goals.

Too many companies go on the web without a set of goals. This is a recipe for disaster, not only for the company but also for the marketing manager responsible. Without a clear purpose in mind, you can be assured that when management looks at the results in three or six months, they will be disappointed because they have no numbers with which to compare activity. You might be thrilled that 100 people placed orders or 1,000 people visited the site to build brand awareness in your niche market, but if management wonders why there weren't 1,000 sales and 10,000 visitors, then your job is history. It is essential that marketers responsible for the web site create clear, achievable goals early in the process and revise them as events warrant.

SUMMARY

The first step in going online is to create a master plan that sets realistic, definable goals. There are many reasons to go online to fulfill a variety of marketing goals. It is essential that the organization get support and input from as many constituents as possible for the web site to be a success.

CHAPTER 4

Corporate Policies for Web Site Content

The Internet is the hot new prize in corporate America. It seems as if everyone in the company wants to control this new status symbol. Yet the issues for effective use of a web site go well beyond turf battles. Serious decisions need to be made to avoid having the Internet turn into a hot potato.

This chapter discusses policies for decision makers and suggests guidelines for a successful Internet master plan.

MANAGEMENT ISSUES TO CONSIDER BEFORE YOU EVEN GET ONLINE

Issue: Who Owns the Web Site?

Marketing wants it and so does the information technology group. My vote is for marketing. Why? Because marketing knows the overall picture of the company, its products, and its mission. Marketing knows where the company is headed. Technology understands the tools to make the Internet operate; marketing knows how to make it sing. Technology departments that have put up web sites in the first phases of marketing have shown they don't understand how to write marketing copy that sizzles without being offensive, don't understand the fine points of tracking return on investment, and have a propensity to add time-consuming toys to the site even at the risk of burning relationships with prospects who have shown that they don't want to waste time watching pictures slowly unfold on their screens. However, marketing must work with technology to understand the new technological tools and toys, their strengths and limitations. The technology staff should be involved in planning meetings to keep the marketing staff up to date on developments, but marketing must call the shots.

Issue: Who Signs Off on Web Site Issues?

Each bit of information on the web site is an official piece of business correspondence and should be treated as an important part of the company's history. If a site is sloppy, filled with typos, or contains out-dated price information, the company's image will suffer both in pub-lic perception and even in a court of law. It is essential that companies create a policy on who has access to updating information on the Internet and who has sign-off authority. Policies will vary based on a number of factors such as company size, status of the marketing de-partment, or charisma of the founder. It isn't necessary to debate the merits of each factor here as long as a clear line of decision making can be used to approve and post pages. Having such a policy in place ensures that disgruntled employees can't malign the company on its web site and that people who don't have the latest marketing infor-mation cannot post inappropriate, inaccurate, or misleading informa-tion.

Issue: How Are Incoming Messages Handled?

The interactive nature of the Internet demands that each site have an e-mail address so customers can talk to the company. The question is, who handles those messages? The answer depends on what kind of com-pany you run and what the mission of the site is. For some companies, the answer is a product manager; for others, a customer support repre-sentative; for larger companies, the answer might be both. In fact, there might be a need for a mail room supervisor to sort the mail to each de-partment. A simpler approach would be to have separate e-mail ad-dresses for each major department, such as media relations, product information, product support, and investor information.

Issue: How Long Should It Take to Answer E-mail Questions?

Autoresponders can send preprinted information within seconds of re-ceipt of the inquiry, so people are beginning to expect this kind of service, which works well for requests for product literature. However, as it is impossible to provide answers to individual questions in seconds, companies can earn brownie points by sending a message that acknowledges receipt of the initial inquiry and a promise to respond within a certain time frame—usually 24 hours.

A recent survey of Fortune 100 firms revealed that many companies respond to e-mail in a way that could irritate customers. Four companies took at least a week to reply to the simple e-mail query, "What is your corporate headquarter's address?" Hewlett-Packard Co. took 23 days. On the other hand, Texaco, Albertson's, and Costco replied within five minutes. Fewer than 15 percent responded within three hours, according to Chuck Williams, chief executive of Brightware, which conducted the survey. He added that 26 percent of the Fortune 100 companies either did not accept e-mail or made their address very hard to find. Twelve companies, including Intel and Motorola, required users to give detailed personal information before sending a message, Williams said.

Issue: How Do Employees Refer to Themselves Online?

Employees have lives; they participate in online activities such as submitting questions and answers to newsgroups and mailing lists. If they identify themselves as working for your company either in their messages or in their signature files, then their views will reflect upon the company, to which this can present a dangerous situation. For instance, do you want the world to know that an employee is a member of a list that your company finds in questionable taste or represents a controversial political point of view?

Another serious issue is employees' participation in newsgroups when the discussion turns to competitors. Do they present the company point of view, or do they report on the discussion to product managers or executives? How do they introduce themselves to the discussion? For example, let's assume that your product manager for the seat belt division enters a discussion about a car manufacturer's performance and offers her views about the safety of the car. Should she identify herself by company and title, as her opinions could be biased? Or is she a private citizen entering the discussion because she is a car nut? These issues need to be addressed by companies before damage is done.

Issue: Whose Budget Is It?

Who pays for the web site? Marketing? Customer support? Public relations? Advertising? A combination of all? The answer will vary based on the company and the size and marketing mission of its web site. Although it is beyond the scope of this book to suggest a hard and fast rule, companies certainly should decide who will pay for the site.

Issue: Relations with Franchisees

For franchise companies, officers must decide if local franchisees can have their own web site and what statements they can make. The design, look, and feel of the local site must reflect positively on the corporate image.

If the franchise decides to offers a host service to local franchisees, it must declare these issues as well as decide how much space to devote to each business.

The method of handling inquiries and referring leads must also be determined.

Issue: What Is the Job Description for the Web Master?

Businesses must write a job description for the web master. Here is the view of Brian Flanagan, supervisor of Internet projects for Molson, the leading Canadian brewery.

My job description is similar in scope to that of a magazine editor and more.

Depending on what you are trying to accomplish and the scope of your site, the responsibilities of your web master will vary substantially.

The following qualities are what I would look for:

- Ability to handle multiple tasks/brands/initiatives simultaneously.

- Ability to manage an existing budget and plan one for the future.

- Being well versed in HTML and understanding technology well enough to work with system administrators, etc.

- Design sense. This will vary with the amount of HTML you do in house.

- Strong communication skills. Report writing is vital to informing the unwired masses!

- Good interpersonal skills, public speaking (if required for presentations), etc.

- Some media background is helpful if you plan to advertise unconventional media.

All in all, a generalist is what you really need. The more experience that the candidate has, the better. I suspect that a production assistant from the film world would have many of these qualities.

Issue: What Role Does the Web Master Play?

Although web master is the coolest title on anyone's business card these days, no one can agree on the role or responsibilities of such a person. At some companies, "web master" is synonymous with "king." At others, the web master is a propeller head who tinkers with hardware and software either to the relief or consternation of the marketing department.

The role of the web master will change radically in the short term, with power shifting from the technician to the thinker. Although HTML programming skills and knowledge of network servers seemed like a task for rocket scientists a few months ago, new software is making these tasks less daunting, even transparent, to many web masters.

The situation compares with that when I was a news editor for the Gannett Westchester Rockland Newspapers, which were the first in the country to have full-page composition systems on their computers (this was years before PageMaker brought the same results to desktop computers). I was among the first 12 editors in the country to use this system. In the beginning we were high-level editors and treated with great respect for our mastery of layout chores that formerly took tedious minutes to accomplish. However, as the technology spread and more editors learned to use the systems, the tasks became routine. In less than a year, a new job category was created for paginators who worked under news editors and merely followed orders to lay out the papers. They had almost no discretion on placing articles or writing headlines. The same will happen to web masters.

GET INPUT FROM VARIOUS DEPARTMENTS

It is essential for everyone in the company to have a say in the online marketing program. This is a fundamental business step. It is not important that everyone agrees on the final results, but it is important that everyone connected with the project feel that their comments were at the very least listened to. From a management perspective, it is important to listen to as many ideas as possible because good ideas can come from any source. If you follow this step, you might avoid ruffling feathers and even sabotage.

DETERMINE BUDGETS

Deciding which departments will pay for the online marketing plan is a tricky issue whose outcome will vary from company to company. Everyone may seem to want to take responsibility for the project because it is new, exciting, and cool, but no one wants to have the money come from his department's budget.

Although it is possible to construct a web site with a software program, Forrester Research, Inc. (www.forrester.com), for $100, there are additional human resource costs for designing and maintaining it. Forrester Research, Inc. (www.forrester.com), reports the figures shown in Table 4.1 as average costs for going online based on interviews with 50 consumer-oriented web sites. It should be noted that many companies run their sites for a fraction of these figures.

Table 4.1 Estimated costs to build a web site

Type of site	Costs ($)	Time to launch (months)
Promotional	304,000	2
Content	1,312,000	6
Transactional	3,368,000	4

Notes:

A *promotional site* promotes a company's product or service.

A *content site* publishes constantly updated news, weather, or entertainment information.

A *transactional site* lets viewers shop, bank, or get customer service.

Source: Forrester Research, Inc.

OTHER QUESTIONS TO CONSIDER

The marketing staff and Internet team need to consider these questions when creating the online blueprint:

- Do your online marketing materials carry the same image, message, and tone as your other marketing materials? Do they add multimedia, virtual reality, and other forms of interactivity that enhance the shopping experience? The online message should be consistent with the rest of the marketing program.
- What materials are needed to support the message? Sales sheets, customer testimonials, reports from testing labs, awards, and the like can help build credibility.
- Why would customers buy online instead of through another channel? You need to create a reason-to-buy-online statement, considering first if you want them to buy online or to go to the store. Will you damage channel relationships if you sell directly? Should online marketing be a stimulus to generate in-store traffic?
- Who will create the campaign, including message, art, and technology? Does your in-house staff have the expertise to plan a campaign, or should they manage an outside agency that understands the nooks and crannies of online marketing? Should part be conducted in house and part farmed out?
- Will the materials be updated? How often? By whom? Updating a print catalog can be expensive, given production and mailing costs. However, online catalogs can be brought up to date with new prices and products very quickly and usually at a lower cost. Sites should have new information added on a regular basis to attract customers and encourage repeat visits.
- How does the message reinforce the company's mission? Is the message consistent with the company's goals? Does the online marketing campaign tie in with the entire marketing program?

SUMMARY

To avoid problems, corporations must set policies regarding mission, content, and public persona before going online.

PART 2

Online Selling

CHAPTER 5

Creating Your Marketing Message: Writing Interactive Ad Copy

Now that you've figured out what you want your web site to accomplish for your sales and marketing program, you need to create the marketing messages that help achieve those goals.

This chapter will help you understand:

- Differences and similarities between paper and online reading behavior
- Why web sites fail: the need for call-to-action statements.
- How to create the correct tone online.
- How to write effective copy for web sites.
- Other tactics for increasing sales.
- Testimonials.
- Upselling.

DIFFERENCES AND SIMILARITIES BETWEEN PAPER AND ONLINE READING BEHAVIOR ONLINE

Does writing style differ on the web? And should it? There is a camp of researchers who say, yes, most definitely, writing for the screen is different than writing for paper, primarily because of the way people read and process information. With a book or newspaper or printed report, you are reading ink on paper; with the web, you are reading electrical impulses on a screen that is refreshing (or redrawing) those images at a very high speed. This difference could lead to all sorts of problems with your eyes and how they process information. For example, when you read a newspaper, you look down. This causes your eyes to tear, which is a good thing because it lubricates your eyes. When you read a computer screen, you stare straight ahead, which forces your eyes to tear less, leading to dry eyes and an uncomfortable feeling. You don't blink as often either, which makes the condition worse, according to researcher Jakob Nielsen (www.useit.com), who also urges people to write short messages that will fit on computer screens. One screen worth of text should be enough, but you might want to add a bit more—it's okay if people have to scroll down a little bit. If more space is needed, he urges people to add another page and continue the information there. That's because on paper, you can move up or down the page with no ill effects, but when you scroll down a screen, that movement could actually make you nauseous, according to researchers. They advocate keeping the message to the length of a screen, although other interface experts argue that the length could be equal to another screen.

Nielsen suggests that page layout is a very important part of the online reading experience. To make sure your copy is read, use tables, bullets, and lists as well as white space to enhance legibility. People surf the web, which means they scan pages and don't read anything word for word. However, others disagree with this assessment. Have you ever written and edited a 10-page report on your computer? Did your eyes get dry? Did you get nauseous? Did your finger fall off after pressing the PAGE DOWN button too many times? Of course not. So why should your reaction be any different on the Internet? After all, it is still a computer screen, no matter how you look at it.

Meanwhile, publishers on the web have adopted the shorter-is-better philosophy. They are likely to write a long article that has a main point and 10 examples, with each example sitting on its own page. This is called "chunking." They justify this on the grounds that people will be able to read and process the information better. However, critics say this is a just way for the publisher to display and garner revenue from banner ads on each of the 11 additional pages. And as a reader, I feel like I am always pressing the icon to load the next page and waiting as long for the page to display as it takes to read the resulting information! It's like those "Film at 11" commercials that promote the 11 o'clock news: We wait and wait and wait for the exclusive material, but when it finally appears (just before the end of the show), we realize the film wasn't worth waiting for.

Professional communicators with whom I spoke about this issue seemed to favor the longer articles over the chunked ones. The benefits of the long article were that people could read it without clicking to read more, which could be a waste of time, and could easily print out the whole article if it were in one piece. For some marketing materials, the longer pages seem to work better because people can find all the information they need in one spot. Testing different sizes and styles might show you which method works best for your company. Furthermore, although it is probably true that many people surf pages, I believe that when they find information they really want and need to know, then they do read every single word.

Public relations consultant Shel Holtz, author of *PR on the Net* (Amacom, 1998), offers the opinion that people will print out longer articles and read the printed copy. However, he says that companies writing instruction or policy manuals might benefit from chunking because people would be able to find the information they needed quickly without having to wade through many pages or paragraphs of irrelevant material. For those tasks, I fully agree.

Only time and more research will tell whether the researchers are right or wrong. In the meantime, it is important to note their claims because they might have some valid points.

INTERNET WRITING FOLLOWS THE DIRECT-MAIL MODEL

When the web first evolved as a medium for sales and marketing, the digerati (that is, the digital literati) said that the web is a new medium that requires a new way of writing and new mind-set about interacting with readers. That prediction was sort of like the prediction about cable TV. When that medium first sprang forth, people said that the airwaves would be filled with educational and community-based programming; as a result, we would become smarter and more informed about educational and civic matters. After all, everyone could be a broadcaster now! In reality, we have 50 channels of reruns of old TV shows and very little community-based programming or educational channels. Oh well, it sounded good.

The same is true with the web. People thought that it would usher in an age in which we could all engage in multimedia experiences with companies that were truly interactive. Instead, experts seem to agree that the Internet is really a direct-response vehicle in terms of sales and marketing. As a marketer, you try to get people interested in your product by having them visit your web site where they read (yes, reading is still the predominant communications form) your advertising copy; their decision to buy is based on what they read. It is very similar to direct response but offers a few new tools, a much lower cost of doing business and generating leads, and a slightly different writing style.

With all the new technology tools and toys available to jazz up a web site, you'd think that successful marketers would be blinking, wall-papering, and Shockwaving their way to success. However, one of the software industry's leading direct-mail copywriters, Ivan Levison (www.levison.com), has a different point of view for making direct sales on the web. He's one of Silicon Valley's hottest marketers, having written successful pieces for Netscape, Adope, Apple, Hewlett-Packard, and Intel. So he knows how to sell in a crowded, competitive environment, and here's what he has to say on this subject:

> The World Wide Web inverts the way communications really take place. I am a writer of direct mail. I knock on people's doors. I push my way in (with logic, benefits, facts, and emotions) and make them a terrific offer, and I'm in the house. The web changes this. The inversion is that I am sitting in my house (my web site). I am the salesman and I am waiting for people to knock down my door. Rather than an aggressive push into their houses, they have to come to me. It is an interaction process instead of an intrusion process. What flows from this is that you really have to attract. From this you need the creativity to get them to come. Because we have to attract, we have to be creative.

This means marketers must return to the basics, he goes on to say: "You will be more effective if you use proven direct response techniques. That means getting people to order now or get more information now. The idea is that immediate action is called for to break through the inertia. You have to force people to act."

And he notes that good writing will always work: "Marketers must be good writers. Spunky writing. Writing with personality. Writing with humanity is what you need. Retreads of your brochures and press releases ain't gonna make it. For example, write, 'Check out my terrific clients.' Don't write, 'See my clients.' "

Multimedia could be a factor in the future, but right now, but not in the near future, he adds:

> For all the talk of the graphics and so forth, the World Wide Web really is a text-based medium. A very important statistic is that 40 percent of net surfers disable their browsers so they never even see graphics because they do not want to wait. They are voting for text, and we have to acknowledge that this is a text-based medium. Right now, you better write well, or the back button is always lurking and you are one click away from oblivion. In the future, when we have giant bandwidth, then they can have full-motion video and audio. But right now most people are using 14.4 modems and they are sitting around knitting while they wait for graphics files to download.

WHY WEB SITES FAIL: THE NEED FOR CALL-TO-ACTION STATEMENTS

Most web sites fail because they don't have a strong call to action. There is simply no incentive to move people from being curious to being committed.

Advertising in print publications works in part because they use off-the-page selling techniques such as coupons, fill-in forms, and irresistible offers. Web marketers can learn a lot from these examples.

Most sites on the web tell you about products using bland words to describe features and benefits. They ask for the order by weak calls to action such as CLICK HERE, ORDER or ADD TO THE SHOPPING CART, or SELECT. These words don't cut it. "Order" is as weak a sales tool as a retail clerk asking "May I help you?" Sounds good in theory; doesn't work in practice. "Select" also sounds good in theory, but what does it really mean? When I asked that question in one of my seminars, one woman said, "Select the product and buy it," while another person said, "Select this icon to read more information about it." The most common words on the web are confusing readers! That spells trouble.

The best call-to-action I've seen in place of the SELECT button read I GOTTA HAVE IT! This button appeared in a sports site selling a team logo uniform shirt. Sure, it sounds informal, but it appeals to the emotions— and that has a lot do with your ultimate success.

Online marketing consists of a series of requests seeking closure, which means different things to different companies. For companies selling products, such as flowers or books, closure is the sale. For more complex items such as insurance and high-ticket products, closure is a request for a salesperson to call the viewer or to put the viewer on a mailing list. Other companies want to create repeat visits so that they can sell the impressions, or advertising insertions the number of times an ad appears on a web site, to advertisers.

Larry Chase, author of *Essential Business Tactics on the Web* (John Wiley & Sons, 1998), is quite blunt in his criticism. "Most Web sites don't go for any closure," Chase says. No wonder their owners complain their sites are not effective. This deficiency might be a throwback to the fear of turning off prospects with a hard sell, but professional marketers seem to agree that the tools of traditional marketing must be employed on the web site to get action.

Marketers must offer incentives to get people to order. Consider these calls to action:

- Order today and get a free dingbat!
- Order today and get two for the price of one!
- Order today and get a second for a penny!
- Order today and we'll pay the shipping and handling!
- Limited time only!
- Supplies limited!
- Exclusive offer for Internet customers only!

Highlight the cutoff date as well to stimulate the urge to take action: "The offer ends December 31 and will not be extended."

Because people on the web don't have the benefit of dealing with you face to face, you must do everything you can to inspire trust and confidence. Offer "an iron clad, no-questions-asked guarantee," Levison says. "If you can live with a 30-day guarantee, why not consider going out to 45 days or 60 days. It is definitely worth testing. If you have few problems with returns, make the guarantee stronger and stronger."

Starfish Software (www.starfish.com) has some of the best copywriting of any web site. Consider this example: "A power-packed collection of over 25 essential utilities. Your choice: CD or download for only $29.95." Try to find a word that doesn't belong in that sentence or doesn't help the sales process. Notice that every price is preceded by the word *only*. It makes the price sound reasonable; in fact, this technique can make almost any price sound reasonable, even for cars that sell for "only $29,995."

Another good technique is to write enticing copy. How many products have you seen that have skimpy or neutral copywriting? An example would be "20-ounce jar of tomato sauce." That doesn't sound appealing in any manner. You might be saying, "But it is a 20-ounce jar of tomato sauce." There's no life in that kind of writing. Think back to a time when you were in a restaurant and read the menu. French fries weren't written as French fries but as "crispy, golden brown french-fried potatoes made from fresh Idaho potatoes." See the difference? Your mouth waters at the second description.

Try to get the consumer interested in the product by personalizing the copy. Show the benefits of the product, not just the features. Show how each feature will benefit the consumer.

Tell a story about the product. Paint a picture of how the consumer will benefit from using it. Place yourself in the shoes of the consumer. Imagine what he would want to use your product for and what fears he has about ordering the product. Now you're in a better position to sell.

Next, you must build trust for your product and company. If you work for a company with a positive brand image, that should be easy. But many of you don't represent well-known companies, so you must craft your message so that it inspires confidence. This can be accomplished by reducing the risks of buying. Offer consumers "a money-back guarantee, no questions asked." That message can allay their fears of buying from a company they had not heard of until a few minutes ago.

Consumers will wonder why they should buy from you instead of a competitor. You must point out the specific benefits of doing business with your company. You might note that you've been in business for a long time, that the product has won more awards than competitor's, or that the product has certain key features that other products lack.

Finally, you must clearly explain the steps the consumer needs to take to buy your product. This step is especially important on the web site, where consumers can get lost or distracted all too easily. Also, because many people are still uncomfortable ordering via the Internet, you need to spell out how they can order by phone or mail. Wal-Mart even displays teletypewriter (TTY) information for people who are hearing impaired. Talk about attention to customers' needs!

If you follow these steps, you should improve your sales efforts substantially.

CREATING THE CORRECT TONE ONLINE

How should your copy sound? In your face, like a Gen-Xer? Warm and friendly? Cool? You have a lot of choices.

If you audience is Gen-X, you could get by with a greeting such as "What's your problem?" However, that won't cut it with an older (and possibly more affluent) group. So consider carefully what you say, because it could affect people's impression of your brand and image. Several years ago Pepsi, trying to court teenage boys, set up its web site as an outhouse where visitors could "squat" and talk to fellow "squatters." It was, of course, referring to a bodily function that occurs naturally after you eat lots of snack foods and soft drinks. Frankly, I found it to be repulsive! However, I was not in the target audience for the site—but I am in the target market for their soda. Pepsi risked the chance of offending me, and frankly, it did! Don't let this happen to you.

Because the Internet started as a medium for scientists and academicians, selling was first viewed as a horrible activity. So web designers purposely toned down their sales messages. They were as subdued as humanly possible. They assumed that if you told your story, people would make an informed decision and buy from the company that best met their needs. Also around that time, the mantra among web marketers at conventions was, "Is anyone making any money." The answer: Of course not, because they weren't trying to sell in a convincing, professional manner.

While no one wants to come across as a loud, crass used-car sales commercial, there are many other tones you can adopt for your web site that gets your marketing message across in a positive way. Ivan Levison offers this advice: "A lot of Internet gurus are giving out lousy advice about writing web sites. They say you should keep the tone of your web copy flat, sober, and subdued. Forget about writing with personality, they say. Keep your copy bone dry and you can't go wrong. Believe me, if you're selling software on the Internet, the last thing you want to do is sound like your software is the new cure for insomnia. Okay. I agree that you shouldn't sound like you're selling Ginsu knives, but let's get real! The web today is a text-based medium and you've got to quickly capture the reader's interest and attention. In other words, as always, you have to establish a relationship with the reader and therefore write with energy, enthusiasm, and personality."

Look at this "flatter-than-a-pancake Web copy" for Lotus Notes:

Lotus Notes has defined a new breed of software called groupware that enables an organization to realize the full potential of its networks and its people. Now teams can work together in smarter, faster, more productive ways, and get more done with fewer resources.

"What a yawn-inducing waste of time. This isn't soft sell—it's no sell!" Levison says.

For an example of web copy that's alive and kicking, check out the lead to Abacus Concepts's page on StatView V4.5:

A statistics package that's easy to use? You've heard this before ... only to realize there's a five-volume library to read before you can get any work done. Not so with StatView. While other packages make lofty claims about ease of use, StatView really delivers. Since 1985, StatView has been the leading statistics package on the Macintosh. And from the very beginning, StatView's goal has been to provide researchers with a software tool that makes statistical analysis a seamless and sensible process. One that works the way you do.

Levison calls this copy "nice and smooth."

"If you're taking text from your brochures and press releases and using it as filler for your web site, you're going about things all wrong. Visitors to your site are looking for an involving, entertaining experience, and if your writing is dead, they'll hit the back button fast!" he says, adding that your lively presentation must extend to the headline of the copy as well: "You'd never, ever write an ad or a direct mail piece that had a lousy headline or no headline at all, yet you see terrible headlines littering cyberspace everywhere. Don't settle for blah, vanilla headers. Give them a little snap and don't be afraid to have some fun."

One of the stories he wrote focused on the College Board. Instead of just throwing away the headline with the boring two words "College Board," he wrote a spunky little headline and subheadline:

HEADLINE: The road to a college diploma starts on the Internet.
SUBHEAD: The College Board puts valuable educational resources online.
COPY: These days, high school seniors aren't just hanging out at the local mall. You'll find growing numbers of college-bound youngsters, their parents, guidance counselors, educators, and other professionals logging on

to College Board Online. It's the exciting new Web site created by the College Board in partnership with the Educational Testing Service....

For the Chicago Board of Trade story, Levison submitted the following copy:

HEADLINE: Good news for bulls and bears.
SUBHEAD: The Chicago Board of Trade helps information seekers cash in.
COPY: At the Chicago Board of Trade (CBOT), information is the most important commodity. Fortunes can be made or lost depending on what you know, when you know it, and how you limit risk. No wonder tens of thousands of people from more than 50 countries visit the CBOT's innovative Web site every day, with more logging on all the time....

"Spirit, energy, personality, warmth, friendliness, and honesty have always worked in print and they will continue to work in cyberspace!" Levison says.

TACTICS AND TECHNIQUES FOR CREATING EFFECTIVE WEB SITES

When you create your page, consider these tactical questions to improve the copy:

1. **Who are you?** Trust is an important factor on the Net. After all, with the exception of Fortune 500 companies, most businesses are unknown entities to online customers. You'd be surprised how many web sites don't list the name of the company, what it does, and how it is unique. Most list this information somewhere on the site but not on the front page. Why force people to find out who you are?
2. **What's in it for them?** Many sites don't tell viewers how they will benefit from visiting the site. Here's a hint: People will stay because you save them time, save them money, inform them, or entertain them.
3. **Is the art appropriate?** Everyone knows not to put large graphics on the site, because they take tooooooo long to display. However, many sites have art for art's sake, even though it has nothing to do with what the company does. I'm not talking

about cute buttons and navigation bars but three-by-five-inch pictures of people sitting behind computers. You can have a funky-looking site by offering a colored background, which takes absolutely no time to load.

4. **How's your grammar?** Typos can make your page look amateurish, yet many pages have grammatical errors, bad punctuation, and erratic capitalization. Check and then double-check. This is a very common problem, even with sites that are magnificent marketing tools. One high-priced consultant actually sent me an e-mail filled with typos. He must have been half-asleep and didn't bother to turn on the spell checker! He looked like an idiot!

5. **Is too much searching required?** One particularly bad site forced users to go from a press release to the site instead of back to the press release menu. Give users the option of where to go. Put a full slate of navigation buttons at the bottom of the page.

6. **Who you gonna call?** Put contact information at the bottom of each page. You never know which page people will print. When they need to contact you, they'll have the information at their fingertips, not at the end of an Internet connection.

7. **Who** specifically **are you gonna call?** The prospect picks up the phone—and winds up in voice mail jail. Tell them whom they should ask for. It could be Jane Smith, director of sales, or Operator 115.

8. **Make sure the important information is at the top of the page.** Don't bury it. If they choose not to scroll, they will get the most important message.

TESTIMONIALS

Testimonials can help you sell products. On the web, no one really knows who you are or how credible you are. Testimonials can bridge the gap. However, a simple "I like the product" will not win many new sales. For testimonials to be effective they must have several elements, and you must employ several strategies to get them.

- **Full names and titles.** No one believes a name like "George from Missouri." That looks phony and probably is because there is no accountability. If people won't give you their full names, don't use the testimonial. Even worse are quotes with no name attached at all. Does anyone believe that an actual person really said them?

- **Aggressively pursue testimonials.** People probably won't write testimonials unless you ask them.
- **Get testimonials for different product features and benefits.** You never know which topic will make the sale. If you have testimonials that praise different features, you have covered all the bases. Don't have all the testimonials sound alike.
- **Have a wide range of professions represented.** People tend to believe people who are like them. So if they read a testimonial from a colleague at a similar company, you have gained more credibility.
- **Let customers write testimonials in their own words.** You might suggest topics, areas, and features if they don't have a clue as to what to write, but let them write the text. That way, each testimonial will have its own flavor and will sound different. If you write them all, they will sound fake.
- **Check e-mail messages for unsolicited testimonials.** Have your customer support representatives, salespeople, and others who read e-mail check for positive comments from customers. You will get them (I certainly do!). Write them back and ask permission to use their quotes. Chances are that they'll be flattered and will grant you permission.
- **Edit the testimonial for content.** It is okay to use long testimonials. However, if the testimonial rambles, cut the extraneous material. No one will miss it.

You can post testimonials on your web site and include them in your e-mail newsletters as well as your print material. Whenever I get a testimonial from a reader via e-mail, I ask if I can use the quote on my book page on Amazon.com! I would never think of asking them to go the extra step and post the message there. I can do it faster. They are thrilled at the idea of being published online.

UPSELLING

Upselling is the marketing function of prompting people who are buying one product to buy additional products at the time of the sale. When the web began to be used as selling tool, merchants were afraid they would lose revenue because they wouldn't be able to upsell customers as they do in their stores. Think back to the last time you bought a pair of shoes. The salesperson probably asked if you would like to buy a pair of shoetrees or shoe polish as well. On the web, businesses feared that people would buy the one item they wanted and leave without buying anything else. This fear is completely unfounded—at least in the view of companies that have studied this issue and have made it easy for customers to buy more products.

To increase sales, smart companies suggest add-on purchases. Music Boulevard's parent N2K found that personal recommendations prompted people to buy 10 to 30 percent of the time, compared with the 2 to 4 percent average for generic information. When consumers search for work by a particular recording artist, its web site shows the names of other artists who might appeal to the buyer. The prospect can view the other artist's works, listen to sound clips, read reviews from professional writers and other music fans, and then may be decide to buy the CD.

Amazon.com (www.amazon.com) recommends books on each page under the headline "Customers who bought this book also bought: ..." and then lists titles of similar books. Amazon.com continues the process by also suggesting books in this subject category.

In retail outlets, the box is the silent salesperson. Many stores don't have enough salespeople—or knowledgeable salespeople who can answer questions—so manufacturers print lots of descriptive information on the box for consumers to learn about the product's features and benefits. On the Internet, there is no box, so manufacturers need to print long, detailed descriptions and offer pictures for consumers to view. Don't force the consumer to guess what the product will do. They will get it wrong every time!

Here are several techniques to improve your upsell:

1. **Recommend products.** When a customer orders a product, post a message recommending other products. A clothing site might recommend an umbrella to go with your new windbreaker.
2. **Entice people with special pricing.** Consider offers like "Because you just bought this rain parka, you are eligible to buy a $29.95 umbrella for only $9.95."
3. **Add special incentives.** Offer free gift wrapping.
4. **Offer special shipping options.** Chances are you receive a deep discount on overnight shipping charges. Consider offering

low-cost shipping. The customer thinks they are getting a $14 delivery service for only $6.95—and you pay only $3.95!

5. **Show pictures of the product.** Auction sites tell their sellers that a picture of a product will lead to more bids and higher sales prices.

6. **Offer to let the buyer hear audio of the CDs or an interview with the book author or watch a video showing the product in use.**

7. **Reduce the risk.** Offer guarantees and state your return policies.

SUMMARY

Writing for the web is both similar and different than writing for print. However, if you want to sell on the web, you need to be engaging, get attention, and inspire the reader to take action. In that way, writing for the web is very similar to writing for print.

CHAPTER 6

Designing Your Web Site to Increase Sales

As an online marketer, you must design web sites to accomplish three things: attract visitors, hold their attention, and gain closure (completing the online sale or fulfilling a request for information, subscription, or exchange of data). Good design is essential for presenting sales information in a comfortable, convenient manner on the Internet. Because the online services are consumer-driven media, it is essential that information be used as the main persuasive and educational tool and thus that it be easy to find and absorb. Good design will build sales; bad design can ruin your credibility.

In this chapter, you will learn:

- How to think like a marketer.
- How to think like a consumer.
- How to create design goals and objectives.
- How to turn goals into reality.
- How to create a web site from a marketing point of view.
- Why information marketers need to put on a web site.
- Guidelines for designing effective web sites.
- Tips for designing web sites.
- Tours of successful marketing sites.
- How to hire a designer.

THINKING LIKE A MARKETER

Imagine you inherit a large, undeveloped tract of land on the beach. This land is beautiful. Everywhere you look is a gorgeous view. Look to the west and you see the ocean. Look to the east and you see the hills. You want to build a house that incorporates the best of both worlds, so you hire an architect to design the house. She hears your wishes, sees the property, and designs a masterpiece on this blank canvas of land.

After six months, she is finished and you go to inspect the house. It *is* a masterpiece! The house is round and uses floor-to-ceiling windows to take in the view. In fact, the central focal point of the house is a winding, spiral staircase to the second floor. From that staircase, you can see the beach and climb a few stairs and see the mountains.

There's only one problem. You're in a wheelchair and can't climb stairs.

That's the story with many web sites that are designed solely by artists and techies. They know all the tools they can use, but they don't have any conception of the customer's needs! If customers have slow modems, large art files on web sites will frustrate them rather than add to the enjoyment of their experience.

It is important to use the skills, experience, and knowledge of the techies and artists, but it is the marketing department that must control the web site. For marketing is whole reason you are online—whether to sell products, provide customer support, or enhance the company's image. Techies don't know how to write or think like a marketer. They probably aren't even aware of new products, price changes, or other communication patterns that the company wants to unveil to the world. Putting them in charge of the web site is a mistake. The web is littered with web sites created by techies that are technological marvels but don't add a penny to the company's bottom line because they don't get the message out! So use the techies and artists when appropriate. Let them translate your messages and themes onto the web. They will know of new tools that will enhance the page, capture user demographics, and allow for secure e-commerce solutions. The artists will know the latest design interfaces, hot colors, and visual trends, which are valuable contributions to the web site—but don't put them in charge.

THINKING LIKE A CONSUMER

The first and most important rule of designing a web site is to think like the target customers. If you build a site that meets their needs, then you'll be able to build your own house on the beach.

Thinking like a consumer should be easy for most of us because we are consumers. We buy things in stores and, hopefully, on the Internet.

We could just as easily use our own experience in shopping on the web to uncover the weaknesses and confusion on web sites.

Customers are being frustrated by stores on the Internet, according to Zona Research, Inc. (www.zonaresearch.com). Nearly 30 percent of Internet shoppers said they have trouble finding products and services. More important, they gave up looking! Instead, they decided to buy from an online competitor or from a store on Main Street.

Bad search tools were cited as the main problem. If people misspelled words, the search engine would turn up nothing. The engine should be smart enough to accept misspellings, or the site designer should be smart enough to code the pages so that misspellings are included. Before you dismiss these errant typists as illiterate, consider that their money is as green as anyone else's. Do you want to lose a sale to a typo?

Another problem is that search engines are not intuitive. If people typed "Do you have a green sweater?" the search engine said, "No." It couldn't reply, "No, but we have it in teal."

Zona Research's study shows that when people gave up shopping at a site, 26 percent bought from another online store, 22 percent bought from a catalog, 12 percent bought at a traditional store, and 5 percent decided not to buy. The report also found that 54 percent of respondents have given up looking for a product because of difficulty from one to five times, while 8 percent gave up six or more times.

Consumers want to be able to find out what you do, how they will benefit, and where to buy it or where to contact someone who can give them more information. One of the first steps you should take in creating the site is to survey your customers and find out specifically what they want.

Kristin Zhivago, editor of *Marketing Technology,* offers this advice:

If your web site is well-designed, customers can quickly get answers to their questions. While the need is still fresh in their minds, they will be transformed from someone with a problem to someone who has identified, and wants to purchase, a particular solution. This compresses the buying cycle and will have a profound effect on marketing practices. Your Web site will be a successful marketing tool only if you organize it to conveniently answer all of the customer's questions. That may seem obvious, but considering how poorly standard marketing materials have provided answers in the past, we are not expecting Web sites to be any better. Organizing the presentation of the information so that it matches the customer's question sequence is particularly important with online marketing because it is an interactive medium. It puts the customer in the driver's seat. The last thing you want to do is make your customer drive all over cyberspace waiting for downloads, and getting lost, locked out, and ticked off.

Call customers and ask them about their buying process. Tell them you are designing your web site and you want it to make sense to them. Listen carefully. By the tenth phone call, the proper structure should be obvious. There will be clear, identifiable patterns. Use this information to design your web site, and you will be rewarded with sales from grateful customers. You will have removed the frustration and confusion from their buying process.... Talking to customers will also make you confident that you are doing the right thing. I guarantee that the customer's view of the buying process is different from your company's view of the selling process. You will have to fight for the customer's interests in internal meetings. If you do not know your customers well, you will not be able to make the logical, fact-based arguments needed to win. The company-centric view will prevail and customers will be frustrated when they visit your site. If you have spoken with customers you will not only know what to do but you will be able to use real-world examples when the arguments start. Anecdotes have an incredibly powerful effect on coworkers, many of whom are holding tightly to cherished but incorrect ideas about who the customers are and how the customers buy.

CREATING DESIGN GOALS AND OBJECTIVES

Another essential step in the planning process is to create your design objectives and philosophy. Here is an example from Ray Poshadlo, owner of Softwrights (www.softwrights.com), a software publisher: "The main purpose of [our] site is to provide enough information for you to see if our products meet your needs and to provide help for existing users of Softwrights's products. Useful information is the focus," he says, "not time/screen-wasting fluff like large animations and large graphics."

After establishing his design philosophy, he then prioritized the goals for the site:

1. Useful, practical, and comprehensive information.
2. Easy to navigate; no more than two levels of menu nesting.
3. Fast loading; don't waste your time with unnecessary waiting.
4. Readable by most browsers old and new; avoid unnecessary new hypertext markup language (HTML) tags.
5. Attractive, easy-to-read layouts; small, fast-loading, eye-catching graphics on the home page.

"Web sites are a mixed blessing. They are great ways to distribute information widely and inexpensively. But they have several layout limitations compared to paper and different browsers support or don't support different features," Poshadlo points out. "Graphics and animations look good, but they take a long time to download. Softwrights decided to keep graphics and animations to a minimum to avoid frustrating delays."

Here are his tips to speed up display time:

- The Height and Width Netscape attributes for images were used. Many browsers ignore these. Because he did not scale these attributes, the graphics look exactly the same in all browsers.
- The Font Color Explorer extension was used on some pages to attract attention.
- The <EM> and <STRONG> logical style tags were used instead of <B> and <I> physical styles tags. This is in the spirit of the Standard Generalized Markup Language (SGML) philosophy of leaving display details to the browser.
- Standard 640-by-480 video graphics adapter (VGA) screen resolution was used as the lowest common denominator because it's the most common video mode in the PC world.
- Tables are great. But millions of browsers don't support them, especially if there are several columns; information gets jumbled out of sequence. Besides, more than a couple of columns cannot be read on most screens without scrolling around.

You can use these steps and tips when designing your site as well.

TURNING YOUR GOALS INTO REALITY

Now that you have your goals in mind and have created the marketing materials to reach those goals, it is time to design a web site that presents those ideas to the public.

Designing a web site is a relatively straightforward process, but how one goes about executing that process is what separates the great sites from the poor sites:

- Design an attractive look that inspires trust and confidence in the company. As I've said before, this look should mirror the colors, typefaces, and logos of the company's print materials so as to integrate the web into the traditional marketing program and help to build brand identity. It is important to create a design that looks good (this sounds obvious). If your site looks good, you will have credibility and will be able to compete on an even footing with larger companies. If your site lacks high production qualities or uses an old-fashioned design, people will subconsciously devalue your site and your company.

- Create a flowchart or site map like the one shown in Figure 6.1. This is a blueprint of the site so that designers will know where to link pages and users will know where to find information quickly. In fact, you should create a flowchart on paper as you begin to design the site and decide which elements should be included.
- Convert the files into an HTML program. Learning to write this code is beyond the scope of this book. For a good reference and tutorial, read any book written by Laura LeMay. Several software programs can convert files or let you paste text into an attractive template.

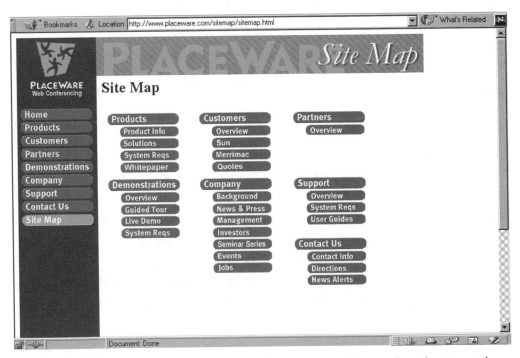

Figure 6.1 This site map shows readers what topics are discussed on the site and includes links to those pages for easy access. (© 1999, Placeware, Inc.)

- Create, rent, or buy the tools for the back-end, office operations infrastructure for e-commerce, database, and security.
- Load the site onto a computer server that is connected to the Internet. Once that step is completed, your site is ready to be viewed by anyone else in the world who has a computer connected to the Internet!

INFORMATION THAT MARKETERS NEED TO PUT ON A WEB SITE

Behind all the cool graphics and clever writing of a web site lies a basic business strategy designed to sell. Good sites have a mission to provide information in an entertaining and interactive manner that helps not only to make a sale but also to create a customer for life.

The opening page (also called the *front page* or *home page*) greets the customer and serves as a table of contents or directory to your store. This opening page is actually longer than a computer screen—perhaps much longer. The advantage is that you can display a great deal of information in a precise location. It is important for you to think in terms of screenfuls of content so that navigation is easy for consumers. Small companies with one product might have only one long page. Companies with more content can use additional pages called *subpages*. The home page and subpages together form the web site.

Although the marketing goal for each web site is different, most companies will find they will need the information shown on Lawrence Ragan Communications's web site (Figure 6.2).

- **Name of company.** Make the corporate identity clear on the home page or first screen. There should be no mystery about who's sponsoring the page. However, it should not be larger than four square inches; logos this size, which are typically graphics based, will take up too much download time, and excessive download time will cause viewers to hit the stop button and skip to another site, says Daniel Sklaire of Systems Research Corporation (www.webanalytics.com).
- **Logo.**
- **Positioning statement.** This explains what your business does, identifies the market it serves, and tells how customers will benefit. A second statement can explain how the company differs

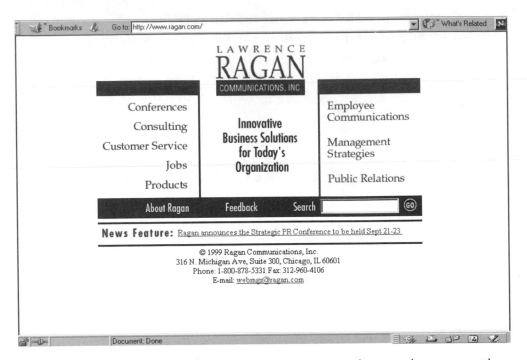

Figure 6.2 Ragan Communications (www.ragan.com) makes searching easy with clear links to content and a search engine to find information quickly on its large site of information for corporate communicators. (© 1999, Lawrence Ragan Communications)

from its competitors. These two statements should be printed in full on the home page. Some companies use their slogan instead.

- **Headlines of the information and products on your site.** These headlines link to descriptions and pictures of products that reside on their own page or set of pages.
- **Notice of special events.** Entice people to visit your store and explore its contents.
- **Sales.** This feature tells people at a glance what the hot buys are this week. This information should be printed on the home page.
- **What's new.** Let viewers know what information has been added or changed. This information should be printed on the home page as headlines and linked to related pages.
- **Message from the president.** This can show the true character and nature of the company, giving it a personal, as opposed to impersonal, feel. This line links to the actual message.

- **Press releases.** These give people a depth of understanding of the company and its products that might not be contained in sales materials. This line links to the press releases section.
- **Sales materials.** These give broad and deep information about the products or services. This line links to the sales materials section.
- **Catalogs.** Show your customers the full range of products in your store, with descriptions, prices, and ordering information as well as transaction capabilities. This line links to the catalog section.
- **Registration form.** Ask people to identify themselves so that you can build a relationship with them. Forms should ask only a few questions, such as name, street address, e-mail address, and the scantiest of demographic material—the more questions you ask, the fewer people will respond. Remember that people value their privacy and might not want to reveal their identities. If you require that people identify themselves before you allow them into your store, they might walk on by. This line links to the registration form.
- **Testimonials.** Reading satisfied customer's statements about your products and services can help convince prospects to invest in your company. This line links to the testimonials section.
- **Employment notices.** These describe jobs that are available at your company. This line links to the employment section.
- **E-mail response form.** Make sure that people can contact you directly and create a one-to-one relationship with you that can last for life.
- **Links to other sites.** List information sources on the Internet that your readers will find interesting. These links tie to a page that contains the links out to other web sites.
- **Coupons.** People can use these when they visit your store on Main Street. This line links to the coupon page, which contains information about offers and can include a registration form that will allow you to learn more about the customer.
- **Fun stuff.** A well-rounded site can include diversions such as contests, trivia, cartoons, and jokes to entertain customers.
- **Registration or log-on information.** Companies that restrict access to the site for privacy or other reasons

(such as banks, stock brokers, etc., who allow you to conduct financial transactions) will post a sign-in box on the front page.

- **Contact information.** Your company's physical address, telephone, and fax numbers should be included on all pages because people print out individual pages, not just the front page. Customers will include your product sheets in their report alongside competing products. It is handy to have the contact data readily available so that they can call to place the order. If they don't know how to get in touch with you easily, you might lose the order.

- **Map.** Show your company's location on a street map along with directions. This can be a link to Mapquest (www.mapquest.com), a free service that allows customers to receive a detailed, turn-by-turn set of directions from their location to your place of business.

- **Date of last update.** People will want to know if anything has changed since their last visit. This item, which was a standard on earlier web sites, seems to be falling out of favor. This seems to be a no-win situation: Unless the page is updated every day, it will appear out of date. And many sites simply don't need to update the page every day because nothing has changed! A service provider, like an accountant or lawyer, doesn't need to update the page every day if the purpose is to be an online brochure that informs people of its list of services and qualifications. Yet the page would give the impression of being out of date if the date listed was six months old. You simply can't win with this item. It might be better not to use it unless there is a valid reason to do so.

- **Search engine.** Allow your customers to find information quickly. The search engine searches your site only; it does not search the entire Internet. In the old days, the design philosophy was that every piece of information should be found within three clicks (this was known as the "three-click rule"). Pages were designed on the menu system, as each page led to other menus or information. As well intentioned as this was, it was slow and clumsy. Search engines allow customers to find information with as few clicks as possible. Just as important, they'll see if something is *not* on the site, which save them a lot of time and frustration.

- **Awards.** If your site wins an award from a recognizable service, such as Cool Site of the Day, you might want to display the award icon on your page. However, be aware that this picture will add to the time needed to load your page displays. I've seen pages with so many awards that loading the pages seems to take forever.
- **Icons from media that have written about your company** (see Figure 6.3). This helps establish credibility. Be sure to get permission to use the logos.
- **Icons from other companies.** Some sites add icons from companies like Netscape, Microsoft, and Yahoo! so that people who visit your site can then leave and go visit their sites. This is dumb! Ask yourself if these icons help you more than they help the other company (these are, after all, unpaid advertisements). The only time you should have an icon for another company is if the company paid you to place their icon there or if you want

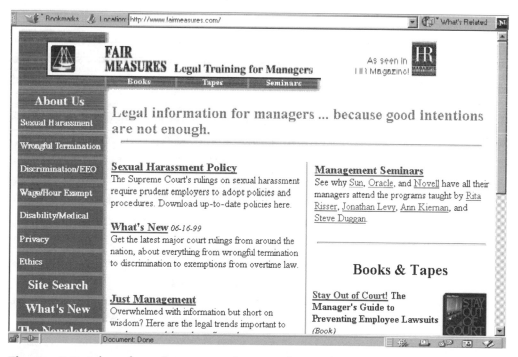

Figure 6.3 A logo from the news media gives the Fair Measures site added credibility. (© 1999, Fair Measures, Inc.)

your customers to download an application software program such as Real Audio so that they can see your audio and hear video. When a link serves a vital marketing function, it should be used. Otherwise, cut it.

- **Copyright notice.** Protects your work!

Remember that links should be set up to take readers from these headlines or condensed bits of information on the home page to the page (or pages) that treat them fully, much in the same manner as the table of contents in a magazine will show the reader on which page she'll find the full story.

STRATEGIES TO DIRECT THE USER'S EXPERIENCE ON YOUR SITE

If you post all of the elements I've just listed on your front page, you will give your customers complete control over their experience with your web site. Most web sites do just that. After all, one of the key differences between the Internet and traditional media is that users can see whatever they want, whenever they want.

However, you might consider directing prospects through the site so that you can educate them in a step-by-step fashion. If you sell a complicated product or want to make sure that they see all your points, this could be a useful strategy.

I consulted with a doctor about his web site. Technically, it was fine. It had all the elements described in the previous section, but, in his case, this amounted to information overload. The doctor wanted to increase the number of patients who wanted a certain type of surgery performed. I realized the consumer had two vital questions: Should I choose this doctor, and is the surgery procedure the best for me? I suggested that he redesign the site so that prospects had only two choices from the home page: about the doctor and about the procedure (no one likes the word *surgery*). All the other marketing and background elements were contained beneath these two elements. This tactic allowed prospects to focus their searches and find the answers to their questions.

Another client asked me to review her site. Her goal was to build a database of prospects. The first element she put on the page was an icon asking people to register. In fact, the front page contained three areas that asked people to register, and if they didn't register, they couldn't see any pages on the site! This was a bad strategy because people aren't going to tell you anything about themselves until and unless you give them a valid reason to share this information. After all, when you go online, is your primary motivation to fill out forms, telling people where you live and how much money you make? I think not! Your prospects feel the same way. I suggested that her company offer some material for free and then ask readers to register so they can delve deeper into the site. They did so and registrations increased.

This case study shows that you really need to consider the ultimate goal of your site and build the site around your expected outcomes. There is no right or wrong answer here. It all comes down to what your goals are and what is the best way to achieve them. But remember—your goals must coincide with the user's goals or you won't succeed.

GUIDELINES FOR DESIGNING EFFECTIVE WEB SITES

A well-designed web site is essential to attracting customers and guiding them to intelligent buying decisions. Designing sites is partly subjective and partly formula. Let's look at some key areas

Content

Time and space are two critical concerns for marketers—usually. When they buy advertising time on a TV show, it is very expensive. When they plan to print a brochure, space is expensive. When they plan a newspaper ad, every word and picture is at a premium. These elements don't matter on the web because space is unlimited.

Therefore, when creating the content for a web site, you (the marketer) must ask different questions:

- What material will you place online? Your entire catalog or just the highlights? If your Internet service provider charges the going rate—which is inexpensive and getting more competitive all the time—you can afford to place every nut and screw in your inventory online. This is a boon to companies with large inventories, such as bookstores, music stores, and technical component suppliers. By using a search engine or other good design elements on your site, people will be able to easily find the one item they are looking for

- How much information will you use to describe the material—a single line, a paragraph, or a full page? Again, with unlimited space you can provide customers with the answers to every question they could think of. You can have both short descriptions written for consumers and pages of technical specifications and schematic drawings for engineers. For example, a stereo speaker could be described with an appeal to emotion, as in "Impress your friends with the best sound available." It can also be sold to the audiophile who demands to know the technical specifications of each component.

- How many pictures will you include? Pictures present a professional image and add to the wow factor. However, they should be small pictures, as large ones take too long to appear on the screen—a turnoff. If you use pictures, create large and small versions of the same pictures and display only the small one. Let the reader know he can see the larger picture if he wants to by clicking on the small one. Pictures saved in GIF and JPEG file formats load faster than those in other formats. People become frustrated if your site sends a large file because it is slow to appear on the screen. Part of this reaction can be circumvented if you let people know how large the file is and how long it will take to transmit. That way they can decide to retrieve it and wait more patiently for it to appear.

- Will sound or video enhance the shopping experience? For an entertainment company or a training company, a video might do a better job of selling than any brochure because the customer can see a clip from a movie or a training session in action.

Interface

An *interface* is the visual display of digital information. It is the way marketers communicate with consumers through the computer. If the interface is fun, exciting, and pretty and if it leads the consumer to a highly interactive experience, the interface is a success. If consumers are confused, the interface is a failure.

A good user interface is critical to the success of a web site, as it is to all forms of sales communications on all the commercial online systems.

Bad interfaces, like bad clothes that stand out and hide the person, detract from the message. Good interfaces, like good clothes that don't draw attention to themselves and don't take attention away from the person, don't distract the reader from the message. A badly designed interface reminds people that they are dealing with a machine. A well-designed interface is so unobtrusive that people can concentrate on the information instead of the computer.

Fortunately, there are keys to good interface design. The best way to understand good design is to browse through web sites and play with them. Make notes on what you like and what you don't. The first generation of web sites used text only with a gray background. The next generation added cartoonlike images or photos. Then designers began using white or colored backgrounds to avoid the ugly gray ones. They are also designing pages to look like magazine pages, including white space near the borders of the screen like a printed page. Another nice look is having text wrap around art. Look at *The New York Times* (www.nytimes.com) for ideas for creating attractive pages. A widespread trend had been to use lots of pictures on the front page, but that trend is disappearing as companies realize that large pictures slow down the page's transmission. If people don't want to wait for the page to load, they will go elsewhere. Many company web sites that used such enormous image maps or pictures have switched to pages that are mostly text or contain only a few images that have been optimized to load quickly. The current trend in 1999 is to create colorful pages full of short text blocks or headlines that link to other pages. Look at Excite (www.excite.com), CNET (www.cnet.com), and PhotoHighway.com (www.photohighway.com) for good ideas.

People hate to wait for pages to display. Some wags have dubbed the Internet "The World Wide Wait." According to research by Jakob Neilsen (www.useit.com), people will wait only 15 seconds for a page to load. If the page doesn't appear, the user will disappear and go to another web site. You might think your company and products are great and that people should wait to see them—but they don't, and they're the ones with the money! You can get a free report on how fast your pages load from Web Site Garage (www.websitegarage.com). The site features a table that presents the load times for different modem speeds so that you can determine if your pages are acceptable from a speed point of view.

An area of concern is the use of colors and backgrounds. A great many web sites sport unattractive and hard-to-read black backgrounds with hideous colored fonts (like purple or brown). Not only are these sites ugly, but they are also nearly impossible to read—a clear case of people who don't know how to market taking control of the site. Another faux pas is the use of busy background images or watermarks, which make pages hard to read. This is an example of people using tools just because they are available, even though the effect is counterproductive. Just think: If backgrounds and dense watermarks were effective presentation tools, don't you think the print world would have adopted them? There is a reason you don't see these devices in magazines and newspapers—they don't work!

Frames are used to display information in three windows on a screen. Although the layouts can vary, the top frame is usually horizontal, and the bottom two frames are adjoining squares. The top frame is used for the corporate logo, the left frame includes a table of contents or directory, and the right frame holds the data. Some designers feel this is an efficient way to display data while keeping the company logo fresh in people's faces; others feel that the frames take up too much space on the screen and don't allow for enough data to be seen at any one time. The frames also take a long time to load and therefore should be avoided if your audience has slow modems or bad phone service. In addition, search engines have problems indexing pages created with frames.

An alternative to frames are tables, which present information in two- or three-column formats. Tables are faster to load than frames and can actually display more information because they don't require the borders used by frames.

If your site requires users to type in a username and password to log on, consider placing that information on the front page. One of my pet peeves is that my online broker forces me to wait for their front page to load. I must then click on a button saying LOG ON. Then I must wait for another page to load. That page actually contains the log-on box. What a waste of time!

Another problem can occur with forms. If users fill out a form incorrectly or leave a field blank, the site will tell them there is an error that must be corrected to get to the next step. The site should redisplay the form as far as the user filled it out, but some sites erase the form, so the user must type everything again! This can lead to frustration, and the user may leave the site without having closed the transaction.

Icons

Because there are no instruction manuals on how to use each web site, icons should be used to help readers find information quickly.

"People recognize symbols rather than text," says Bill Linder of Columbus PBX, a one-stop information resource center that creates web sites in Columbus, Indiana. "Imagine seeing a road sign from 100 feet away. You notice its size, shape, and color. Is it a stop sign or perhaps a yield sign? You begin to act on that information. As you get closer to the sign, you see the word STOP but you've already begun to apply the brakes.

"To complete the analogy, think of the international symbol set. Even without a word, you know that a picture icon means, for example, skiing or no parking. The same is true with icons on the web. Customers understand their meanings faster and make decisions faster with pictures."

You don't have to design a page from scratch. Numerous icons, buttons, and backgrounds are available as shareware, which means you can test-drive the material and pay for it if you decide to continue using it.

"Iconize the most important subjects on the page, thereby prioritizing them for the reader," says Dan Sklaire, president of SRC, Inc., a research company. "The largest icon should bring the viewer to the content that the sponsor feels is most important. Keep icons simple and not too large, again reducing download time."

Menus and Search Engines

Menus are an easy way for customers to find information. Successful strategies include creating an overall menu that leads customers to deeper levels of information. Each menu should also have information on ordering so that once the customer is convinced she should buy the product, she can do so without having to wade through additional materials.

When you design product menus, put your best products at the beginning or the consumer might never see them. Remember that a page can be longer than a screen and that anything below the bottom of the screen will not be seen unless the reader scrolls to it or hits a link. The best way to do this is to create a menu that has a short description of each major product area. For example, an appliance store could have menu listings for irons, toasters, blenders, coffee makers, and can openers. Each item could lead to another menu that lists the brand names of each of five models. If the customer selected blenders, he would see listings for five different models, complete with pictures of the units and a two-line description that included the price. If he wanted more information, another menu could reveal such information as operating instructions, recipes, and comparisons to other models.

Each menu should have information on how to purchase the item. This can be offered as an online ordering form that can be completed and returned to the store either through e-mail, fax, or snail mail (e.g., "To order, call 1-800-555-1212 or e-mail to orderform@estore .com").

Menus should also give users a link to return to the top of the page.

As web sites get bigger and contain more information about more products and services, it is important to create navigation tools to make finding data fast. You can use a site map, which looks like the tree structure used in outlining. Another way to find information on really large sites is to use a search engine. Users type the term they want to find, and the search tool finds all references on the site.

Test-Drive for Usability

To ensure usability, the web site should be tested before it goes online. A test-drive will show you whether the typical user understands the icons and can follow the scheme of things. For the best results, let a nontechnical person try to use the system. Be sure to test the site with different browsers to ensure it displays properly because each browser displays text, color, and spacing slightly differently. You must test your site against the leading programs to ensure that the browser doesn't frustrate your artist's scheme by pushing text off the screen, putting table columns out of alignment, bumping pieces of artwork into one another, or causing other unforeseen problems. As different browsers print text in different colors, be sure not to confuse your readers by saying "If you click on the green text, you'll see the related information." The text might actually appear in red on some browsers. Instead, refer to highlighted—italicized—text.

TIPS FOR DESIGNING WEB SITES

"You'll be amazed at how many sites confound rather than clarify. They force you to search for content subordinated by the bells and whistles of gratuitous animations and wall-to-wall competing text. These all-out assaults on the sensibilities can drive traffic from a site as fast as it comes in," says information architecture consultant Dr. Ron Sheer (www.ronsheer.com) of Los Angeles. He has studied the way people use the web and has compiled a list of pointers for web designers. "These tried and true methodologies will help you design for clarity, not chaos."

- Direct the reader's eye. In the West, we read from left to right and from top of the page to the bottom. This fundamental axis dominates most design decisions in print and on the web. For example, printed page layout makes the top of the page the most dominant location, but on web pages the upper page is especially important, because the top six inches of the screen is all that is visible on a typical computer monitor.
- Assume the user easily gets lost. It takes considerable effort to mentally map a site while exploring it. Users can quickly lose a sense of where they are and where they've been. A system of consistent and clear navigational markers can help users quickly recover their bearings.
- Assume the user is a web novice. Although the population of web users is growing, a large percentage will continue to be just that—novices. Their web skills will be few, and much that expert users take for granted is counterintuitive to the newcomer.
- Anticipate the most likely user interactions. Make a list of all the tasks that a user can perform at your site. Remember that users don't only search for information; they also want to compare facts and make judgments. Remove obstacles that make any of these tasks less than utterly easy. Make the most frequent tasks easiest.
- Avoid using the same site for multiple audiences. As this is not always possible, be aware that each set of users has a different set of tasks and wants to accomplish them without confusion or hesitation. Structural boundaries should prevent users from crossing over to other areas.

- Be flat if you can. A comprehensive array of content choices at the highest level of organization (e.g., the home page) gets users where they want to go with few clicks. Web sites seem to run into trouble when their organization is deeply hierarchical or vertical. Requiring users to drill down invites navigational problems.
- Build in shortcuts for expert users. For users familiar with your site or with web site logic in general, provide options that let them move around with a minimum of steps.
- Respect web conventions. Unless you have an inarguably good reason for doing so, don't build a site that runs counter to what web users tend to expect. For example, use the standard colors for links.
- Don't waste clicks. Be mindful of the tedium of separating start points and destinations with multiple pages.
- Make each page identifiable out of context. Thanks to the technology of the web, users can arrive at any of your pages directly from some other site. You want them to immediately know where they are and what they are looking at. So each page should be labeled with the name of the web site and a title describing its content.
- Test. Don't just trust your own judgment. If you think you've got all the bugs out, don't believe it. The most obvious problems are usually invisible, and watching someone new use your site can quickly reveal them. And try several users—testing by individuals looking for problem areas on web sites shows that even usability experts can disagree widely on what needs fixing.
- Do regular tune-ups. As content changes and grows, layers of complexity creep in. Keeping a site simple and easy to use requires regular maintenance.

GUIDED TOURS OF WEB SITES

The best way to understand the World Wide Web and its implications for shopping and to begin thinking about organizing your web site accordingly is to visit several existing sites. This section will take you on a guided tour of several web sites that clearly illustrate how to make shopping interesting, fun, and interactive. The examples come from a variety of categories that show that the web can be home to many different companies specializing in things as diverse as consumer products, business-to-business and professional services, mass-market items such as film and hot sauce, and business market products such as real estate, software, and consulting.

Case Study: Best Software

Best Software (www.bestsoftware.com/pay) has a web site (Figure 6.4) that is a perfect example of how to explain a difficult concept. This problem is one shared by many business-to-business companies: How can we make our story interesting and tell it properly? They have created a slide show of their accounting software program and posted it on the web. Prospects merely hit the NEXT button to see additional information, which is broken down into simple, bite-sized pieces and illustrated with graphs and screen shots.

Users must feel like they are in control, so at the top of the screen you will notice icons for stopping the demo, starting over, going back or forward, or getting a free trial. If prospects like the product, they can stop the demo and jump to the free trial; if they want to check information on a previous slide, they can control the action and go back. This is a great idea when you have a complicated story to tell.

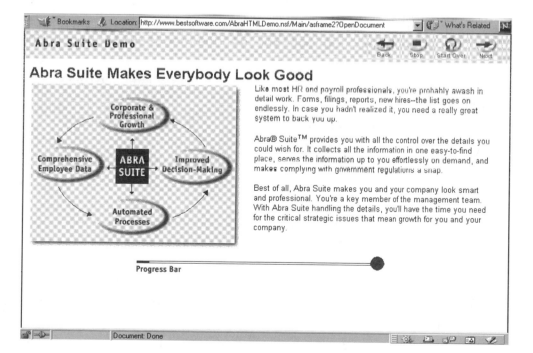

Figure 6.4 This guided tour demonstration explains a difficult concept in an easy-to-understand manner. (© 1999, Best Software, Inc.)

Case Study: Health4Her.com

Health4Her.com (www.health4her.com) is a site that sells vitamins and nutritional supplements (Figure 6.5). There are many companies like this on the web, but this site stands out because it is clearly focused on a niche—women. Fortunately, this is one of the largest niches you can find! Selecting a niche is important because people want to think the site is just for them. Any site can sell vitamins to anyone, but if you are a woman, you know this site has been designed with your specific needs in mind. It addresses issues of concern, such as menopause, pregnancy, and cellulite, which is a very good marketing idea. The marketing positioning statement reads "Natural Nutrition for Today's Woman." This positions the site for its target market and incorporates its key feature, natural products.

The site conveys this concept visually by showing several pictures of active, vibrant women engaging in a variety of interesting activities—exercising, walking the baby, laughing with a friend, and relaxing in the water. The pictures also show women of different ages and different life stages. These pictures say, "We include you." It is a very warm and appealing montage.

The first headline reads "Healthy Tips" and offers advice on several topics. This follows the web practice of giving away information for free. It is a great way to build confidence in the site and to encourage repeat visits, as people come to expect to see useful information posted here. Further down the page (see Figure 6.6), readers can subscribe to their newsletter by filling in their e-mail address. Notice that the company doesn't want or need extensive demographics from its readers, so it doesn't waste time by asking for irrelevant demographics.

One headline reads "April special: Buy two get one free." There is no doubt this site wants to sell and is asking for the order right up front. But it doesn't appear aggressive in this context because it is offering you a sale!

The site tries to personalize its service in the headline reading "Free Analysis." The body copy reads: "No two women's bodies or lifestyles are identical. Get vitamins customized for your personal needs. Click Here for free recommendations based on your diet and lifestyle." This section shows that the company wants to begin a personal relationship with the prospect and turn her into a customer for life.

Along the left side of the page, you see text links to the lowest-price guarantee and for safe and secure ordering—two important marketing factors that will boost sales. There's also a text link to its board of medical ad-

Figure 6.5 The pictures illustrate this site's target audience—active, vibrant women. (© 1999, Health4Her.com, Inc.)

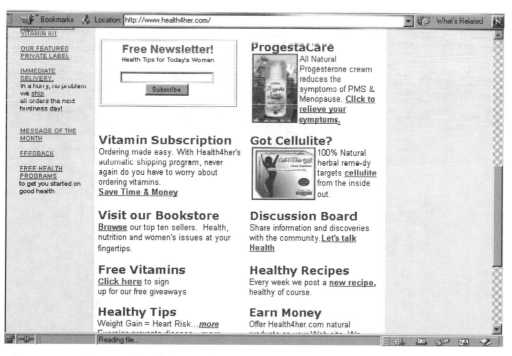

Figure 6.6 This site blends free information alongside sales messages. (© 1999, Health4Her.com, Inc.)

visors. This is a nice touch to persuade skeptics who wonder about the quality of such products. Marketers know it is always a good idea to handle objections.

Further down the page, you'll see the headline "Popular Sellers." This is a great feature for a consumer site with lots of products for sale. As you might have guessed, this listing steers people to the most popular products. You could also use this idea to move your featured items, including products you need to move owing to the end of the season or overstocking.

Case Study: Royal Sonesta Hotel

The Royal Sonesta Hotel (www.royalsonestano.com) in New Orleans is one of the finest hotels in the country and the most sought-after hotel in that city. Its location in the heart of the popular French Quarter is a prime asset. The web site (Figure 6.7) takes advantage of this by showing a terrific picture of the hotel and its outstanding architecture. A smaller picture to the side shows revelers at Mardi Gras, which reminds viewers about the charms of New Orleans, the city that care forgot!

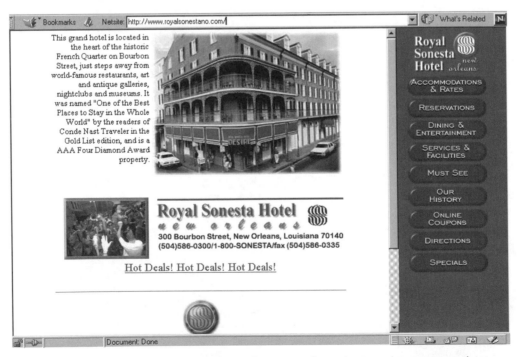

Figure 6.7 Clever copywriting and good pictures show the Royal Sonesta as the place to stay in New Orleans. (© 1999, Royal Sonesta, Inc.)

The body copy extols the virtues of the hotel's proximity to tourist activities and fine restaurants and also makes mention of awards it has received from important reviewers. Readers can scan this page and get a great first impression from the text and art. The navigation buttons on the right let surfers dig for deeper information and make reservations.

A line at the page bottom offers "Hot Deals," a must on the web to help build relationships.

Case Study: Ivan Levison

I've already interviewed direct-mail copywriter Ivan Levison (www.levison .com) in this book, so it seems like a good idea to review his web site (Figure 6.8) as well to see if he practices what he preaches. Sure enough, the graphic on his home page looks like a coupon, the visual embodiment of copywriting. The red checkmark really catches your eye. This graphic element is repeated in the links to contact him or read articles he has written and posted on the site. This is a good example for a service provider to follow.

Figure 6.8 Clever artwork that looks like a coupon conveys what Levison does at a glance. (© 1999, Ivan Levison and Associates)

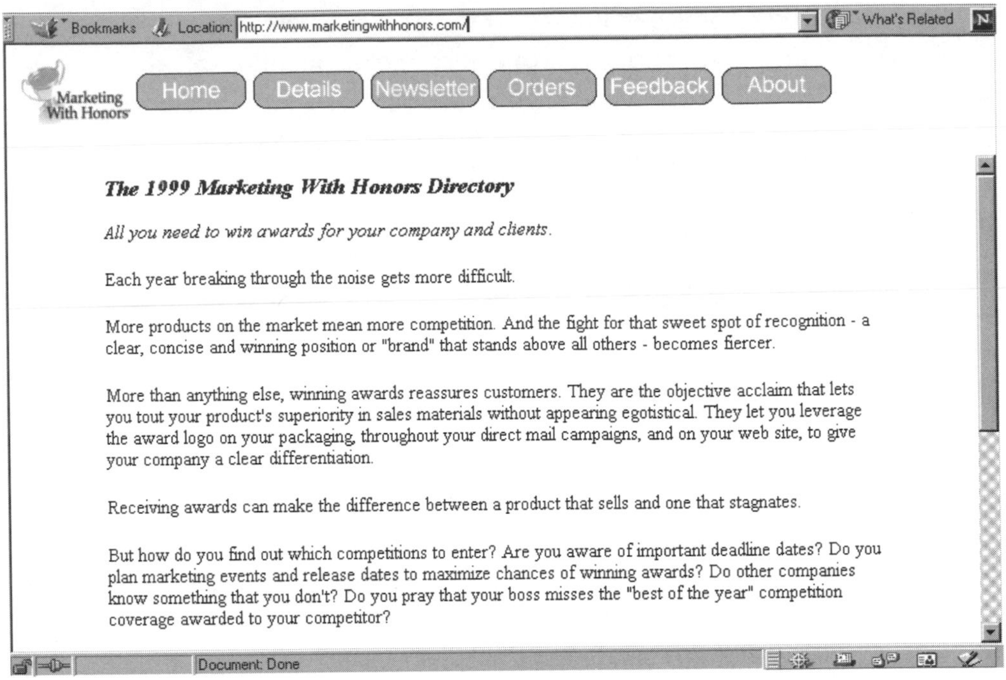

Figure 6.9 The front page is a complete sales flyer for this directory of information. (© 1999, Marcus + Company, Inc.)

Case Study: Marketing with Honors

Marketing with Honors (www.marketingwithhonors.com) sells a directory of awards presented to computer hardware and software companies. Looking less like a web site and more like a letter, this web site (Figure 6.9) is among the growing number of pages that start telling their story and sales pitch immediately. Some pages even look like flyers. This page presumes you want to know what the company does and how the product will help you. It doesn't force you to go deeper into the site to find this out. This strategy is very effective for selling products. It grabs attention and dispenses information. If you need more information about the company or want to see a sample report, you can dig deeper.

PhotoHighway.com

PhotoHighway.com (www.photohighway.com) is a portal site that focuses on a large vertical market—amateur photography. An important task for companies with a site like this is to identify users so they can create customers

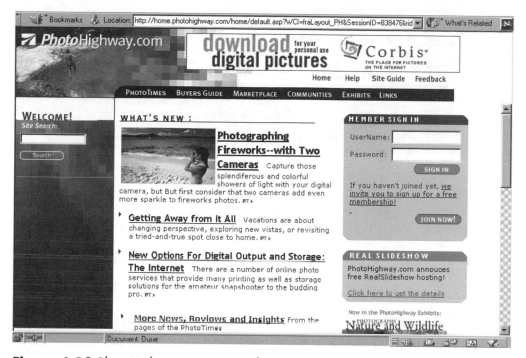

Figure 6.10 PhotoHighway.com is a perfect example of a portal site that offers original content and an easy way for visitors to become members of the community. (© 1999, PhotoHighway.com)

for life and collect demographic information. This task is accomplished with the registration box at the right-hand side of the screen and accompanying text that points out the benefits of becoming a member (Figure 6.10).

A large site with a great deal of information, PhotoHighway.com helps readers find articles quickly with a search engine that is located on the left-hand side of the page.

Readers can see what is new on the site in the wide center column, which highlights new articles, contests, and reviews. A colorful picture helps steer the eye toward this column.

Case Study: Insight.com

Insight.com (www.insight.com) is a leading seller of computer hardware and software on the Internet. Its front page (Figure 6.11) looks like a flyer you might see in a Sunday newspaper for a computer store. This is a good analogy; they know you want to buy a product, so they show you their featured items.

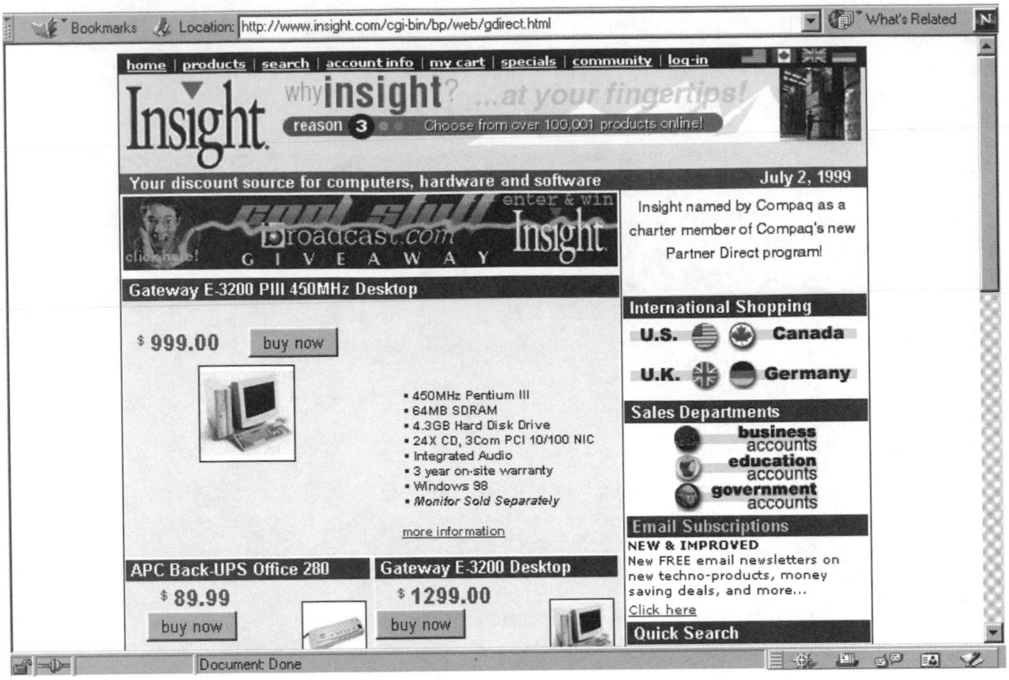

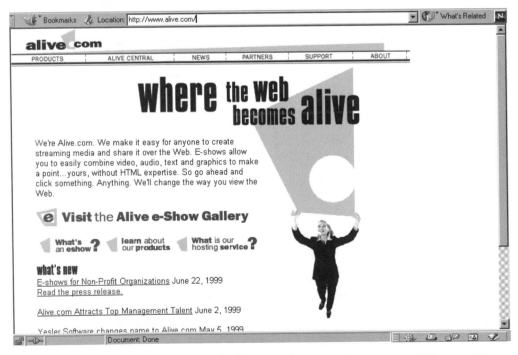

Figure 6.11 Highlighted products on a catalog site direct users to featured items. (© 1999, Insight Enterprises, Inc.)

Figure 6.12 A front page that looks like an ad conveys the company's image. (© 1999, Alive.com, Inc.)

Case Study: Alive.com

Alive.com (www.alive.com) sells a software program that creates multimedia presentation for the web that can be used in sales, marketing, customer support, and training applications. The front page (Figure 6.12) is interesting because it looks like a magazine ad with its large picture, good use of white space, and a catchy headline. Yet it still looks like a web page with its attractive navigation tools. Although the company claims the product is easy to use, prospects might not believe this claim, so Alive.com has added a multimedia event that shows how to use the product to create a presentation, step by step.

Case Study: Tools for Exploration

Tools for Exploration (www.toolsforexploration.com) is a leader in the alternative therapy market. It wanted to create a web site that helps maintain and enhance its leadership position. The solution was a fully customizable electronic commerce web presence (Figure 6.13).

Web developer Ariesnet (www.ariesnet.com) created an intuitive interface rich in graphics and content. "The site expands and develops the com-

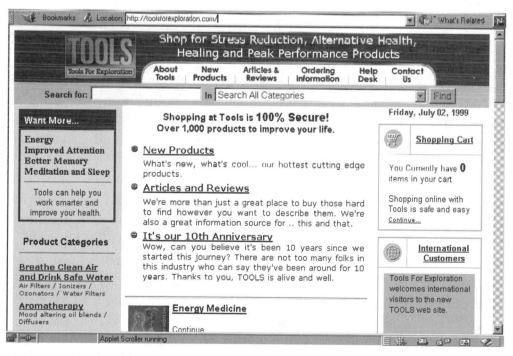

Figure 6.13 This information-rich site fulfills its marketing goals. (© 1999, Tools for Exploration, Inc.)

pany's customer base by reaching new audiences and providing products and services to current customers with the convenience of the Internet," says Cruce Saunders, principal of Ariesnet. "Not only does the site present products and services in a clear and perceptive way, but it also encourages customer feedback."

Users can access information about the company's products by browsing the easily updated electronic catalog and e-commerce solutions.

"The site not only allows for an easy and insightful shopping experience for customers, but it also greatly empowers the company, giving them control over key aspects of the web site. The company can update their product catalog, make changes to content oriented sections in the site and review customers information," says Saunders.

The web site has reached its goals of developing new channels for sales and customer acquisition, collecting user data, creating a vehicle for consumer ideas and opinions, and providing conveniences for customers, he said.

HIRING A DESIGNER

Should you create the site yourself, use an in-house team, or hire an outside firm? That's one of the stickiest questions on the web, and unfortunately, there is no one answer. Every company has different talents and expertise.

Large companies with marketing departments, technology departments, and designers will probably want to do the work in-house because they have so much talent and knowledge. Also, many people in corporations really want to create the web site to show off their talents or to establish their own political agenda inside the company.

If you are a one-person company or are in a very small business, you could create your own site easily by using a software program that includes templates of well-designed pages. Products such as Microsoft's Front Page, Ixla's Web Page Designer, and others present fill-in-the-blank templates that require absolutely no knowledge of programming language to build an attractive web site. Higher-end products such as Net Objects Fusion let you break out of the template mold and add your own artistic endeavors. For competent programmers, HTML programs like HotDog, HotMetal, and HomeSite let you create your own look and feel from scratch. Several companies sell software that let you put an entire catalog online, complete with order-entry and credit card verification abilities. Yahoo Store, a division of the ever-popular search engine/portal, is a complete turnkey solution for companies that want to get online quickly and sell products. You should be able to do this all by yourself.

If you are not comfortable with the technical and artistic aspects of creating a web site, don't worry. Outside companies can handle all these details so that you can concentrate on doing what you do best. After all, you didn't install the electricity or plumbing in your office. You hired contractors to do that. If you are unfamiliar with the web but an ace at selling insurance, then you should concentrate on the efforts that bring in the most money. Hire the pros to do what they do best.

A cottage industry for creating sites is springing up. These companies offer complete site creation and supporting materials. The advantages of hiring consultants to create these materials are plentiful. As they already know how to use the software, they save you the time, expense, and hassle of learning it. Their familiarity with it enables them to use the software to its fullest potential so that your products are displayed in the most advantageous manner available. For the same reason, consultants are able to create and complete the project for you quickly. Because they have designed projects for other companies, they will be able to draw on that experience to create a better presentation for you. Finally, because their business depends on their being well informed, consultants know about the latest technological improvement and how these can help you.

Select a site designer as you would choose any consultant: Ask for referrals from your colleagues, ask the consultants for references, look at their previous work, determine your level of rapport, and ask for the price structure. After you've selected the top two or three consultants that you feel can do the job, begin negotiating their fees. Bear in mind that you don't want to cut the price to such a low point that they will not want to work with you or will have to cut corners to complete the task.

"Before a contractor goes about building an office space, their architect first works with the client to create a blueprint of the outcome. Without a blueprint, the construction process would be a mess, with little clarity as to what goes where, and what the final product will look like," says Cruce Saunders, principal of Ariesnet. "But with a blueprint, a clear direction has been set, engineering details have been worked out, client design approval has been sought, and the construction begins geared towards success. That's why we've created the Blueprint, a strategic, practical, logistic, and creative web development plan custom-crafted for your company."

This blueprint can help you build your company's web site and negotiate details and responsibilities with the design firm:

Site flow chart. A complete diagrammatic outline of the site that shows all pages and links within the site. It also includes a description page detailing the contents of each section.

Creative concepts. Creative style sheets presenting proposed fonts and color palettes for your site. Also includes layouts and roughs for different looks/feels for the splash page, navigation design, and if applicable, storyboarded animations.

Production schedule. GANNT charts serve as the calendar for your web development project showing who is responsible for what and when. Itemized by actions.

Cost analysis. A detailed spreadsheet of costs itemized by job and team member. Info on hosting expenses, domain setup fees, and external fees is included. Finally, maintenance estimates and expansion options are discussed.

Initial Request for Information (RFI). This section goes over the various raw materials needed from the client to begin production. The RFI is itemized by section and time.

Custom market research. Online market research and analysis, including information on competitive sites, an analysis of the competition, and a synopsis of the ways in which Ariesnet will help differentiate your company online and reach your audience most effectively.

By following the Ariesnet blueprint, you'll have a better chance of reaching your goals, while greatly reducing causes for confusion with your designer.

BUDGET CONSIDERATIONS

Budgeting for the creation of the web site must include line items for creating content, converting it to HTML format, and connecting it to the computer server. Here are important factors to consider:

- **Creating content.** Creating content can be done in house with the marketing team determining which products and messages to feature. In-house artists and graphic designers can create the visual elements. Companies that don't have artists can hire consultants.

- **Creative and technical consulting.** Consultants can help companies create web sites from start to finish or just complete parts of the puzzle. For example, large companies with in-house advertising departments may be adept at creating text and graphics files but may lack the expertise to convert files to HTML format or to place the files onto a computer server and connect to the Internet. That might be the time to call in a consultant.

  The cost of hiring a consultant varies greatly depending on the size of the material you need to create and the negotiating ability of the consulting firm. If you have a simple site with few items and links, the consultant might be able to complete the job in a few hours. A more intricate job could take days or weeks. As with any immature industry, prices have yet to become standardized. Consultants can and will charge whatever they think the market will bear. Prices vary across the country, ranging from $50 to $125 an hour plus expenses. The time to create a web site for a small or home-based business could range from 6 to 100 hours depending on the complexity of the project.

- **Updates.** A key benefit of electronic information is that it can be changed easily whenever you want. However, each time you change information, you have to pay for the artist's time. Most companies have dynamic information; it changes with each modification in the product line, price, or availability. Your budget should account for time to update material. If you decide to undertake this task in house, you have to account for training and actual time spent on this function.

- **Copyright.** Who owns the work product? The artist or your company? You must negotiate this point in your contract. Obviously, your company should retain the copyright. If you don't you might find that your web designer is laying claim to the site and demanding a fee every time you or she changes anything on the site. This scenario is no different than most wedding photographers. Although you hire them to shoot your wedding, they own the rights to the pictures and you must pay them whenever you want additional prints.

SUMMARY

To make the sale, build credibility, or ensure a successful transaction, good design and content are essential ingredients of any web site. This chapter showed you the basic ingredients needed to create a site for marketing purposes. The next four chapters will discuss sales issues and show how companies selling consumer products, services, and business-to-business are using the Internet with great success.

CHAPTER 7

Strategic and Operational Issues for Online Selling

Merchants have a ground-floor opportunity to build brand identity and make sales to an online audience that is wealthy, growing, and eager to buy products online.

In this chapter, we will explore:

- The World Wide Web: interactive selling at its best.
- The benefits of online shopping.
- Security for online ordering.
- Online malls.

THE WORLD WIDE WEB: INTERACTIVE SELLING AT ITS BEST

Clearly, the most exciting interactive sales and marketing tool to date is the World Wide Web. The web lets you create a virtual shopping experience through a combination of text, pictures, and sound that consumers can access to learn more about your company and its products and to place an order. A web site can be compared with a catalog or a store because customers can read about products, see them in action, and place an order. A site will usually include an overview of the company as well as point-and-click access to product or service information, online catalogs, product order forms, and other literature.

The web is tailor-made for interactive sales presentations because your prospects will select the information they are interested in.

Customers can pick and choose the products they want to see, read as much information as they want, ask questions (and find answers) at any time of the day or night—and place an order from anywhere in the world. They can do this by pointing and clicking on designated words and graphics in a document located on a computer miles, or countries, away. They can place the order on the spot or can go to discussion groups and ask others about their experiences and recommendations.

Because of this high degree of interactivity, companies have the luxury of creating sales presentations tailored to each customer's individual needs. Also, marketers can create multiple selling propositions—a different reason to buy for each customer. In this manner, everyone who visits the web can get personal treatment. At its best, the web creates a personal selling experience. Customers can see a demonstration of the product in full color. If you're in the food industry, they can hear a step-by-step explanation of how to use your products to cook a better meal, listen to the eggs cracking, and watch a happy family eating the food.

Best yet, creating a web site doesn't cost an arm and a leg. With the right tools and training, anyone can design a site and have it loaded onto a computer server for the whole world (literally) to see. The web is truly every person's printing press.

BENEFITS OF ONLINE SHOPPING

The exciting promise of online marketing is the ability to make the sale. The Internet and commercial online services can deliver this today! Whether it be a trip to the virtual mall or a browse through an online catalog, marketers can use online services to make money.

Online shopping offers several advantages over shopping in person:

- Comparison shopping is quick and easy.
- Consumers can order directly from the comfort of their home or office, 24 hours a day, from anywhere in the world.
- The store never closes.
- There are no traffic jams, no parking places to fight over, and no waste of time.

Shopping has never been easier for consumers. They can order products directly from the merchant by using a computer and a modem. They can browse at their own pace and can't be hassled by pushy salespeople. Orders are paid for by credit card, which merchants can verify before processing the order. Many companies offer toll-free telephone order services for customers who prefer them. Delivery varies by merchant but is usually made by a recognized carrier such as Federal Express or UPS so that companies can track receipts.

Online information can be delivered immediately to consumers via e-mail. They don't have to wait three weeks for a catalog to reach them by mail. They can view the information and make a buying decision immediately. In this way, online services help fulfill demand.

Merchants benefit as well:

- They gain an additional distribution channel for their products.
- Online shoppers tend to have more disposable income than the average consumer.
- Online marketers can keep track of their best customers and alert them to sales and special promotions.
- Vendors can build relationships with customers through online sales, support, and service.
- The flexible publishing platforms of the Internet and commercial online services offer the marketer the chance to build relationships by publishing unlimited amounts of information for consumers to devour at their own pace.

SECURITY FOR ONLINE ORDERING

Using a credit card on the Internet was once something few people were willing to do. Now it seems that people have become comfortable with using credit cards as they buy books, CDs and items at Internet auction sites. It should be pointed out that although many people feared having their credit card numbers being stolen on the Net, no such cases have ever been reported. There have been cases where hackers broke into the accounting systems of companies, but that is another issue entirely. Security experts have told me that it is virtually impossible to steal a credit card number as it goes over the phone lines. You have a better chance of having your credit card stolen in a restaurant. However, it is important for merchants to win the public's trust by posting notices that they have secured servers and other devices to protect credit card orders.

Merchants should make it easy for customers to buy products in the manner they prefer: calling their order center via a toll-free number, sending an e-mail note, completing an online order form, or printing out their order form and sending it via fax or phone, putting it in the mail, or using cash on delivery (COD).

The specter of fraud exists for merchants as well. They might receive calls from thieves who are placing orders with stolen credit cards. Good business practice calls for merchants to call a credit card authorization center to make sure the card is valid. However, fast thieves can place many orders online before the card's original owner realizes the card is missing and calls in to report the disappearance. By that time, many merchants could be liable for a lot of money.

Merchants can protect themselves from fraud by following these steps:

1. Send the product by a carrier that gets a signed record of delivery. Customers can't claim they never received the product. If they honestly didn't receive the product, the shipper's records can be traced.
2. Call a credit card authorization center to verify the credit card number before shipping the product.
3. Ship the product quickly. People change their minds and then claim they never ordered the product.
4. Ask for the customer's address for verification purposes. This is especially important for online orders of information products or other products that are transmitted to the customer over the online system, such as newsletters, software, or research or consulting services. In those cases, the merchant or consultant probably wouldn't have thought to make a record of the address because he isn't mailing or shipping anything over a normal shipping route to the customer.
5. Ship the package COD.
6. Request payment in advance.

Online marketers can employ other strategies to fight fraud. Companies like CyberSource (www.cybersource.com) will process the transaction against their security fraud screen and guarantee the sale.

ONLINE MALLS

Virtual malls on the Internet are gaining in popularity and scope. Many companies are creating their own electronic realty offices and opening malls, which are collections of businesses accessed by the consumer through a common address. According to Forrester Research (www.forrester.com), there are 601 malls, with an average of 18 stores per mall, representing 7,500 merchants. Mall owners take 5 to 15 percent commission.

Malls can be based on a number of similar elements:

- Products.
- Industries.
- Geographic regions; chambers of commerce or visitors and convention bureaus might be likely to sponsor a mall based on a geographic region.

Malls can also be based on dissimilar products. This should be avoided, because they might not be able to attract the people who are interested in your products or services.

Pros and Cons of Joining a Mall

There are many reasons why merchants might want to be in a mall:

- A large amount of traffic comes to a mall site because people know they will find related types of products.
- Merchants can take advantage of a business structure that handles technology as well as accepting and verifying orders. Malls should have designers available for hire who can create and update your site.
- As mall operators upgrade equipment, merchants benefit as the costs are spread out among many players.

On the down side, if mall operators don't promote the site or are bad landlords, your store will suffer. Before joining a mall, ask yourself if it is providing benefits that you couldn't provide for yourself. If the site becomes very big, customers might never find you.

How to Select a Mall

A good mall provides management, marketing, and security for its merchants. If you decide to select a mall, make sure it offers these features:

- Affordable, high-quality connectivity lines—and lots of them, if the mall has many merchants. As more merchants sign on and more consumers join, the transmission times slow considerably. If the mall doesn't offer fast access, your consumers could get turned off by long transmission delays.

- Attractive and easy user interface.
- Software tools for providers that make it easy to put up and maintain the site, or access to technicians who will update the sites for you at a reasonable cost.
- Security mechanisms, including authentication and encryption.
- Experience in the business. Many start-up companies bill themselves as malls but don't have the depth of knowledge, expertise, or hardware needed to help merchants.
- Experience in publicizing and promoting the site.
- Reliability of hardware systems and the ability to fix hardware problems quickly. If the site is down, no one can buy from you.
- An easy-to-type address. For example, an easy address is www .mycompany.com. A difficult address is www.somemall.com /level2/eastwing/mycompany.

Compare mall operators on the basis of how much commission they take, transaction charges, download or access charges, and payment schedules.

SUMMARY

Sellers of consumer products and business-to-business products can build their sales by expanding their markets on the Internet. Security for online sales has proven that ordering is safe, and surveys suggest customers are more than happy to order products online.

CHAPTER 8

Selling Consumer Products and Services Online

Companies in many industries are selling products and services to a willing online audience. This chapter continues our examination of examples and strategies.

In this chapter we will explore:

- What's wrong with sales offers from consumer companies.
- The online catalog.
- Case studies.
- Channel conflict.
- Selling your products on the auction block.
- Tips for increasing sales during holidays.

WHAT'S WRONG WITH SALES OFFERS FROM CONSUMER COMPANIES

Maybe the Godfather had it right when he said, "We'll make him an offer he can't refuse." If only web retailers took his lead! In the past few weeks, I've been victimized by incompetent merchants making offers that were all too easy to refuse. I say "victimized" because these merchants had promised me one thing and delivered a much lesser value. So I could have been mugged on the Net if I had actually followed through and made a purchase!

Let's look at these three incidents:

United Airlines (www.ual.com) has a great offer. Subscribe to their free e-mail newsletter and you'll receive information about how to fly at radically discounted rates. Imagine flying from San Francisco to New York for $174 instead of $400 plus! What a deal. Then you read the small print. You must fly on Saturday and you can't return on Sunday. That sort of limits your options by a factor of 100.

Let's say you decide to take United up on its offer. You get on the 10 A.M. flight, and you arrive in New York, all fresh and ready to go—at 7 P.M. The day is shot! And if you have to be back at your desk on Monday morning, then you are out of luck because United won't let you fly back until Tuesday! That's an offer you can refuse!

Autobytel.com (www.autobytel.com) promises no-hassle, low-cost cars. Guess again. My mother wanted to buy a new car and got a quote from a Toyota dealership near her. I told her we could do better on the Net, so I contacted Autobytel. The local dealer promptly let us know that the car would cost *more* than the quote given by another dealer. Autobytel.com also includes links to car information services, such as price guides, so that we could actually see what a "good" price was. The local dealer would have benefited by reading this information as we did. She did buy a car at that same dealership that offered her the higher quote. But she bought from another salesperson, in person, who offered her a lower fee. Another offer you can refuse!

My mother doesn't know how to turn on a computer, but she wanted to get one when her local supermarket offered her "web bucks" coupons. I went on the web to find that several supermarkets are using this interesting marketing concept. Here's how it works: You go to the supermarket's web site and start a brilliant one-to-one marketing process. You type in your zip code to find the store that is closest to you. You select a page containing specials and select the items you want to purchase—and see how much you'll save with the "web bucks" coupon. There is an impressive list of items, from baby products, to food and health and beauty aids. And they offer nice discounts of a dollar or more. So far, so good. When you are finished, you print out the page, which contains your selections, your name, and a nice bar code. Now the store knows who you are and what products and brands you like. They can use that information in many ways: to market additional products to you, to offer you coupons on competing brands, and to see buying prefer- ences and trends in regional markets—a brilliant move. And when you go to the store, the salesclerk scans the page so he can complete the process—they know that you have followed through. Now they have accountability to their marketing system.

Ah, but here's the rub. You don't actually get the discount on THAT visit. If you buy the products, then you get the web bucks, which will be good for discounts on FUTURE visits. This deal isn't so bad: You do get the discount, and the store is assured of two visits from you, which might help make you a customer for life. It is just that the wording on the offer is confusing. I'm sure that some people who don't read the small print will be offended when the cashier tells them the discount applies to the NEXT visit. This type of offer might blow up in your face!

All the world loves Amazon.com, Reel.com, and CDNOW, which offer books, movies and CDs at discount prices. However, once you add in the shipping price, you might not be getting the bargain you thought you were—again, an offer you might be able to refuse.

Now, I'm not saying you should give away the store, or offer prices that are so low you can't make money. However, the web should offer merchants enormous savings because of the lowered cost of doing business; reduced needs for inventory, financing, and salespersons might cause consumers to expect a discount—and a fair one.

If you make an offer they can't refuse, you might find extra dollars in your bank account instead of a horse's head staring at you in your bed.

THE ONLINE CATALOG

Online data can be seen as an electronic version of the company catalog, complete with pictures that entice the eye, words that inspire the imagination, and prices that don't make consumers think twice. Electronic information is less expensive to deliver than catalogs: There aren't any printing or postage costs. Online marketers with wry senses of humor are fond of saying they don't like to spend money mailing dead trees to customers.

The lowered cost of doing business online means that some merchants can enjoy a larger profit margin, while others pass the savings along to consumers in the form of lower prices. Still others view the online systems as another distribution channel that features the same pricing structure as catalogs or direct mail.

Merchants can change information, product lineups, and pricing immediately to take advantage of market trends, price tests, and the like.

Some companies, of course, would like to move quickly but can't because of internal operations, though at least the promise is available.

Print isn't outdated yet. Hard copy catalogs can display color more attractively than computers. Print catalogs can be read on the bus or in the bathroom. Also, consumers can flip through pages more easily and see several pieces of information at once. This is handy when, say, they are looking at the order form and then need to flip back to page 20 to find the product number for the kite they want to buy. Yet online consumers can find information quickly by linking from one page to the next and can order directly from each page. Regardless, the elements of proper advertising must be present for online marketing to work effectively.

Creating a catalog was an expensive proposition until very recently. Expensive software dominated the field. However, the introduction of Yahoo! Store (www.yahoostore.com), a turnkey storefront, has simplified the process and lowered the cost for small businesses.

Case Study: 1-800-FLOWERS

1-800-FLOWERS (www.1800flowers.com) is one of the most successful direct sales businesses on the Internet. The site also helps its integrated marketing program, says Donna Iucolano, the manager for interactive services.

Consumers are greeted at the site by a cheery message—"Welcome to our world"—and an equally cheery image of the entrance to a nursery. They then select SHOP OUR STORE. In that section, they can choose from four main categories:

1. Seasons' Best, an assortment of bouquets with enticing names like Fields of Europe, Fresh Noble Fir Wreath, and Dried Floral Winter Centerpiece.

2. Shop by Occasion, including birthday, anniversary, congratulations, best wishes, thank you, new baby, get well, and sympathy offerings.

3. Shop by Product Category, such as flowers, roses, plants, gift baskets, gourmet items, balloons, and decorative keepsakes.

4. Shop by Price Range, from under $25 to $65 and over.

Each product is accompanied by a photo and enticing descriptive catalog copy. Each arrangement can be ordered in small, medium, or large sizes. Prices and shipping charges are clearly visible.

To purchase a product, consumers select the product and quantity. They then click the ADD button. After each selection, an invoice pops up showing the products ordered, total price, and service charge. When they've finished selecting, consumers click the GO TO THE CHECKOUT LANE button to pay for their purchases by filling in their name, address, phone number, and credit card information. If they make mistakes, they can reset the form to empty their shopping basket.

Q: What was 1-800-FLOWERS's mission in going online?

A: The original reason for going online was to pursue new media and showcase our products online using interactive media. Our first interactive project was in 1992 with CompuServe. Since that time we've made substantial investments in the interactive services division.

Q: Has it met its goal?

A: We are at $25 million as a division. I think we are doing all right. That figure represents 10 percent of company sales. We are on 16 electronic ventures, all major commercial online services, interactive TV trials, multimedia kiosks, PDAs (personal digital assistants, hand held computing devices), wireless, and cellular.

Q: How did the idea get started?

A: As a company we are pretty innovative and big technology users. We saw this as a new and innovative thing. We run a very state-of-the-art facility on the telecom side. We embrace technology.

Q: How has the cost of technology affected your product costs and consumer prices?

A: We realized that technology reduces the costs of service, and we pass along the savings to customers. It is less expensive to order online than over the phone. We made a decision very early on that savings would be passed along to customers.

Q: Was it difficult to get approval from corporate to go onto the web?

A: Not really. We came to the Internet in April after spending three and a half years online. It wasn't our first venture online. A lot of companies are having trouble selling it [a web site] internally because they don't have any experience online.

Q: Which department has responsibility for maintaining the site?

A: Interactive marketing, which is a hybrid of marketing and has a staff of 12 with a wide variety of skill sets.

Q: Was the site created internally or was an outside contractor hired?

A: It was created with an Internet development company, Fry Multimedia, for the back end and Erin Edward for the creative.

Q: What criteria do you look for in a vendor?

A: We certainly want them to have experience with the Internet, multimedia art and design, and transactional applications. They should be able to support our marketing efforts and work with our larger ad agency of record. We look at their work for other clients and check referrals. We also ask for recommendations.

Q: What would you do differently?

A: We are constantly rebuilding the page. That is very important because a month or two in this environment is a long time. New developments happen all the time. We make changes daily. As new technologies are available, we are comfortable making enhancements and changes.

Q: What role does the site play in the integrated marketing program for 1-800-FLOWERS?

A: It has a big role. It is more than just a shopping application. We have a lot of floral info online. We promote our retail stores and post help wanted information. It is a comprehensive application. It talks about the company as a whole and allows us to publish information about the industry, flower giving, and gifts.

CHANNEL CONFLICT

Companies that sell online as well as in retail outlets face a serious problem: channel conflict. Retailers won't be happy to find they are competing against the manufacturer to sell products. Another problem to consider is that the manufacturer might actually sell the product at a lower price than the retailers!

In the case of software publishers, nearly every company sells software at its site, in direct conflict with retailers. In addition to this, online software retailers also sell the product. Because software can be downloaded from the Internet directly to the customer's computer, the company and online retailer have sold the product with a minimal cost of goods sold. Additionally, if software publishers don't sell their products from their web sites, other online retailers will! So customers might find a lower price on the web than in the retail world anyway. Their only expense is the credit card transaction and verification (and the cost of creating the e-commerce site). Meanwhile, brick-and-mortar retailers deliver a box, disk, and manual that cost more to create, ship, store, and sell!

There is no easy answer to this question. Software publishers—and other manufacturers—will have to weigh the relative risks and rewards of direct selling in competition with their retailers.

SELLING YOUR PRODUCTS ON THE AUCTION BLOCK

Are you looking for a new way to sell your products? Consider offering your wares at the auction web sites. These incredibly popular sites are attracting millions of bids for hundreds of thousands of products each day! Your investment to sell the product is small, and the return can be great.

You can still sell products on your web site, but adding this new channel of distribution opens up a wide new universe of potential buyers for your products. Best yet, you don't have to spend a fortune on marketing and promoting your web site, because the auction sites do a great job of attracting lots of people who are ready, willing, and able to buy your products! So let's take a look at how they work.

You've probably heard of the most popular auction sites, such as eBay (www.ebay.com), Onsale (www.onsale.com), and Amazon.com. These are great places to sell anything from Beanie Babies to model scale railroad engines. But you'd be surprised to learn that these sites also sell new and refurbished computer equipment, cameras, stereos, and even airline tickets and vacations. Then there are more specialized auction sites that only sell one commodity, such as wine (www.winebid.com), coins (www.coinuniverse.com), golf clubs (www.golfclubexchange.com), and even collectible cars (www.livebid.com).

Each auction house works in pretty much the same way. They charge the seller a modest fee for posting the product online. They also charge a fee to the seller based on the final sales price. At eBay, the rates are $2 for an item selling over $50. When the product sells, eBay also charges what it calls a "final value fee" ranging from 1.5 percent to 5 percent of the sale price. In exchange for those fees, you get the right to post your product online. Customers can find the product easily by typing in the item or category of product on the auction's search engine. So if a customer types in "hair loss remedy," he'll find your auction page.

How can you improve your chances of selling the product? Here are several tips from eBay taken from www.ebay.comlaw.faq.html seller:

- Provide a complete description of the product.
- Add a photo so that people can see the condition of the item.
- Disclose all terms for payment and shipping so there are no unanswered questions.

I'd like to add another tip: Provide a guarantee that the product is in the quality and condition described. If there is one complaint against auctions, it is that some people are advertising ripped and discolored products and claiming the items are in "near perfect condition." You'll avoid angering a lot of customers if you tell the truth straight out!

Here's another tip: In the description of the product, let the prospect know that you have a web site that offers even more products. That way you get more advertising bang for your buck. Not only could they bid on your product, but they might also go to your web site and see all the products you have for sale!

When people bid on items, their e-mail addresses are listed along with the price they bid, so you can keep track of how well your auction is doing. And here's another marketing tip: You can look at other auctions and send e-mails to the bidders to let them know that you have similar products and better prices! This actually happened to me when I bid on a Beanie Baby. I received several e-mails from other vendors letting me know that they had the same Beanie Baby and were willing to sell it to me for less than I had bid on the auction site. That's really prospecting!

When I proposed that idea in my newsletter, one person asked if that was an ethical way to market because you would be stealing customers away from the auction house. Although I don't want to steal business from the auction house or the seller, consider this scenario. The seller has one item for sale. He gets a high bid and sells it. However, 31 people are disappointed because they lost the auction. Those 31 people still want to buy the product, and the seller can't accommodate them. It is your ethical duty to sell the product to them at a mutually agreeable price.

Merchants need to protect themselves from fraudulent customers. eBay maintains a deadbeat file of people who win auctions but never pay. You can also check on the reputation of buyers if they have bid on previous items. eBay also maintains a large database that provides sellers comments on buyers. You can see if they pay on time and if their checks clear. Coincidentally, a database of sellers exists so that customers can check on your reputation as well—so be sure to ship your products quickly and provide great customer service. That way you'll get a good reputation.

If you are thinking about buying items from an auction site, The National Fraud Information Center (www.fraud.org) has several tips to protect you against fraud. Some of the best ones are:

- Be wary about claims about collectibles.
- Understand how the auction works and what your responsibilities are.
- Check out the buyer.

You can find additional tips at the National Fraud Information Center http://www.fraud.org.

TIPS FOR INCREASING SALES DURING THE HOLIDAYS

Consumer buying picks up around the December holidays and special events such as Valentine's Day, graduation, and Mother's Day. Here are suggestions for improving your sales at these times:

- Provide a variety of gift wraps for free or a nominal fee.
- Offer several shipping options, including overnight and second day. People want to save money on shipping if time allows. If they wait until the last minute, they want to be sure the gift will arrive in time.
- Explain your privacy policy. People won't buy from you if they think you will sell their names to list brokers.
- Send a confirmation note via e-mail.
- Let people track the progress of their orders. You can do this by linking to the Federal Express or UPS web sites.
- Create one-click shopping for repeat customers. This service retains the customer's mailing and credit information so they can order quickly.
- Provide a toll-free number in case customers have questions or aren't comfortable ordering via the Internet.
- Create a gift registry similar to a wedding registry in a retail store. Think of events, such as birthdays, graduations, and anniversaries, and invite people to list the gifts they'd like to re-

ceive at those times. Send the web address of the web store to guests on their invitations. Clinique has a wish list on its site.

- Offer incentives on a time-limited basis. American Express and Gap Online offered a discount to web shoppers over a two-week period after Thanksgiving.

SUMMARY

The Internet offers a great many tools to reach consumers to make sales. However, many merchants still don't understand how to take advantage of selling online. In some cases, they are myopic; in other cases, they don't offer real benefits to users. Finally, they might be afraid of hurting their traditional sales channels and partners. However, by using the new tools and techniques offered by the Internet, merchants can sell many more products to satisfied customers.

CHAPTER 9

Business-to-Business Selling Online

Many people believe the Internet's greatest benefit will be to businesses that sell to other businesses because companies can study product offerings at their convenience and form relationships with those vendors that meet their needs. This chapter rounds out the advice given throughout the book on how to use the Internet to build relationships and sell products. Because every business claims to have its own unique obstacles, no one chapter could possibly be all things to all people. Therefore, this chapter will present highlights of business-to-business selling through statistics and case studies. We trust you will be able to glean a few tidbits from other industries to help make you a success.

In this chapter, you will learn about:

- Business-to-business selling opportunities online.
- Who's doing business online.
- Virtual trade shows.
- Additional marketing strategies.
- Problems with sales personnel.

WHO'S SELLING BUSINESS-TO-BUSINESS

Companies in virtually every industry are using the Internet to create relationships with prospects and customers and to sell products. Searching through Yahoo! on your industry will yield invaluable links to other companies whose strategies you can explore on your own. Here are examples of how companies are using the Internet to sell products to businesses:

123

- Career Mosaic (www.careermosaic.com), a job listing service, receives more than 4.4 million visitors a month.
- AMP (www.amp.com) features 90,000 computer and stereo parts. It attracts 200 new customers a day and repeat customers are growing by 15 to 20 percent each month. The company is one of the more sophisticated sites on the Internet; it offers such options as asking a customer to type in her language, country, and company to produce an interface that will, for example, account for the person's language, local shipping costs, and preferred pricing lists.
- Softbank, operator of the Comdex computer trade show, allows business people to register via the Internet, thus saving the company the costs of postage and labor to type information.
- Dell, a computer manufacturer, sells more than $16 million of products a day from its web site.
- IBM's "Seminar in a Box" provides qualified leads for resellers. It has grown 10 times in less than a year—without any need to hire more personnel to supplement the two original employees who manage the site.
- VerticalNet (www.verticalNet.com) owns and operates more than forty business-to-business vertical web communities on the Internet. It builds, develops, and maintains the editorial and community-building functions for such diverse industries as insurance, safety, and communications. The goal of these sites is to attract prospective buyers and sellers with news, information, job postings, and networking opportunities. Any company in that industry can post its own web site inside that vertical area so readers can learn about the company and start a business relationship.

Marketing on the web can cut costs for business-to-business firms. The Direct Marketing Association says a sales call may costs $700 depending on the industry, while an online communication program can cost 5 cents to $1.50 per contact.

Forrester Research (www.forrester.com) predicts that by 2002, 98 percent of large businesses and 45 percent of small businesses will do business online. Internet business-to-business commerce will grow to $327 billion by 2002.

VIRTUAL TRADE SHOWS

Many companies are finding they can attract qualified prospects by becoming a sponsor of a virtual trade show (VTS) on the Internet. These trade shows can take one of two formats. In one, a trade show in the real world adds an online component that allows vendors to buy advertising space on its web site. Companies can sponsor the online site or the real world site or both. The advantages are that companies can reach more prospects. The prospects who come to the show can do their research online before the event. The ones who can't afford to go to the show can learn about your products as well. After the show is over, the web site usually stays up for a while so prospects can refresh their memories by visiting the site. The other format for VTSs exists only online. The success of both formats depends entirely on the promoter's ability to generate traffic to the web site. This type of event can be a boon to companies that can't afford to sponsor booths in the real world or don't have the human resources available to attend a great many shows.

For small companies that can't afford to attend a real trade show or that would be lost in the crowd if they did attend, a VTS is an excellent opportunity to get noticed. The audience is highly targeted and you have interactive marketing capabilities. Furthermore, you can begin selling your products long before the show starts and long after it closes.

You should select a VTS that matches the demographics of your target audience. In the case of competing shows (e.g., Internet World or Internet Expo) that all reach your target audience, you might want to be on both. Consider it as just another ad; that's all a VTS really is anyway. You are advertising to reach a guaranteed audience for a set price. Call it anything you want, it is still an ad.

You might be wondering if a VTS adds more value than your web site does. After all, if you have web site, you can present much more information than on a VTS site for less money. However, a VTS can draw many more people than your web site could. You would also benefit from the synergy of customers from related companies. Smaller companies that might get looked over online would stand on an equal footing on a VTS site. Smaller companies would also be exposed to customers who didn't even know they existed before going to the VTS.

ADDITIONAL MARKETING STRATEGIES FOR BUSINESS-TO-BUSINESS

It is vitally important for businesses to qualify the people who come to their site so salespeople can follow up, as no one will ever buy a piece of capital equipment solely over the Internet. Companies must require the prospects to identify themselves by title, purchasing power and authority, and other factors relevant to their industry.

Here are two strategies to add to others found throughout this book:

1. Require registration for access to the site's meatier subjects.
2. Offer a form for a free evaluation. The evaluation is really a sales call with information provided by the user and helps the company to qualify the user.

PROBLEMS WITH SALES PERSONNEL

Although companies might love direct selling to their business clients, some salespeople might find the Internet to be a major drain on their income. Their clients and potential clients can buy directly from the company and bypass the salesperson. There are many stories of salespeople who do not tell their customers that information is online. They might have gotten away with this tactic several years ago, but most customers these days know to look to the web to see if they can get a better deal there.

Companies can respond to this issue in several ways, depending on their overall goals and strategies:

- Not sell on the web to protect their sales reps.
- Provide a commission to the sales reps and distributors who refer customers or whose accounts they normally service.
- Sell on the web in direct competition to reps and distributors.
- Sell on the web, but at full list price so reps and distributors can sell at a lower price.

SUMMARY

The Internet is a viable source of commerce for companies in the business-to-business area. Not only are companies doing a landmark business today in terms of sales and sourcing, but projections also call for this trend to continue as more companies and prospects go online.

CHAPTER 10

International Marketing Online

People from around the world can access information about your company and its products as the Internet turns commerce into a global marketplace.

In this chapter you will learn:

- The opportunities for worldwide sales.
- Fifteen steps to increase marketing efficiencies internationally.

THE OPPORTUNITIES FOR WORLDWIDE SALES

We all know the World Wide Web, but how many of us underscore *World* and appreciate the Internet as a medium that reaches surfers in Australia as well as in Hawaii?

The truth is that a goodly number of leading-edge consumers and companies log on to the Internet in countries around the world. The marketer who doesn't appreciate this fact is losing out on opportunities.

Software publishers realized long ago that overseas sales can account for 50 percent of revenue and a large percentage of the growth of their product line. The same can be true for producers of other products as well.

International consumers generate 30 percent of gross sales for Fatbrain.com (www.fatbrain.com) because books are cheaper to buy in the United States than in their own countries, even with shipping costs.

AMP added Japanese, Mandarin Chinese, and Korean versions of its online catalog already available in English, French, Spanish, German, and Italian. The result: Visits in these new languages accounted for 2 percent of the total number of visits after just one month.

The Milne Jewelry Company (www.xmission.com/~turq) of Utah found a ready audience for its products in Japan and Germany, where customers place larger orders than U.S. residents. It offers its pages in several languages.

FIFTEEN STEPS TO INCREASE MARKETING EFFICIENCIES INTERNATIONALLY

What can you do to increase sales internationally? Here are 15 tips:

1. **Make your site available in several languages.** On the site, add buttons that allow customers to select the language of their choice. To be culturally sensitive, don't label the button GERMAN but DEUTSCH. Have the page written or edited by a native speaker who will catch errors in usage, connotation, and denotation.
2. **Be considerate of cultural differences.** What you take for granted might be offensive to people in other countries. For example, a woman's bare leg or arm could be seen as pornography in Muslim countries. A U.S. businessperson was tossed in jail in one such country for showing tapes of *The Love Boat* TV show, which featured women in bikinis walking in the background of sets.
3. **Be conscious of word choice and idioms.** We've all heard the anecdote of the Chevy Nova not selling in Mexico because *no va* means "doesn't go." I've also heard half a dozen versions of the negative connotations that the Coca-Cola red and white logo has in China.
4. **Be aware of colors.** Certain colors and combinations that are effective in the United States don't mean the same things or stir up the same feelings in other countries. Red, white, and blue mean patriotism here but don't say anything in Brazil, whose national colors are green and yellow.
5. **Be aware of international laws.** In Spain, you can't use the country's flag in ads. In Germany, it is against the law to compare your product with a competitor's product.
6. **Make it easy to take money.** Put your prices in local currency. Be sure you account for the change in exchange rates; update these figures regularly.

7. **Make it easy to accept your customers' money.** Although many Canadian companies have bank accounts that draw on U.S. dollars, many other prospective buyers don't have such ready access. Make transactions easy by accepting credit cards, which are payable in U.S. dollars at the current exchange rate. You might not need to be as concerned with international buyers' reluctance to share credit card information over the Net as with U.S. customers'. I've received credit card orders for my books from people in Germany, Australia, and Israel. I can't recall a single order from the United States that included a credit card. Still, offer your phone or fax numbers as ways to accept orders.

8. **Make sure you can do business in other countries.** Do you need a license? Can you sell your products internationally without violating U.S. law?

9. **Refer business to local operatives.** It might be easier to send international business to your local distributor or office. Be sure to list the local addresses and phone numbers. Be sure to remove toll-free numbers that work only in the United States.

10. **Create the right product mix for an international audience.** If your U.S. catalog lists bikinis, sweaters, and ski parkas in equal ratio, you might want to reconsider the offerings for a page viewed in Norway or Ecuador. Hard to find items seem to sell well on the Net, so a New England jam that is a slow seller in the United States might find a ready audience in a country that doesn't have maple trees.

11. **Be attentive to sounds.** The beeps in Lotus 1-2-3 were considered offensive in Japan. Lotus had to change the sounds to sell software in that country.

12. **Test the page with local speakers.** They understand the language far better than a staffer in the United States who studied the language in high school.

13. **Test the page with a browser that displays the appropriate alphabet set to ensure that the text is readable.** One good program is Internet with an Accent by Accent Software.

14. **Don't use a lot of images.** People in most countries on the globe have spotty, expensive phone service with noisy lines. Tell your story with text; you'll have a better chance of getting your message across without encountering a disconnect.

15. **Create forms for addresses that use the appropriate headings.** For example, Canada doesn't have states; it has provinces.

SUMMARY

Marketers can generate additional sales by selling to the worldwide online community. However, they must be prepared to conduct business internationally and to be mindful of the differences in culture and customs across borders.

PART 3

Promoting Your Web Site

CHAPTER 11

Promoting Your Web Site with Search Engines

There are hundreds of thousands of web sites on the Internet, and they are all fighting for attention. Without a concerted marketing and promotion effort to promote it, your web site could resemble a ghost town. This chapter and the next will explain numerous strategies for getting attention and show you how to get the best possible results step by step. Most of these methods are free, except for the employee time needed for execution.

This chapter will focus on search engines and these strategies for using them to help you:

- Register on Yahoo!
- Register under the appropriate category on Yahoo!
- List your Yahoo! registration in two additional categories.
- List your site in Yahoo's! geographic editions.
- Consider using Yahoo! friendly names for your products.
- Add the META tag to your web site.
- Create compelling keywords.
- Create descriptions.
- Create a title for each page.
- Put keywords near the top of your page.
- Create specific pages for each major search engine.
- Register each product from your site.
- Buy keywords in search engines.
- Register with location-specific search engines.
- Register with topic-specific search engines.

- Check to see where your site is ranked.
- Create a list of links.
- Link to complementary sites.
- Register with automated registration tools.
- Hire a professional to register and optimize your web site.
- Subscribe to Search Engine Watch.

SEARCH ENGINE REGISTRATION TACTICS

Have you ever used a search engine? If you have, chances are you found 2,000 listings you didn't want. That's because search engines are not smart. They are literal. If you type "demolition" because you want to find a company to knock down your building, the search engine will show you web sites for demolition derbies and a rock band called Demolition.

So if it is hard for you to find a company, imagine how hard it is for your prospects to find a company like yours. Let's look at search engines from a prospect's point of view and then use that information to create your winning tactics.

If prospects know your company exists, they type in the URL directly. They probably saw the address on your business card, in an ad, or simply typed in your company name and added *.com* to it. Lucky you if that worked! They don't need a search engine. But if they don't know your URL, they would use a search engine to find it.

Most people who use search engines, however, do so to find products and companies that they don't know exist. They know they want to buy a product that cleans rust from driveways, but they don't have a clue what the name of that product is or who makes it. They want to find a company that can move their household from their old house to their new one, but they don't know which companies service those markets. They want to buy antique beer signs, but they don't have the faintest idea who sells them. So they go to a search engine and type in their query. Maybe they find you, and maybe they don't. That's what happens in most cases.

Search engines and directories are the number one way that people find new web sites, according to several research reports. Of all the traffic in search engines, Yahoo! gets the lion's share. It is imperative that you register your web site with the leading search engines so your clients can find you easily. There are many tips and strategies for designing your pages so that the search engines will rank your web site ahead of others, although there are no guarantees; the search engines change their criteria for ranking all the time. Keeping track of these changes is almost a full-time job. This section will show you the most efficient strategies for getting noticed.

Register Your Web Site on the Search Engines

Purpose: Build traffic.

Discussion: Search engines are the *TV Guides* of the Internet. They are vast databases of sites that can be searched by company name, industry, or keyword. Many people use search engines to begin their relationship-building experiences. By registering with search engines, people who didn't know you existed five minutes ago can visit your site. This service is free; the search engines generate revenue by selling advertisements.

There are two kinds of search engines:

1. *Directories* require you to register your site. Editors check the site and decide whether to include it in their listings. Yahoo! (www.yahoo.com) is the most well-known directory and the most used. Others in this category include Snap (www.snap .com) and Looksmart (www.looksmart.com).

2. Search engines per se explore the web for new sites and list them automatically. You don't need to register your page at these sites; in fact, you might want to search these engines now and see if your company is listed! However, you can ensure that these search engines look at your site by registering. Unlike a directory, human beings do not select the content for inclusion. Every site stands a good chance of being listed. The most popular search engines are:

- AltaVista (www.altavista.com).
- HotBot (www.hotbot.com).
- Infoseek (www.infoseek.com).
- Excite (www.excite.com).
- Go (www.go.com).
- Google (www.google.com).
- Lycos (www.lycos.com).
- WebCrawler (www.webcrawler.com).

There are several hundred search engines on the Internet; for listings and descriptions, refer to the WebStep Top 100 (www.mmgco.com /top100.html). However, the ones listed here get most of the traffic from consumers. Some search engines or directories might focus on your industry, and you should make a special effort to find those and register your web site with them. Search a major search engine with the words *directory* or *free links* to find additional promotional opportunities.

Search engines can be extremely effective tools to get people to learn about your company and go to your web site. Lawyer Steven L. Kessler promoted his web site on only one search engine, Yahoo!, and received more than five hundred visits a month from highly qualified prospects. Those visitors included several lawyers who wanted to network and a request from a trade magazine editor who asked him to write an article.

Action: Register your site on the search engines. This chapter will show you how to do this.

Register on Yahoo!

Discussion: Yahoo! is the most frequently used search tool on the Internet. It is imperative that your company be listed here.

Action: Registering your site is a simple process that involves a few easy steps. Here is the process for registering on Yahoo!:

- Write the name of your site, for example, My Company.
- Write the URL, for example, www.mycompany.com.
- Add a two-sentence description of what your company does and what people will find at your site. For example, Joe's Travel Agency, specializing in vacations to Hawaii, offers readers a coloring book and 10 tips on how to cut travel costs.
- Yahoo! is organized like a directory or yellow pages. Each business is listed by category. Select the category you want to be listed in, e.g., Business_and_Commerce:Public Relations Agencies. You can search for categories by using the main menu and selecting the industry your company is in.
- List your contact information (your name and e-mail address).
- Submit your form by clicking on the SUBMIT button.

- Your site could be registered in a few days, weeks, or months. There is no set time limit. If you want to guarantee your business site will be listed in two weeks, you need to pay $200. Otherwise, registration is free.

Register under the Appropriate Category on Yahoo!

Purpose: Ensure that prospects can find you easily.

Discussion: Yahoo! maintains a strict categorization of companies. This is good for marketers as all competitors are listed in the same area so customers can comparison shop.

Action: Go to Yahoo! and take these steps:

1. Find the category under which you want your site listed. If you are not sure which category is appropriate, type the name of your closest competitor and see which category it is listed in. That might be the same category you should use.
2. Go to that category and make sure this is where you want your site located.
3. Click on the ADD URL image and enter all the pertinent information.

List Your Yahoo! Registration in Two Additional Categories

Purpose: Increased exposure, making it more likely for prospects to find you.

Discussion: Yahoo! lets you list your web site in a total of three categories. This is beneficial for companies that sell multiple products. If you sell cookware, cooking books, and cooking supplies, you can list your web site in all three categories. It also helps companies that sell to multiple audiences. For example, a software company selling children's software could be listed under software, educational software, and games. You might find it useful to see under which categories your competitors are listed. To do that, type in the name of your competitor. Yahoo! will display the categories.

Action: Go to Yahoo! and

- Browse through Yahoo! to find the proper wording for each of the categories under which you want to be listed.
- Write down the categories exactly as they appear. Register with Yahoo! There is a fill-in box on the registration form that asks for the titles of the categories to be listed.
- Write them in.

List Your Site in a Geographic Edition of Yahoo!

Purpose: Get targeted traffic from your local audience.

Discussion: Yahoo! has special editions of its directory for different cities, such as San Francisco, Minneapolis, and many others as well as many countries. Most businesses don't know about these special editions. Therefore, these directories don't have thousands of entries as the main directory does. Consequently, your company can stand out because there is less competition.

Action: Go to Yahoo! Look at the top and bottom of the front page for links to the geographic editions. Follow the instructions for adding your web site.

Consider Using Yahoo! Friendly Names for Your Products.

Discussion: When someone goes to a search engine and types *pasta* and finds 2,000 listings of companies selling pasta on the Internet, you'd like your site to be ranked first. Yahoo! lists all companies alphabetically, so you have no chance of being ranked first if your name is Ziti 'R' Us. You'd have a much better shot if your company were called Angel Hair Pasta, Inc.

Action: Obviously, you can't rename your company or products. But you can give serious thought to the names of new products.

The following tactics work with the other search engines.

Add the META Tag to Your Web Site

Purpose: Aids search engines in identifying your keywords.

Discussion: META tags are HTML commands that some search engines use to index your site so prospects can find your web site. The META tags consist of three elements: keywords, title, and description. Figures 11.1 and 11.2 show what the search engine sees and what the reader sees on the screen. Customers don't see these commands. They are part of the HTML code, which is hidden from their view. The syntax is:

<META name = "description" content = "We specialize in grooming pink poodles.">
<META name = "keywords" content = "pet grooming, Palo Alto, dog">

The search engine will:

- Index both fields as words, so a search on either *poodles* or *dog* will match.
- Return the description with the URL. In other words, instead of showing the first couple of lines of the page, a match will look like the following:

```
</script>
<meta name="description"
content="corporate and e-commerce web design, marketing and search engine registration services".
<meta name="keywords"
content="design, web, designs, site, logo, professional, page, graphic, corporate, website, marke
<title>Custom graphic corporate web design, marketing, tracking, ranking, and submission
services. See what it takes to own a top 10 site.</title>
</head>

<body MARGINWIDTH="0" MARGINHEIGHT="0" topmargin="0" leftmargin="0" bgcolor="#BEBEAB"
background="images/nav/bkgd.gif">
<div align="left">

<table border="0" cellspacing="0" cellpadding="0" height="1">
  <tr>
    <td valign="top" align="left" height="1"><img src="images/nav/newlogo2.gif"
    alt="Custom graphic corporate web design, marketing, tracking, ranking, and submission servic
    WIDTH="217" HEIGHT="163"></td>
    <td valign="top" align="left" height="121"><p align="center"><img src="images/nav/top.gif"
    alt="design web designs site logo page professional" WIDTH="20" HEIGHT="119"><img

    src="images/nav/top.gif" alt="corporate web design internet marketing services" WIDTH="20"
    HEIGHT="119"><img src="images/nav/top.gif" alt="promotion marketing design" WIDTH="20"
    HEIGHT="119"><img src="images/nav/top.gif"
    alt="design web designs site logo page professional" WIDTH="20" HEIGHT="119"><img

    src="images/nav/top.gif" alt="free promotion submission search engine" WIDTH="20"
    HEIGHT="119"><img src="images/nav/top.gif" alt="corporate submission design professional"
    WIDTH="20" HEIGHT="119"><img src="images/nav/top.gif" alt="stop looking at my html"
    WIDTH="20" HEIGHT="119"><img src="images/nav/top.gif"
    alt="web design 3d designs marketing commerce" WIDTH="20" HEIGHT="119"><img
```

Figure 11.1 The search engine sees this. (© 1999, Web Wolfe Designs)

Figure 11.2 Your readers see this. (© 1999, Web Wolfe Designs)

- ◦ Pink Poodles, Inc.
- ◦ We specialize in grooming pink poodles.
- ◦ www.pink.poodle.org/—size 3k—29 Dec 99.
- Index the description and keywords up to a limit of 1,024 characters.

Action: For a complete description of how to insert a META tag into your web site, read instructions in the Advanced section of AltaVista (www.altavista.digital.com).

Create Compelling Keywords for Search Engines

Purpose: Help your target audience find your web site more easily.

Discussion: Search engines list sites by how well they rank in relation to the user's request for information. Users might type *Alaska* and get 10,000 responses ranging from hotels to job opportunities. This is clearly too many sites to look at. So they add another keyword to narrow the search, such as *Alaska cruises.* Now they see a handful of sites and can look at a manageable list. This process is all controlled by keywords. You can create these keywords and put them in the META tag area of your HTML page.

When creating keywords, most businesspeople think of nouns, (e.g., travel, airplanes, cars, and hotels). To go one step beyond your competitors, think like your customers and create keywords based on benefits. For example, a travel agency might use the keywords *travel, vacation, adventure, romance,* and *relaxation.*

Use these keywords as well: your company name, each product name, names of competing products, and names of competitors. That way, if a prospect types the name of a competing product or company, she will see your company as well as the intended company. Many consumers, especially business-to-business consumers, will look at your site to see how it compares to the intended company. If you offer better quality or prices, you might get an order from a person who didn't even know you existed a few minutes ago! You can find the keywords that your competitors use by going to their sites and using the browser's commands to view the document source.

Another tactic is to include typos of your company or product because people either don't know how to spell it or frequently hit the wrong key. Try typing *amazom* instead of *amazon* and see what happens!

Another strategy that worked at one time but is no longer effective is to list the top search terms several times. Search engines used to list the finds in order of how close a match there is. For example, a site that lists the keyword *publicity* five times will show up as a better match than a site that lists the same keyword only once. That no longer works.

Your site's log files also will contain a list of the keywords that people used to find your site.

Action: Create the keywords and then list them on your META tags (described in the next section).

Create Descriptions

Purpose: Helps your audience find you.

Discussion: Search engines use the "description" META tag to index sites. The description could be your positioning statement. When people type your company name, they will see whatever your leading lines are. For example:

My Company provides helicopter tours of Hawaii.

Action: Create one sentence that really grabs your prospects.

Create a Title for Each Page

Discussion: Search engines read the HTML tag title to rank your site. If your titles are descriptive, they can lure people to your site. Consider using your company name and a brief description of what you do or a key benefit, for example, Widget Company, the leading manufacturer of widgets. If you have a lot of good information, consider using this format: YOUR COMPANY: How to save money on taxes. The command looks like this:

<HTML>

<HEAD>

<TITLE> Widget Company: The leading manufacturer of widgets
</TITLE>

If you do this, searchers will find out exactly what you do and will have a reason to go to your site. This tip might make the difference between someone visiting your site or a competitor's site.

Action: Create title descriptions for each of your pages.

Put Keywords near the Top of Your Page

Purpose: Improves site rankings with search engines.

Discussion: Some search engines read the first few sentences or paragraphs on the page (not the HTML tags) and determine your ranking.

Action: Place the keywords in the first few sentences.

Design Your Web Site without Frames

Benefit: Improves rankings in search engines.

Discussion: Frames and search engines don't mix. Search engines can't read and index sites created with frames. If your site has frames, consider creating a new front page and new pages for your key products without frames so search engines can index those pages. Then you can link to the rest of your framed pages.

Action: Redesign your site or create new pages.

Revise Your Key Pages

Benefit: Improves rankings in search engines.

Discussion: Several search engines return results of searches based on the date the page was last saved. This helps users see the most current pages first. However, you might have pages that have not changed in a while because the information is still current. Yet the date will appear old even if the material is fresh.

Action: Open the page and save it. The computer will put the current date on the file. Send the file to your server. The next time the search engines index the site, they will recognize the edited page as more current than the one they have on file and will replace it.

Create Different Home Pages for Each Major Search Engine

Benefit: More traffic.

Discussion: Because each major search engine uses a slightly different technique for ranking web sites, you might want to create a home page that is optimized for each search engine.

Action: Study the search engines' rating methods. Create pages for each one based on their exacting criteria.

Register Each Product from Your Site

Purpose: Get multiple exposures on search engines.

Discussion: Instead of merely registering your home page, register each product that has its own page on your web site. People can find out about more products more easily this way.

Action: Create a page for each product. Register each page using the tips from this section.

Buy Keywords on Search Engines

Benefit: Deliver advertising banners to your target market to increase visits.

Discussion: Advertisers can buy keywords on search engines to increase their exposure. When a consumer types in a keyword, such as *computers, airplanes,* or *hotels,* he will see a banner ad paid for by an company that sells computers, airplanes, or hotels. This is a great concept because users are identifying themselves as being in the market for those products at that time. This is one of the great advantages of advertising on the Internet.

There are two parts to this advertising strategy. The first part is that the consumer sees the banner advertisement. The second part occurs when the consumer clicks on the banner. They are connected to your site, but where in your site? That's the key question. For a long time, advertisers led consumers directly to their home page. However, this is not necessarily the right place for them to be. If you have a good many products, they will have to wade through the clutter to find the material that related to the ad. It is like going to a hotel to attend a seminar. You arrive at the hotel lobby, search for the roster of the day's events, find the room where the seminar is located, search for the elevator, get off at the right floor (and make a wrong turn), and eventually find your way to the room. The same scenario applies to the Net. If someone comes to your front page, they might not make it to the advertising page because of all the confusion.

The answer is to link the banner to a specific page on your site. That way, when the consumer clicks on the ad, they will see a message created just for them. An ad for a hotel might read: "Hello, traveler, need a place to stay?" That is so much better than "Welcome to Our Hotel Home Page. Click on any of these icons to read about us, our mission statement, a message from our chairman, letters from our guests, press releases, and a list of our properties." Whenever you have an ad linking to a site, it should link to a specific page.

If you are really clever, you will create different pages for each ad so you can track the effectiveness of each ad in the sales process. After all, if everyone sees the same ad, you won't know if readers from ad A are more likely to buy than readers of ad B. Of course, the ad can be the same; only the URL needs to be different. This concept is discussed in detail in Chapter 13, "Measuring Return on Investment."

Register Your Web Site with Location-Specific Search Engines and Directories

Purpose: Increased exposure.

Discussion: If your web site serves the residents or tourists in a specific geographic area, you should register your site with a search engine that meets the needs of that area. For example, businesses in Iowa can register with Iowa Online (www.iowa.net/links). Check with your chamber of commerce and your visitors and conventions bureau as well. These strategies can bring new customers to your site who are planning to vacation in your area, start a new business, or are searching for specialty items from your neck of the woods.

Action: Use the major search engines to find these specific search engines. Register your site.

Register Your Web Site with Topic-Specific Search Engines

Purpose: Increased exposure.

Discussion: Many professions and industries have their own search engines, indexes, or list of links. By registering on these tools, prospects will find your business. An example of this is FindLinks (www.findlinks.com), which offers links to many different types of businesses and services.

Action: Use the major search engines to find these topic-specific sites. Register your site.

Check to See Where Your Site Is Ranked

Discussion: An online tool called Rankthis! (www.rankthis.com) shows you where your site is ranked on various search engines. That is, when people type *pasta,* you'll find out exactly where you stand. If your ranking is low, people probably will not wade through hundreds of listings and learn about your site. If this is the case, you can use this information to your benefit by taking additional steps to improve the site's ranking, such as adding titles, keywords, mission statements, and other tactics described in this chapter.

Action: Go to the Rank This! site and use the service. It is free.

Create a List of Links

Purpose: Increases attention and return visits.

Discussion: People love links. They love to follow links and find new things. Now you may be wondering why you should create links that allow people to leave your site after you've spent so much time, energy, and money to get them there in the first place. After all, Macy's doesn't have big signs in its shoe department pointing the way to the Thom McAn store in the mall. However, on the web, you can be sure of one thing: People will leave your site. You can make that fact a pleasant experience by creating a list of invaluable resources for them to pursue. Obviously, you don't want to link to your competitors, but you can link to associations, news sources, and other related sites. By doing this, you are creating an invaluable resource for your readers, who will come back to check for updates. They also will tell their friends and colleagues about this resource. If you are concerned that people will leave your site and won't return, use the <target="parent"> tag, which will open a new browser window for the new site while leaving open the one in which your site is viewed. If you use frames, the second page will open the page to which you're pointing in your own web site.

Action: Create the list of links. Use a search engine to find relevant sources.

Link to Complementary Pages

Purpose: Increases exposure to prospects.

Discussion: If I sell Italian suits and you sell Italian shoes to the same audience, then we can complement each other by telling our customers about each other's services. We can each leverage off the investment that the other has made in attracting and building an audience. Further, we don't risk losing these prospects to the complementary site because they are not competitors. (Don't link to another site selling suits, of course). There is no charge for this service if you find friendly sites. The standard has been to give free links. However, as paid advertising becomes more prevalent on the Net, some companies are charging for this service.

Action: Find complementary pages by looking in the search engines. Send a short message to the web master, the person who runs the web site, asking if she would be interested in a reciprocal link. If she is, place a link from your site to hers.

See Which Sites Link to Yours

Discussion: Some search engines will rate your site higher if it is listed on more engines. This is called "popularity."

Action: You can see which sites have links to your web site by using the AltaVista search engine (www.altavista.com). In the empty search box, type the following code, substituting your company name for mine:

link: www.janal.com

Then press the SUBMIT button. You'll see a list of the sites that link to your site.

Register with Automated Registration Tools

Purpose: Saves time.

Discussion: Several software programs and services on the Internet automatically register your web site with other search engines. The key benefit is that you can reduce the amount of time needed to register with dozens or hundreds of search engines. A possible disadvantage is that the page might not be registered accurately in these one-size-fits-all remedies. For the maximum return on your time, register with the top eight services by hand and consider using a service to do the rest. Companies offering this service for free include:

- Submit It. (www.submitit.com).
- SelfPromotion (www.selfpromotion.com).

Action: Complete forms.

Hire a Professional to Register and Optimize Your Web Site

Benefit: Higher rankings.

Discussion: Because there are so many search engines and so many strategies, you could spend your whole life trying to figure them out and registering (and reregistering) your site every time a change takes place. Consider hiring a consultant who can perform this service for you. I have used Michael Krois of Web Wolfe Designs (www.webwolfe.com). His clients have appeared at the top of search engine rankings on a consistent basis. I was skeptical at first of anyone who could make this claim, but seeing is believing.

Subscribe to Search Engine Watch

Discussion: Search engines change their ranking procedures periodically. You could go crazy trying to keep up with all the changes. By subscribing to Danny Goodman's Search Engine Watch (www.search enginewatch.com), you'll learn the latest tricks. Other good resources are:

WebPromote.com (www.webpromote.com).
WebPosition.Gold (www.webposition.com).

SUMMARY

There are many ways to promote your web site. Search engines are only one major part of that strategy. The next chapter will show you how to use publicity, advertising, and promotions.

Promoting Your Web Site with Publicity, Advertising, and Promotions

Search engines play an important tactic role in enticing people to visit your site. In fact, the number one question I hear in the online marketing seminars I conduct for assocations and corporations is, "How can I get my site listed higher on the search engines?" Hopefully, you learned how to do that in the last chapter, but that shouldn't be the only tactic you employ. There are many other ways to draw people to your web site that involve publicity, advertising, and promotions.

This chapter will show you how to incorporate these tactics into your integrated marketing program:

Publicity Strategies

- Notify the press about your new site.
- Notify the press about new content additions.
- Notify the press about new awards and distinctions.
- Encourage sites to reprint your informational articles on their sites or create links to your articles.
- Create a signature file.
- Post notices in newsgroups and mailing lists.
- Answer questions in newsgroups and lists.

Site Management Strategies

- Ask viewers to bookmark your site.
- Make your site the starting point for your customers.

- Create a personal mailing list and send updates to subscribers.
- Create a domain name that is easy to remember.
- Hire a professional firm to promote your site.

Advertising Strategies

- Advertise the site on the net.
- Advertise the site in traditional media.
- Send direct-mail postcards to your customers or prospects.
- Create joint promotions with complementary sites.
- Pay commissions to other sites to refer people to your site.

Promotion Strategies

- Print your URL on all marketing communications materials.
- Offer free products.
- Offer free information.
- Contribute funds to charity for each visit your site receives.
- Create your own awards.
- Use novelties to keep your URL in front of people.
- Add fun stuff.
- Personalize the site.

Strategies to Promote Return Visits

- Create compelling content.
- Create a Cool Tip of the Day page.
- Update information on your page.
- Notify people via e-mail when you update content.
- Notify people via e-mail when you find information or offer new products they have requested.
- Create an insiders-only area that requires registration.
- Operate surveys.
- Conduct contests.
- Require an offline activity to be performed before proceeding online.
- Give coupons, discounts, and rebates.

PUBLICITY STRATEGIES

Notify the Press about Your New Site

Purpose: Gain phenomenal exposure to new audiences.

Discussion: This is one of the best methods to attract people to your site because it reaches so many people. If you send the press release to the media in your industry, you will reach a highly targeted audience as well. Major newspapers such as *USA Today, The Wall Street Journal, The New York Times,* and many others print listings of new web sites every week.

Action: Write a press release. Find your target media by browsing publications or by using Bacon's Media Tracker (available in libraries, or you can order it by calling 1-800-621-0561). Send the release to them via e-mail or regular mail. Business Wire and PR Newswire can send a press release to the media on a cost-effective basis.

Press Release Primer

The *headline* tells the gist of the story in five or six words, written in active style and centered in larger type than the rest of the press release.

The *lead paragraph* tells the essence of what is new and answers the questions who, what, when, where, why, and how. It also points out the benefits of the site to the reader.

The rest of the press release gives more explanation and examples of what is contained at the site.

The last paragraph includes background information about the company, such as when it was founded, what it is known for, awards it has received, and other memorable achievements.

Be sure to include the URL in the first paragraph so reporters can find the site quickly.

Follow the style in this example by substituting your own information, and you'll have the basics of a good press release.

Sample Press Release

For immediate release

Contact
Your name, phone number, and e-mail address

My Company Creates Web Site on the Internet

YOUR CITY—TODAY'S DATE—Mycompany, [short positioning statement], today opened a store on the Internet at http://www.mycompany.com. The site contains information about the company and buying products online, by telephone, or by visiting the company's real store on 123 Main Street. Guests will be able to read the company's history, its annual report, and about its role in the community. They also will be able to find out the latest specials, prices, and discounts on products. Children will be able to retrieve free games, contests, and coloring books. Current customers will be able to find answers to common problems and get customer support online at any time of the day, seven days a week.

"We are providing our customers with more information and service that helps make their lives more productive, interesting, and fun," said Big Boss, president of Mycompany.

Company backgrounder.

####

Notify the Media about New Content

Purpose: Increased exposure.

Discussion: As news about new web sites become old hat, the media will increasingly report on what is new on existing web sites. If you have a new game, article, sample, or the like, you could get coverage. Neuberger and Berman Management, Inc., a no-load mutual fund firm, commissioned a survey that showed baby boomers were not saving enough money to send their kids to college. They issued a press release with this information in conjunction with the launch of their web site (www.nbfunds.com), which features a worksheet for estimating the cost of a college education. The press release was printed in daily newspapers, including the *San Francisco Chronicle*.

Action: See steps in previous strategy.

Notify the Press about Awards and Distinctions

Purpose: Increased exposure.

Discussion: The media could cover news of your new awards and distinctions, like being named one of the Cool Sites of the Day.

Action: See the steps in the previous two strategies.

Encourage Sites to Reprint Your Informational Articles on Their Sites or Link to Them

Purpose: Draws people and increases word of mouth from satisfied browsers.

Discussion: The more people who see your article, the more chances you have of gaining new clients and customers.

Some people have a hard time with this one. They are concerned about copyright and think that anytime anyone uses their work, those people must pay. Let me say this: You cannot pay people enough to post your work on their site. They are giving you a third-party endorsement, much in the same way as newspapers and magazines would be if they did something similar. You can't pay for that kind of credibility.

Action: Write the article. At the top of each article you write, post the following message:

> This article can be reprinted on your web site or in your print publication provided you.
>
> - Print my name and contact information.
> - Print the copyright notice.
> - Print this message.
> - Notify me of the publication date.
> - Send me a copy of the printed article.

You can send e-mail to complementary sites that would attract your target audience or wait for enterprising souls to find your articles

Create a Signature File

Purpose: Useful in creating an identity for your soft-sell image in newsgroups and mailing lists.

Discussion: Targeted newsgroups and mailing lists are comprised of your potential audience members. You need to communicate with them, but netiquette forbids the posting of advertisements in these areas. The first step to using these areas effectively is to create a signature file, also called a sig file. This is a four- to six-line message that tells people who you are, where you work, what you (or the company) do, and how they can contact you.

Action: Create your signature.

Example:

```
 > > > > > > > > > > > > > > > > > > > > > > > > > > > > > > > > > > > > > >
```

Daniel Janal * Janal Communications * 510-459-7814

Author, Speaker, Marketing Consultant

Dan Janal's Guide to Marketing on the Internet • *Risky Business: Protect Your Company from Being Stalked, Conned, or Blackmailed on the Web* http:/www.janal.com/ dan@janal.com

```
 > > > > > > > > > > > > > > > > > > > > > > > > > > > > > > > > > > > > > >
```

Post Informational Articles in Newsgroups and Mailing Lists

Purpose: Increase exposure to your target audience.

Discussion: This strategy can be dangerous if used incorrectly. Newsgroups and mailing lists do not want to be commercial areas and forbid notices of a commercial nature. If you send a commercial announcement, you will receive hundreds of flames or hate mail. People could boycott your site and encourage their friends to do the same. So don't do it!

However, you can post notices that you have just created a site that would appeal to members of newsgroups or mailing lists or have information on that site that would enhance their professional or personal lives.

Here are examples:

- *Not acceptable:* The Fly Fishing Store has opened a site on the web at www.fishing.com. Come to our store and find the lowest prices on the web!
- *Acceptable:* The Fly Fishing Store has opened a site on the web at www.xyzfish.com. Come and read about the best places to fish in Montana.

> >

John Smith * Fishing Store * 800-555-1212

Complete Supply of Everything for the Enthusiast

http:/www.xyzfish.com/ john@xyzfish.com

> >

Action: Find appropriate groups. Write messages. Post along with signature file.

Answer Questions in Newsgroups and Mailing Lists

Purpose: Builds credibility and exposure.

Discussion: Many people post questions of a noncommercial nature in mailing lists and newsgroups, such as "Where is the best place to go fishing in Montana?" You can build credibility and exposure by answering the question; even if the question doesn't benefit you directly, answering it will benefit you because thousands of people will see your name and company information in the signature file. This strategy complies with the Net rule of being a good "netizen," or Net citizen, by contributing to the community and offering something of value for free.

Action: Look for appropriate newsgroups and mailing lists. Search for questions you can answer. Answer them. Attach your signature file.

Example:

> Dan Janal writes:
> Where is the best place to go fishing in Montana?
Try the Old Man's Fishing Hole 30 miles east of Bozeman.
Happy trails!

> >

John Smith * Fishing Store * 800-555-1212

Complete Supply of Everything for the Enthusiast

http:/www.xyzfish.com/ john@xyzfish.com

> >

Special note: Don't subvert the system by having a friend post a leading question such as "Can you recommend a telephone answering machine?" if you sell that equipment. You could answer the question, but someone will find out that the question was a plant and will expose you. Even worse, you don't control the conversation, so unhappy customers could vent their frustrations, thus exposing your product to damage. People who use competing products could also tell how much they like other products, so you just can't win if you use this bad, inappropriate gimmick.

SITE MANAGEMENT STRATEGIES

Ask People to Bookmark Your Site

Purpose: Encourages repeat visits among prospects and customers.

Discussion: A bookmark is a software tool that automatically loads the page to which it refers. If people visit your site once, they might visit again if they see a reminder in their bookmark section.

Action: Place a notice on your home page or subpages saying "Bookmark this page!"

Encourage People to Mark Your Page as Their Starting Page

Purpose: Builds repeat visits to your site; builds brand awareness.

Discussion: Netscape Navigator and Microsoft Internet Explorer default to their home page when viewers sign on each session. However, this default can be set to any page. If you encourage people to set the start-up to your page, they will see your news and updates every time they sign on.

Why would they want to do this? Perhaps you can offer a contest or coupons that make it worth their while to see what you are up to. Be creative! Although this might be difficult to do if you are in a business that people will use only once in their lifetimes, organizations that have a need for regular communications with their customers, employees, or members will not find this task difficult. For example, a trade association of human relations professionals offered free software to its members and set the start page to be its web site. Members found this useful as they needed to be kept up to date on their industry's affairs.

Action: Post a message on your home page asking people to change their starting page to yours. Offer them benefits. Explain how to perform this function.

Create a Personal Mailing List and Send Update Notices to Subscribers

Purpose: Encourages repeat visits among prospects and customers.

Discussion: People may visit your site once but never again because of the competition for attention. Even if people place a bookmark for your site, they might not necessarily visit it often.

If you ask people to join your mailing list, you can send them e-mail notifying them of new articles and offerings at your site. This strategy can build repeat traffic from people who have identified themselves as being interested in your company. Another strategy is to simply send the newsletter out to your subscribers, thus saving them the activity of going to your web site. This tactic also reaches out effectively to people who have e-mail systems but don't have access to the World Wide Web, which is a fairly common practice at many organizations.

Action: Add a form to your site that asks people to subscribe for free to your update service. Compile the list. Update the page. Send out the notices.

Case Study: Flying Noodle Pasta

We are a gourmet pasta and pasta sauce retailer; we have been on-line since December 1995, and our site generates 30 percent of our total sales. The remainder is from direct mail.

A commercial web site should focus on many things; two of the most important are bringing new people to the site and giving all visitors a reason to return.

The main reason to update your site is to keep your site interesting for repeat visitors. First-time visitors don't know how fresh your information is and, frankly, don't need to know.

Hence, there is no point in updating your site unless you have a means to tell previous visitors that you have added new information.

What we, and many other sites, do is offer a free e-mail newsletter to help drive people back to the site. Every two months we send out a newsletter with the following information:

1. Prizewinner name.

2. Article relevant to food/pasta.

3. Recommended food site.

4. "Noodle News."

5. Sale items.

6. How to order.

7. How to get off this list.

The hook to get people to subscribe to our newsletter is the drawing from our subscriber list for a free month in our Pasta Club.

The article gives the publication credibility and gives the reader something useful. Recent articles have dealt with olive oils, balsamic vinegars, what makes one pasta better than another, how to jazz up boring supermarket sauces, and so on.

The recommended food site is often a place that we have traded links with. Generally commercial, always food-related. Often the other site will mention us in their newsletter.

Then we get to the good stuff. The Noodle News section deals with updates to our site, new products we are offering, recent publicity on our company, and any other newsworthy happenings.

The sales items are offered for a limited time to subscribers of the newsletter only and are different from the sales items on our web site. We always refer people to the web site sale items as well.

Other two items are self-explanatory.

When the newsletter goes out (we have around two thousand subscribers), there is always a flurry of new sales and our visitor stats take a jump for a few days.

We find that sending the newsletter out every two months is often enough without being intrusive and isn't so often to be a logistical problem. So by all means update your site; just don't do it in a vacuum.

Raymond K. Lemire, The Big Parmesan, flying@ici.net (www.flyingnoodle .com).

Create a Domain Name that Is Easy to Remember

Purpose: People will come to your site more easily if they remember its name.

Discussion: A domain name is the name by which the Internet user finds your site. An example is http://www.janal.com. *http* stands for hypertext transfer protocol, *www* stands for World Wide Web, *janal* is my company name, and *com* stands for commercial (or business). Your first choice should be to pick your company name to be your domain name and register it with Network Solutions (www.networksolutions.com), the central registration agency of all domain names on the Internet. If that name is taken, you might be able to use a variation of the name. For example, if Janal were taken, I might have used Janal-Communications instead, or Janalcompany or Janalinc. If a product is more well known than your company, you might register that instead, such as Tide instead of Procter and Gamble. Some companies use their slogans, like Southwest Airlines, which uses http://www.iflyswa.com. This is memorable only if the customer remembers your slogan. You can also register your category if people think of that first. For example, I helped Cambridge Publications, Inc., a company that writes documentation for computer software companies, register the domain http://www.documentation.com.

Action: Register your domain name or names by calling your ISP (Internet service provider) or Network Solutions. It costs $70 to register your domain name for the first two years and $35 a year thereafter.

Hire a Professional Firm to Promote Your Page

Purpose: Saves you time.

Discussion: Most of the techniques described in this chapter are so simple that anyone can effectively promote his site. However, you might want to hire a professional company that specializes in this service to save time and gain leverage from its expertise. It might make sense to hire an expert so you can concentrate on running your business, selling products, or doing whatever it is that you do best. Also, if the task involves conducting a lot of online research, such as reading newsgroups and mailing lists for opportunities to mention your product or contribute to the community, then a professional might be more economical.

Action: Hire a firm. Check Yahoo! for companies in this category; ask for references and check them out. Compare prices.

ADVERTISING STRATEGIES

Advertise the Site on the Net

Purpose: Ads expose your message to new audiences.

Discussion: Banner ads are becoming more evident on the Internet with each passing week. By placing ads on search engines and sites that attract your target audiences, you can convince them to visit your site as well.

Action: Create the ad banner. Study the demographics of various sites to find the right fit. Negotiate the advertising rate. Study the number of hits you receive and whether they result in leads or sales. Read Chapter 23, "Buying and Selling Banner Ads," for more information.

Advertise the Site in Traditional Media

Purpose: Increases exposure.

Discussion: More and more companies are displaying their URL in classified and display advertising sections of daily newspapers, business publications, and trade media. Advertisers range from small tax preparers to large car companies. Even TV ads are featuring web addresses. Nearly every movie from Hollywood has a web site filled with games and press materials. The studios run the typical ad for the movie but end it with the URL. Companies like MCI, Toyota, and IBM list their URL on their TV ads as well.

Action: Talk with your advertising department or agency to include your URL on all ads in all media. Buy advertising in a publication that reaches your audience.

Send Direct-Mail Postcards via U.S. Mail to Your Customers or Prospects

Purpose: Increases attention.

Discussion: If you don't have the e-mail addresses of your target audience, you can send them postcards via the U.S. mail to let them know about the creation of your web site and all the new features and free services. If they are not online, your wealth of offerings might convince them to get accounts!

The Wall Street Journal announced its interactive edition by sending a 5.5-by-8.5-inch postcard (presorted, first-class rate) to subscribers of their noninteractive print edition. The postcard offered two months for free if people signed up before a certain date. The teaser read: "After that, it'll pay for itself." Subscription prices followed as well as a toll-free number for more information and how to access the web.

You can send electronic postcards through e-mail as well. Go to a postcard site such as Blue Mountain Arts (www.bluemountainarts.com) and send your advertising information in the postcard; include a picture. Suggest they visit your site to get a free item or free information. This idea is still novel, so you might gather a good many visits.

Action: Create the postcard and send it to your mailing list.

Create Joint Promotions with Complementary Sites

Purpose: Increases traffic to both sites.

Discussion: If I sell shoes and you sell hats, we can agree to post coupons of discounts that would lead people to each other's sites. This can be done in any number of ways: Mention my site and get a discount; buy something at my site and get a discount at the other site.

Action: Find complementary sites. Offer a promotion. You are limited only by your imagination.

Pay Commissions to Other Sites to Refer People to Your Site

Purpose: Increase traffic.

Discussion: If a complementary site has done a good job of attracting qualified prospects, you might be able to lure those readers to your site by paying to put a link or ad on the complementary site. Prices for this type of service are very elastic, so negotiate heavily.

Action: Find complementary sites. Send e-mail to the web master with proposal.

PROMOTION STRATEGIES

Print Your URL on All Marketing Communications Materials

Purpose: Exposure to people who use your products.

Discussion: Companies print their web addresses on their marketing communications material and anything that doesn't move (and some things that do!). Print the address on your press releases, brochures, advertisements, letterheads, envelopes, and business cards. Molson prints its URL on a billboard leading from the Toronto airport to downtown. Joe Boxer weaves the URL into the waistband of its underwear and on roadside billboards (which yielded 15,000 e-mail requests in San Francisco and Los Angeles). Other companies print the URL on trinkets such as pens, mouse pads, and Frisbees. Distinct Corporation printed its address on coasters given to trade show attendees.

Action: Call your graphic artist and incorporate the address into appropriate materials. Be creative!

Offer Free Products

Purpose: Draws people and increases word of mouth from satisfied browsers.

Discussion: If *location, location, location* are the three magic words in real estate, then *free, free, free* are three magic words in online marketing. You can lure people to your site by offering them free samples or information.

The Seattle Filmworks Company (www.filmworks.com) lured people to its site by offering them two free rolls of film. Not only did this have the intended effect of drawing people to the site, but it also meant that people had to divulge their names and addresses to receive the film! SFW went a few steps further to build customer support by offering a free screensaver that would turn their pictures into images that would appear on their computers. Everyone who uses the Internet has a computer and loves the idea of getting more software for it, especially if it is free. Software companies are changing the way their products are being distributed by offering software that runs for a short period of time via the Internet.

Software companies also release demo versions of their software for free, hoping satisfied users will buy the full version of the product.

Action: Contract to create these files and post them on your site. Post notices of their availability in appropriate newsgroups, mailing lists, and forums.

Offer Free Information

Purpose: Draws people and increases word of mouth from satisfied browsers.

Discussion: Information-based companies, such as those that print reports, can post a press release announcing a major news item. Many research companies do this on the Net, as they realize their audiences will be attracted to the headline, but need deeper levels of statistics and explanation than are included in the press release.

Companies not in the information industries can also post files that help enhance the lives of their customers and prospects. If you sell gas grills, list dozens of barbecue recipes.

Consultants and speakers also post information articles. My site (www.janal.com) provides my latest thinking on online marketing topics. Prospects and clients can read the articles for free. If they know that the site will be updated regularly, they come back periodically and tell their associates.

Action: Write articles and post them on your web site.

Create Your Own Awards and Issue Them to Cool Sites

Purpose: Creates exposure on complementary sites; positions your company as an authority.

Discussion: Because everyone and his brother are creating awards, why not create one yourself and notify the happy winners? You will be seen as an authority and will build traffic to your site from people who are looking to find previous winners.

Action: Search for the sites using Yahoo! or another search engine. Read and rate the sites. Create a clever logo. Notify the winner. Create an index of all top winners so people can link to them as well.

Use Novelties to Keep Your URL in Front of People

Purpose: Increases impressions of your company while providing a useful device for consumers.

Discussion: Putting your web site address on something that will be seen often is a great benefit. Although the easy options are mouse pads and coffee cups, other companies are getting very creative without spending a fortune. Smart Business Supersite (www.smartbiz.com), which offers thousands of free documents for marketers, keeps its name on desks by offering a free tent card with space for people to write their user ID and passwords for a dozen sites that require this information. At the top of the list is Smart Business Supersite. When I first received the card, I thought it was a dumb gimmick—until I couldn't remember my codes! Then it became invaluable and earned a spot on my desk.

Action: Brainstorm! Or talk to your novelty sales person for ideas.

Add Fun Stuff

Purpose: Create word of mouth.

Action: Brainstorm over an idea that is fun and relates to your product or service.

Personalize the Site

Purpose: Build relationships.

Discussion: Every portal site now includes personalized news, sports scores, stock quotes, and even e-mail for its members—for free. These services help to encourage repeat visits.

Action: Brainstorm!

STRATEGIES TO PROMOTE RETURN VISITS

Create Compelling Content

Purpose: Encourages repeat visits.

Discussion: If the purpose of your site is to create brand awareness or if people usually buy your products only after numerous impressions, it is essential that you convince prospects to return. If you give people great content or clear benefits for visiting your site, they will come back. Great content could be interesting and useful articles, such as L'Oréal offering hints on makeup and skin tones (www.loreal.com). UPS (www.ups.com) allows you to check the status of a package. Wells Fargo Bank (www.wellsfargo.com) permits you to find the balance on your checking account. Many sites offer free stock quotes and news. The History Channel (www.historychannel.com/today) shows you what happened on this day in history.

Action: Brainstorm to think of the kind of content you can create for your site.

Create a Cool Tip of the Day Page

Purpose: Encourages repeat visits.

Discussion: A Cool Tip of the Day page includes a neat new tip that enhances the reader's personal or professional life. It might be a sentence or a paragraph in length. It could offer information such as how to be a better gardener or how to repair something around your home or how to market something on the Internet. If readers know the site will be updated every day, they will come back for more information every day. Meeting Planner Tips (www.meetingplannertips.com; Figure 12.1) provides information for people who plan conventions and meetings.

Action: Create content and update the site every day.

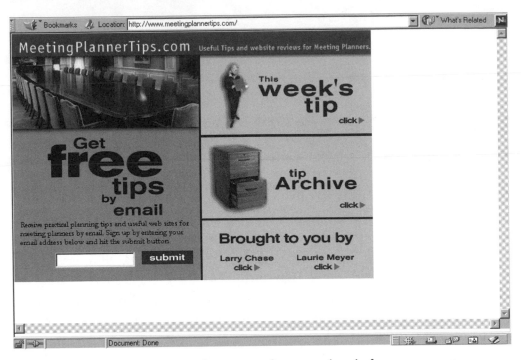

Figure 12.1 This tips site is a clever way of staying ahead of your prospects on a regular basis by offering them news they can use. (© 1999, Chase Online Marketing Strategies, Inc., and Programs Plus International, Inc.)

Update Information on Your Web Site

Purpose: Maximizes repeat visits.

Discussion: Adding new articles, games, and other content will increase the number of visits by prospects. No one knows how often a site should be updated. A good rule of thumb is once a month or once a week if you adopt a magazine approach. If you offer time-sensitive information, such as stock or mutual fund quotes, you need to update the page every few minutes. If you operate a business-to-business site that offers a solitary line of products and don't want to devote a lot of time to it, then you might update it only when new pricing, products, or specifications are announced.

Action: Update as often as necessary.

Notify People via E-Mail When You Update Your Web Site

Purpose: Maximizes repeat visits.

Discussion: People won't know that your site has been updated unless they take an active step and visit (which could be frustrating to them if you don't update the site as often as they check it). To encourage repeat visits, send out notification by e-mail whenever you post new information. You can gather e-mail addresses by asking visitors to register.

Action: Create forms to gather e-mail addresses, store names, and send out information.

Notify People via E-Mail When You Find Information or Offer New Products They Have Requested

Purpose: Builds sales.

Discussion: For companies that sell products, consider asking customers to let you know what products they are interested in should those products be out of stock or not yet created. You notify them when those products appear. Using this tactic will also let you build a database of customers' needs and desires.

Example: Amazon.com asks readers to fill out a simple form about their interests or tastes so that the company can notify them when books from a particular author, genre, or topic are published. (Companies that sell videos, music, magazines, and the like can also use this strategy.) When they find a book that matches your criteria, they send a note that reminds them that they asked to be notified, and of the name of the new book—along with a link to a web page containing information about the book and how to order it.

Action: Build the form.

Create an Insiders-Only Area That Requires Registration

Purpose: Helps create a sense of exclusivity.

Discussion: By creating a password-protected area on your web site, you give people the feeling of belonging to a special community. You can also gather demographic information from the members.

Action: Decide what content should be cordoned off. Talk to your web site designer to implement the password system. Talk to your marketing staff to determine what demographic material is needed. As people don't necessarily like to fill out this information, create a priority of needs so that you get the most important information.

Conduct Surveys

Purpose: Encourages repeat visits.

Discussion: People like to see what other people are thinking. That's why presidential polls are so popular. Web sites can survey their readers on issues of the day or topics in their industry. Surveys serve the additional purpose of gathering useful statistics from your target audience to use in marketing research. If the information is newsworthy, you can issue a press release announcing the findings.

Several search engine/portals offer daily surveys. Readers can state their preferences on issues of the day and see the results immediately. By tabulating results instantly, people get instant gratification.

The granddaddy of all polling firms, Gallup, maintains a polling site on the Internet (www.gallup.com) that lets people enter their opinions and read the results of famous surveys. Excite (www.excite.com) and ESPN (www.espn.com) also feature many surveys.

Action: Create a survey that ties into your integrated message or reinforces your company mission.

Conduct Contests

Purpose: Creates widespread attention and repeat visits.

Discussion: At any given time there are more than one thousand companies offering contests to draw people to their sites. Prizes can range from $1 million in CompuServe's Hunt to two free tickets to a minor league baseball game sponsored by Commonwealth Bank in Virginia. Sunny Delight offered college-bound students an Internet scavenger hunt and a chance to win a $10,000 scholarship. This ploy received nationwide attention in *USA Today.*

Accutrade, an online discount stockbroker (www.accutrade.com), created a stock market trading game. Every participant was credited with $100,000 in play money. The person with the most valuable portfolio at the end of the game wins a free trade every day for life.

Microsoft created a contest for people who used its Front Page program to create home pages. This is a great idea because it caused people to buy and use the program to have a chance at winning.

Contests are best when they reinforce the sponsoring company's mission or core values. For example, Amazon.com, conducted a contest in which customers wrote a segment to a short story begun by literary icon John Updike. The company awarded $1,000 a day to each winner and entered all winners in a $100,000 lottery. More than two hundred eighty thousand entries were received, which averages out to nearly nine thousand entries per day!

Crayola conducted a contest for adults to draw artwork with its crayons. The contest was judged by children. The company regularly conducts contests for children to create greeting cards, for example, for Mother's Day. This type of contest helps encourage the use of the company's products, a very smart marketing move.

Contests can be conducted simply, for example, by asking people to identify themselves by filling in a form stating their name, street address, phone number, and e-mail address so they can win in a random drawing or can be as involved as a challenge or test of skills, as in the Crayola coloring contests, trivia contests, and essays and photo contests.

One clever strategy could be to create a contest that asks people to explain why they desperately need a new copy of whatever you are selling. Give away a certain amount as prizes. The rest of the entrants become leads for your sales staff—equipped with the prime buying motive as stated by each prospect!

Another benefit of all these types of contests is that winners can be promoted on local newspapers and television. In the case of Amazon .com, which has daily winners, there are numerous opportunities for publicity in many local markets on an ongoing basis.

Action: Create a useful contest. The more the contest relates to the company's products and mission, the more effective the overall result will be in reinforcing the marketing mission. For example, the Crayola coloring contest requires children to use crayons. This act reinforces sales and use of the company's products. A contest involving children to write an essay about the use of crayons in folk art would not be as effective.

Case Study: Hotel Discount

Hotel Discount (www.hoteldiscounts.com) sells hotel rooms via the Internet. To stimulate traffic to their site, they created a contest in which they asked business travelers to write about their "Trip from Hell." The prize was a weekend vacation in Boca Raton, Florida.

More than thirteen thousand people either entered the contest or read the entries. All entries were posted online. The site was so popular that 50 people a day still visit the site even though the contest ended months ago.

The contest helped the company create a brand name and increased traffic, which resulted in sales.

"It was so successful, we will do it again!" said Larry Chase, president of Chase Online Marketing Strategies (larry@chaseonline.com, www.chase online.com).

They intend to run banner ads on the search engines with the headline: "Just when you thought it was safe: Trip from Hell 2."

Case Study: *Reader's Digest*

When I created a contest for The Reader's Digest Association to promote the new Complete Do-It-Yourself Manual on CD-ROM, I discovered a number of factors that must be considered before committing a company to a specific type of contest.

At first we thought it would be a good idea to have people submit something to win the grand prize, such as a short letter about the funniest thing that ever happened to them doing a home repair. We nixed the idea when we thought people wouldn't have the time to write or might not be comfortable with their writing skills.

Then we thought about having them submit before and after pictures of their home repair. That idea didn't pan out when we thought that people might not have taken pictures of their work.

We then realized that any kind of contest that required a submission would also require judging. That meant we had to line up a panel of judges, a human resource burden.

Even worse, we thought of the tremendous number of people that would be needed to open envelopes of submissions, take out the material, and sort it—let alone read the material to pick a winner!

We then decided that the easiest tactic would be to ask people to fill out an entry form online. They didn't have to submit anything but their name, e-mail address, and street address—after all, how could we send them the prizes if we didn't know where they lived?

The next step was to create a site to showcase the product and allow for order taking. To lead people to the site, we created a Cool D-I-Y (Do It Yourself) Tip of the Day page with 60 tips for the two-month run of the contest. Press releases, reviewer's quotes, and product information added heft to the site and credibility for the CD-ROM. We also added a quiz about home repair that showed off the content of the product. However, we didn't require anyone to fill out the quiz to enter the contest. It was just a fun thing to do. The quiz changed every week.

The contest met the company's goals of introducing the product to the online world and generating sales in the 1 to 2 percent range.

Require an Offline Activity to Be Performed before Proceeding Online

Purpose: Ensures repetition of the brand name.

Discussion: The web site for the movie *Jumanji* hosted a multipart game (www.spe.sony.com/Movies/Jumanji/contest.html). Users could download a part of it and play it offline. When they solved the game, they received a password that they could then use to go back online to get the next segment of the game. This activity ensured that children visited the site over and over.

Action: Create a game, quiz, or test that encourages this type of repeat visit.

Give Coupons, Discounts, and Rebates

Purpose: Encourages repeat visits.

Discussion: People will come back to your site when they know you offer coupons, discounts, rebates, or other money-saving incentives. Casual Male, a retailer of clothing for big and tall men, stated that 23 percent of the 30,000 visitors to its web site (www.thinkbig.com) downloaded coupons worth 25 percent off apparel. The Hyde Park, Massachusetts–based firm uses the site to lead buyers to the chain's 400 retail stores. L'eggs, the leading hosiery manufacturer for women, offers a

50 percent discount on its products to people via online ordering. Rail Europe (www.raileurope.com) offers special prices for online consumers. Go (www.1800batteries.com) offers a $2 discount for online orders.

Action: Create the incentive and promote it on the Net and other media.

SUMMARY

There are many ways to publicize your site and draw people to it. Most strategies are free except for your time and energy.

If you have ideas for promoting a web site, please send me the strategy, action steps, and results. I'll be happy to include the strategy on my site and put a free link to your site there, too!

Measuring Return on Investment

Every action on the Internet can be counted, tracked, and traced. No other medium allows for such a precise technology for measuring the effectiveness of every piece of text or image. Unfortunately, most companies online have neither implemented these tools nor instituted measurement and tracking systems to test the effectiveness of their marketing campaigns. The online industry also needs to establish standards of measurement, performance, and metrics as well as create an unbiased, objective source to verify web site demographics and statistics.

This chapter will explore:

- Why companies need to track their messages across all communications platforms.
- The problem with hits.
- The next generation of web site measurement.
- Benchmarking the web.
- The direct-response web site.
- Expanding on the direct-response model.
- Accountability and metrics for online communications.

WHY COMPANIES NEED TO TRACK THEIR MESSAGES ACROSS ALL COMMUNICATIONS PLATFORMS

Is your home page hot?

Is your web page cool?

Does it really matter?

I am sick and tired of hearing these phrases!

What do they mean? Really?

Cool is a 50s term.

Hot is a 60s term.

Beatniks.

Hippies.

What do they—or their pony tailed, goateed, tongue-pierced progeny—know about marketing? These groups are the very antithesis of marketing. Do you want Maynard G. Krebs and Abbie Hoffman designing your web site? Yet their terminology and supposed marketing strategy are taking over the Net. How did this happen? How is it possible that dull, boring, geeky technology has suddenly been transformed and reframed like the ugly duckling into a medium that is cool—or hot?

That's a rhetorical question. No answer is needed. What is needed are data. Hard, cold facts that answer the real question: Does my web site meet my marketing goals? Does it sell? Does it provide customer support? Does it build and enhance the relationship between customer and company?

These are the questions companies need to ask—and answer.

Case in point: As I mentioned before, everyone loves the Ragu site. You can't go to a marketing conference without hearing a speaker extol its virtues. Hundreds of thousands of people have been exposed to this pasta sauce through the web and from conferences. But no one asks the vital question: Is anyone buying Ragu? Have its sales increased? Has its market share increased? Has even its share of the people on the Net who buy spaghetti sauce increased? No one has these answers.

Although everyone loves cute Mama—including me—why isn't she part of the integrated marketing campaign for Ragu? Why isn't her inviting, motherly face beckoning to us from the label of the bottles in the supermarket shelves? Why is Ragu not taking advantage of its most famous—cool—asset while she is—pardon the expression—hot? These omissions would not be made by professional marketers.

In the pursuit of knowledge, I sent an e-mail to Mama and her minions to find out the answers and told them that I planned to write about the site as well as mention it in my speeches around the United States, Canada, and Mexico. I promptly received an e-mail from Kathy

McNally and Mama, who wrote, "We have had many requests on just these same questions. Unfortunately, due to confidentiality, we are unable to answer them." When I informed them that I intended to write about this, they wrote, "We are so glad that you liked our web site. Unfortunately, we cannot respond due to the amount of requests received."

That sounds like a form letter—not what I'd expect from a company that prides itself on one-to-one marketing! Your company doesn't have to have that same experience.

Fortunately, the Internet provides powerful tools for marketers to extend the integrated marketing program to the electronic media.

Question: Can you be hot and cool at the same time?

Answer: No, you can only be lukewarm.

As the Net enters the next phase of its marketing maturity, professional marketers will demand answers on the issues of accountability, return on investment, and message consistency. They will set up reliable tests, surveys, and benchmarks to justify their existence on the Net and to provide the quality of service and information that their customers seek in a web site.

Won't that be groovy?

Scenarios like that of Ragu are replayed in many places where I speak and conduct online marketing seminars. Marketers want to know how to find the return on investment. But there are problems with methodology that confound marketers at every step of the way. Consider this case: During a seminar I conducted in Des Moines, a delegate asked if anyone had ever bought anything over the Internet. In the crowd of 70 people, about fifteen raised their hands.

I asked one of them what he had bought. It was a Kodak digital camera. When I asked him to describe the steps he took in buying this expensive piece of equipment, he said he had first read about it in a magazine.

I asked if he had been reading an advertisement or an article. He said he didn't remember. (Marketers, note that people do not always remember how they heard about your product.) While reading, he saw the address for Kodak's web site and went online. He read more about its family of products and decided which one to buy. Kodak has a policy of not selling products directly to consumers; instead, it supports its dealer network with its ads, both in print and online. So he found the toll-free phone number of the nearest dealer, who was in Chicago; called the number, and placed the order.

Notice how many different media he used: magazine, the Internet, and telephone. Internet marketing was but one piece of the marketing puzzle.

Now let's go back to the actual transaction. When the dealer picked up the phone, were his first words "How did you hear about us?" or "What's your credit card number?" You bet it was the latter! He didn't know or care how he got the order as long as he got the order.

Let's go to the next scene: It is the next day at Kodak headquarters. The director of marketing calls the person charged with Internet marketing and asks, "How is our Web site doing? Is it making any sales? Is it paying for itself?" Unfortunately, the Internet manager has no idea that Kodak just sold a thousand-dollar piece of equipment via the Internet because no one asked the buyer or the dealer!

Therein lies the fatal flaw of most online marketing activities today. No one is tracking sales, let alone tracking brand awareness or image or goodwill. These web sites might be doing marvelous jobs in reaching those goals, but no one will know if they aren't counting—and counting over all media platforms!

THE PROBLEM WITH HITS

The first measurement technique you've probably heard of in relation to the Internet is "hits." Your friends probably asked you how many hits your page gets, or you might have seen a web page displaying an odometer that shows how many hits the page has received since a certain date.

These measurement techniques are dead wrong.

Hit is very misleading term in this context. A normal person would assume that a hit refers to a person visiting a web site. In reality, it merely means the number of times a file on a web page has been accessed. So if your front page has one text file and four picture files, that adds 5 hits to your counter. If the person goes to read your press releases on a new page and returns to the front page, there are 5 more hits added to the counter. What happens if she leaves the page after the third file loads? Are we at 15 hits or 13 hits? And what difference does it make anyway? Hits don't buy things; people do. If you look at your hit counter, you'd think 15 people visited the site and only 1 person bought anything. That's not a very good percentage. But in reality, only 1 person visited your site and she bought something. That's a pretty good percentage. Unfortunately, you'd never know it by looking at hit counters.

BENCHMARKING THE WEB

By Katharine D. Paine, CEO and founder, Delahaye Medialink Communications Research, Inc. (www.delahaye.com), 603-431-0111 © 1998. Reprinted with permission.

The Basics of Measurement

Yes, Virginia, there is a way to measure it.

The simple answer is that you measure your Internet activity the same way you measure any other communications activity—you get everyone to agree on objectives, you establish specific criteria, you measure those criteria, you look at the results, you take action, then you measure again.

And really, it's just as simple as it sounds.

Before we get into the specifics of measuring online marketing, let's review the basics of measurement. No matter what you benchmark, your success depends on following six basic rules:

1. **Establish objectives.** Reach an agreement between all the parties involved about what you are trying to achieve.
2. **Determine criteria.** Define success specifically—number of hits, percentage of people more likely to purchase, rave reviews in *a magazine*. At the end of the day, what will convince you and your superiors that your web site is a success? Decide upon a benchmark. Benchmarking above all is a comparative process. If you tell me that 1,000 people a day are hitting your site, you haven't told me anything of value. I have no way to know whether 1,000 is a good number or a bad number until I know how many hits you received last month or last year and unless I know how many hits the competition gets. And how do those numbers compare to the number of people reading your ads?
3. **Select a benchmark.** There is no shortage of criteria against which you can benchmark your progress. The key to valuable benchmarking is your choice of the right criteria. Are you going to compare your progress to yourself over time, compare yourself to the competition, or compare the web to other forms of communications? Select the right measurement tool! Only after you've identified your objectives, criteria, and type of benchmark can you really decide what technique you should use to benchmark your program.

4. **Compare your results to objectives.** Once you've conducted your benchmark, don't get carried away by numbers. Instead, examine them in relation to your original objectives to decide if your online marketing has succeeded.

5. **Draw actionable conclusions.** You've received one million hits a day, but what do you do with that information? No one in business today needs more numbers. They need interpretation of numbers to know what actions will help them become better, more efficient, or more cost-effective.

6. **Deliver on time.** Work backwards from planning sessions, strategy meetings, or quarterly review meetings. Don't just pick an arbitrary time period to measure. Pick one that will give you critical information for your upcoming meetings.

Now, with those rules in mind, let's get into the specifics of Net benchmarking.

Definitions of Success

To know if your web site works, you have to know its specific purpose. Otherwise, you can't define what marks its success. Why is your company bothering to put up a web site? What do you want to accomplish? In the past few months I've been boggled by how many different things companies try to do with their web sites. Here are a few examples:

- **The "Hello, I'm Here" Site.** Some companies believe that it's better to have something out there than nothing at all. Frankly, I can't argue with that logic. It's what I call your basic place holder—something out there so that someone can call up widget.com and find you. This type of online presence typically includes some basic company background information, a list of products, maybe a newsletter and a feedback form. Success in this case is measured by evidence that no one is flaming you and that you're not on anyone's worst-of-the-web list.

- **The customer service substitute.** Most fully operating sites probably originated from customer service departments to answer customers' questions online and therefore ease the workload of customer service phone banks. Success for these is measured by the reduction of wait time on phone lines and increased number of people contacting you for very efficient help.

- **The "Hello, I'm Cool" Site.** Some companies (or technowizards within companies) decide that the web is the coolest thing around and they're going to join cool by putting something on it. Whether such a site is consistent with anything else in the company's communications program is irrelevant. Success for such an objective is measured by whether the site tops the best-of-the-Net in *Wired* magazine.

- **The image-enhancing site.** Image builders also appear in web sites. These companies see their presence on the Net as part of their larger image. They use their sites to enhance their other communications strategies. Success for them is measured by consistency of messages across various media, from publicity to newsgroups to advertising. Ultimate success is measured by users' awareness of the company's key messages and preference for the company's products.

- **The international marketing site.** Actually, this web site goal is redundant because by its very nature the web is the most international of communications media. Companies that don't bear this in mind can get into major trouble. Witness the small instrument company that, after putting up a web site, was instantly flooded with international orders years before it planned international distribution. But if your primary purpose for a site is to target international customers, your site design and definition of success will be quite different.

- **The revenue-producing site.** Some companies see the web as a new advertising medium. Although sites make information available to a phenomenally large population, the web needs a lot more time to develop and a lot more T-1 lines (a designated Internet connection) before it can substitute for *Murphy Brown*. But never underestimate the power of Coke's and Ford's marketing departments. For these folks, success is measured by the Web equivalent of gross rating points and/or audited circulation figures. Trouble is, we haven't quite figured out what the equivalent is yet.

The So What Department

There's no shortage of ways to collect data, nor is there any shortage of data to collect.

The real shortage occurs in analysis of what all that data means. To determine what it really does mean, you have to return to your original objectives. What do you do if you're getting 100,000 visitors a week, your server is overloaded, and you need a $100,000 investment to upgrade? First, you have to look at who those 100,000 people are, what percentage are in your target audience, what percentage are asking for more information, and what percentage are ready to buy.

Maybe your results are right on the edge. You're getting good, but not great, response. The numbers are good, but you're trying to decide whether or not to put other types of information on the site. Now you need to look at your competition, what else is available to your target audience, and what revenue potential exists for those additional products or services. You also need to assess the quality of other ways you reach your target audiences, and at what cost. Then you can determine cost per contact so that you can compare the effectiveness of your online marketing to other forms of marketing.

The point to remember is the specific value of benchmarking: Whether you benchmark online or with more traditional forms of marketing, the process enables you to use the data you collect to improve all segments of your communications program. If your data doesn't do that, you're collecting the wrong data.

THE DIRECT-RESPONSE WEB SITE

By Bob Vogel, ICI Solutions (softmail@icisolutions.com, www.softmail.com, 518-283-3791), © 1998. Bob Vogel. Reprinted with permission.

The web site is fast becoming an additional selection in the call-to-action response vehicles, right there by the phone, mail, and fax options. Unfortunately, in the rush to construct these web sites—usually in some vain attempt to beat the competition and claim First in Cyberspace—most companies do not carefully think through exactly how best to integrate the Internet into their overall sales and marketing programs.

Now this is not surprising when you look at who within most companies is given the responsibility to create the site. Most often, it is one of three types:

1. Technical consultants, who provide advice on web site content based on what the Internet culture was, not what it is or can be.

2. Graphic designers and advertising types, whose focus is generally sizzle rather than content, and generating hits rather than generating results.
3. Computer programmers who have no clue about marketing communications, or marketing people who have no clue about web site programming and flow chart diagrams.

It's not surprising that only a handful of islands in the ocean of web sites have any true economic value to their owners.

From where I sit, as a direct marketer of 15 years serving technology clients, the paradigm for creating a successful, meaningful, and profitable web sites is crystal clear: the direct-response web site.

The operative word here is *response,* and the underlying key is to design and structure the site as a response vehicle to all other forms of outreach, including advertising, PR, mail, telemarketing, even the Internet itself.

While I may have invented the term *direct-response web site,* I did not invent the time-proven direct marketing techniques behind the concept, namely.

- Carefully target your market.
- Create a compelling offer to get people to respond.
- Use graphics and copy to direct the flow of the message.
- Build fail-safe mechanisms for measuring response.
- Test. Test. Test.

Carefully Target Your Market

As I'm a direct marketer, I'm not so much concerned with the number of hits at my site as I am in accomplishing a clearly defined sales objective, whether that is closing a sale or creating a qualified lead or something in between.

With direct mail and telemarketing, this starts with selecting the best lists that match the profile of your target market. For direct-response TV, radio, and print ads, it means matching the demographics of the program, time slot, or circulation to your target market. For the Internet, it means linking your site only to those places where your target markets might be poking around.

There is no magic to this. In fact, if you are doing your job right with your conventional direct-response tools—advertising, direct mail, telemarketing, trade shows, PR, and the like—adding a conspicuous URL for your web site is probably all you need to do to get started.

Create a Compelling Offer to Get People to Respond

If you have done your targeting job correctly, you'll want to capture the name and at least contact information of every person who visits your site.

Unfortunately, the way the Internet is structured, most people can visit your site pretty much anonymously. You can tell what server they came in from but not necessarily the identity of the individual.

Most companies have a so-called guest book as a standard feature, where people can voluntarily put themselves on a mailing list (or "opt in," as they say in the mailing list world). But there is usually no compelling reason for them to do so, especially if the promise is a vague indication of keeping them informed of new developments.

Again, there's nothing magic or new about how to accomplish this: The very same tricks of the trade we've always used in conventional forms of direct marketing work on the net, too. Try contests, premiums, sweepstakes, promotions, special prices, and the like. Just be sure to structure your offer in such a way as to generate a qualified prospect—not every Jane and Joe in the world who happens to be wired.

Remember, as the Internet is so open, the URL you carefully targeted to a limited audience could quickly get passed on through e-mail and newsgroups to an enormous number of people in no time. And if you're giving away free T-shirts, for example, you'll probably end up giving away the one off your back before you are through.

Here's a good example of how to keep control: To promote a new service being offered by SoftMail Direct, we might take out an ad in a trade publication offering a free web site critique—a $1,000 value. We would offer it to 100 people selected at random from all people who visited our web site between December 15 and December 31 and registered at the special URL mentioned in the ad. Qualified prospects would jump at this opportunity, as they would otherwise have to pay $1,000 for our critique. Anyone who doesn't have a web site for us to critique, or sees no value in having the site critiqued, is not a prospect.

Use Graphics and Copy to Direct the Flow of the Message

Unlike any other response vehicle—like phone, fax, or mail—there is no practical limit to the amount of information you can provide your prospects and customers once they hit your direct-response web site.

Think how much more effective your sales communications would be if you could afford to send the answer to every possible question about your product or service that the prospect might have. Wouldn't it be great if you could afford to send a one-inch-thick color brochure, a three-inch-thick color catalog, or a five-inch-thick technical manual to every single qualified prospect?

Thanks to hypertext and the low cost of electronic storage media, the amount of information you can post is limitless. But this is both a blessing and a curse. If you put the wrong kind of information on your site or if it's not perfectly segmented and linked, you will quickly overwhelm (or underwhelm!) your prospects, and they'll jump off your site with the click of a mouse button.

When building (or revising) your web site, take a look at every single page as a stand-alone entity. Ask yourself how this page is furthering your marketing objective. Then carefully inspect each link on each page. Every single link should move the prospect one step closer to your objective, be it capturing a name, closing a sale, further qualifying the prospect, or expanding awareness of your product, company, or brand.

Also, contrary to conventional wisdom, it is a big mistake to make it easy for people to leave your site by embedding links in your web pages to other sites. Many people put links to other sites as a hook or feature to attract people to their sites. That's the worst kind of incentive you can provide. They should come for your content, or they're probably not worth knowing.

Build Fail-Safe Mechanisms for Measuring Response

Even if you do a great job of targeting your outbound activities, you will find dramatically different costs and response rates associated with each. As with any form of direct marketing, you want to be able to measure response by source of the inquiry or sale.

Most people designing web sites today create a single home page address that they use in all marketing and communications activities. That's like using the same source code for all mailing lists, direct-response ads,

PR hits, and so on. Direct-response web sites have many home pages, all identical in every way (or maybe not) except for their URL.

The best way to track response by source is to create a separate URL or home page for each place you advertise your web site, including the Internet itself. This is incredibly simple. All you have to do is make a copy of your current home page and save it as a new filename in the same directory as the original.

For example, the standard URL for SoftMail Direct is www.soft-mail.com/index.html. However, in the previous example with my special offer for a free web site critique, I could have a duplicate home page at www.softmail.com/NewPubAd.html. That way, when I get my hit report, I know exactly how many people came to my web site as a result of my ad in *DM News*. If I send out a direct-mail piece with the same offer, I would create another home page (e.g., www.softmail.com/NewMail .html), giving me a clean way to measure cost versus response for each outreach vehicle.

And if I'm really smart, I won't send my carefully targeted and segmented prospects to my home page at all. Other things go on there that could distract them from taking the action that drove them there in the first place. Instead, I'll send them to a special page relating to my offer and then give them the option to jump to the home page after taking the desired action (say, completing a form).

Creating unique URLs for each offer may sound cumbersome. But the data is critical, and it's a lot easier, less expensive, and much more accurate than creating unique telephone extensions for phone orders or separate P.O. boxes for mail responses.

Test. Test. Test.

The amount and level of data you can obtain about what people do when they get to your direct-response web site is unprecedented in the world of direct marketing. Imagine sending out a direct-mail piece and being able to find out exactly how many people actually opened the envelope, how many read the letter (and which pages they read), how many read the brochure, which pictures they looked at, and how many people looked at the order form—all of this, even if they never responded to your piece. Wow!

With these finely calibrated measurement tools at your disposal, you have a unique opportunity to test product positioning, offers, and creative materials, that is, ads—in real time!

In addition to setting up separate URLs for separate sources, you can set up separate URLs for different offers, creative, and product positions—just about anything. And if you already have a lot of traffic at your site coming to a single URL, you can turn it into a direct-response web site by measuring the hits for the current offer, creative, or product position and then making a change to one of the variables and measuring what happens.

Again, using my example of our free web site critique service, I might create a new ad with a more generalized promotion such as "Visit our web site and qualify for a super deal on our new Web Site Critique service." (I have set up a special URL for this test—www.softmail.com /Weboffer.)

For the first week of response, I use my control offer of a free web site critique. Then, after one week of response, I might change the offer of 50 percent off a web site critique—just $500. The next week I might offer the web site critique at the standard price, with a $1,000 rebate off our regular fees if we are subsequently retained to redesign the web site.

Depending on your normal web site activity, you might be able to change promotions daily (or even several times a day). The important thing is that whether you are talking to consumers, a technical audience, or business-to-business, you keep testing different parts of your site, removing parts that are not working hard for you, and retaining and enhancing those sections that are.

EXPANDING ON THE DIRECT-RESPONSE MODEL

As good as the direct-response model offered by Bob Vogel is, it only gets better. Once you have people coming to your direct-response sites, you know how many people are coming from each ad. Now you have the starting point for creating relationships with each customer and for measuring the effectiveness of each magazine's readers. For example, let's say you have placed three ads in *Fortune, Business Week* and *The Wall Street Journal.* Readers are from the same demographic profile, so you have one ad message, copied to three distinct URLS: www .mycompany.com/F1, www.mycompany.com/BW1, and www.my-company.com/WSJ1. You place counters on each page, so you know how many people are coming in from each magazine ad. You finally have a tool that measures cost per lead.

On one level you now know how effectively each ad pulls. If 10,000 came from *Fortune,* 1,000 from *Business Week,* and 100 from *The Wall Street Journal,* you'd have a good idea that *Fortune* is the magazine for you to continue advertising in!

However, that might not be the case. Let's take the next step in creating a relationship. You ask each reader to take action: Ask for a sample or download software, read more about the product, have a salesperson call, or buy the product. Now let's look at those figures. How many readers from each magazine took which course of action? You might find that *The Wall Street Journal* readers, who were fewer in number, actually bought more product than the *Fortune* readers! You can now track the cost per sale for each magazine.

It gets even better. You can now compare the average profit per sale from readers of each publication to see where you are really making money. Take this one step further and you can measure the lifetime value of the customer by seeing how much that person buys over the course of months and years.

Let's take this a step further. If you are in charge of public relations at your company, you can tag each press release with a distinct URL so that one newspaper tells its readers that more information can be found at www.mycompany.com/pr001 while a second paper sends its readers to www.mycompany.com/pr002. Now you can track leads and sales by publication. Finally, public relations can show its impact to the bottom line!

ACCOUNTABILITY AND METRICS

You can employ several formulas and tactics to measure the effectiveness of your online marketing campaign.

WebConnect suggests that its clients spread their advertising dollars over several web sites, tracking the click rates for each site where their ad is placed. Within a month, they can see which sites are most effective for their particular purpose and concentrate their money for greater effectiveness.

The banner ad itself needs to be tested, as a slight variation might double the click rate. Some web media brokers allow clients to test various banners for a somewhat higher fee.

Here is a set of measurement metrics developed by Delahaye Medialink:

- If your objective is targeted exposure, count:
  The percentage of visitors from targeted audience.
  The percentage more inclined to purchase.
  The cost per minute spent with prospect.
  The cost per qualified lead.
  The cost savings for literature and mailing.
- If your objective is to strengthen customer relations, count:
  The cost savings of literature, support, and printing.
  The percentage of positive and negative postings.
  The percentage of visitors in target audience.
  The percentage of positive vs. negative feedback.
- If your objective is to improve internal communications, measure:
  The cost savings of literature, support, and printing.
  The percentage of personnel accessing the site.
  The impact on productivity, loyalty, and turnover.

Objective	Criterion	Tool
Reach new markets	Percentage of visitors in target audience	Track visitors' demographics
Sell ad space	Influence of page on purchasing habits	Track visitors' habits
Create affinity between brand and event	Visitor opinion of brand	Survey visitors
Sell product	Dollar volume of web page sales	Isolate and track web page sale
Be cool	Placed in Yahoo!'s "what's hot" list	Track number of mentions in hot lists
Convey information	Amount of literature sent	Isolate and track web page sales

Source: Delahaye Medialink. © 1998. Reprinted with permission.

MEASUREMENT/RETURN ON INVESTMENT

Customer Support

Measure the costs of a support call in the real world. Compute the cost of creating and maintaining a online support center. Divide the cost of the system by the calls handled to determine the cost of service on the web. Compare that figure to the office costs.

For example, FedEx receives 300,000 calls a day from people who are tracking packages, which costs about $3 to $4 to handle. That equals about $200 million a year when you factor in typical labor and equipment costs. With a web site and tracking software costing an estimated $5 to $7 million, FedEx can make its investment back in less than a year.

Netscape pays $10 to a service company to handle telephone customer support calls. If customers use the web, there is no human cost. If the company gets 3,000 calls a day, that's $30,000 for support costs. That figure goes along way toward paying the price of the web site.

Saving Customers' Time

One of the hidden costs and benefits of the Internet is the time that companies save for their customers. Instead of hanging in voice mail jail on the phone, customers can find the answers they need by themselves on your web site. This could also translate into improved customer satisfaction and increased brand loyalty.

Measure Customer Satisfaction

Each piece of e-mail to FedEx is coded. Complaints, compliments, and the like are all assigned codes. The web master can quickly gauge consumer attitudes by counting the numbers in each coded category. The responses are then matched against similar codes to telephone surveys to check for trends and discrepancies.

Customer Education

Companies can save a great deal of money by providing educational material, such as brochures, white papers, press releases, and the like online. If the price of printing and mailing collateral is $10 per prospect and the price of creating online versions is $1,000 per page, the payback comes after only 100 visits.

Lead Generation via Advertising

Advertising can provide several ways to measure effectiveness. The cost per lead model takes the amount of dollars spent on advertising and divides it by the number of leads. For example, if you pay $3,000 for the ad and get 3,000 leads, the price per lead is $1.

Another measure is the sales per lead. To find this number, take the amount spent on advertising and divide it by the number of orders. For example, if you pay $3,000 for the ad and receive 300 orders, the cost for each order is $10.

A third tool is the profit per sale, which might be the most important figure because profit is what you are really seeking. To find this number, take the amount of money spent on the ad and divide it by the profit per order. If you spend $3,000 for the ad and make $21,000 profit, you have a seven-to-one return on your investment. In other words, for every $1 you spent, you received $7 in return.

Online Sales

The figure for online sales is easily computed by measuring the number of sales or the profit for all sales. Divide that figure by the cost of your web site and you will see if your site if profitable. For example, you've sold $1 million of products with a 50 percent margin, so you've netted $500,000. If your site cost $250,000 to build and maintain, you've made $2 for every dollar invested.

Public Relations

You can measure the effect of public relations on the company by creating a chart showing the number of visits per day and overlaying bullet points showing the announcement of news, such as product introductions, earnings reports, or management changes. The chart you produce will probably show spikes at the time of those events. If that's the case, you can show your management that public relations is having an effect on the interest in the company.

Another way to use the web for public image management is to review comments made on newsgroup postings. Do the recurring themes contrast with the company's key messages? What percentage of the posting is positive, negative, or neutral? What issues are on the top of user's minds? Are these issues long term, or do they appear only once or twice? "By analyzing comments made in chat rooms and news groups, you might identify issues that need to be addressed, such as customer support. After making changes to that area, you can then go back to the users and see how and if they are commenting on the topic," says Katharine D. Paine of the Delahaye Medialink.

SUMMARY

An effective online marketing program is one that can be measured, tested, and improved based on specific number targets and realistic objectives. The testing field today is in its infancy, though new tools are being developed to accurately record consumer response. This chapter presented several realistic techniques, including benchmarking and the direct-response web page, to give marketers useful tools for determining the effectiveness of their online marketing programs. It also explored various metrics for determining success.

After it is all said and done, remember this quote from Larry Chase of Chase Online Marketing Strategies: "It is not about numbers. It is about conversions."

Creating Customers for Life with One-to-One Marketing Programs

Creating Customers for Life with One-to-One Marketing Programs

This chapter will help you understand:

- What one-to-one marketing is and what it means to you.
- How to create one-to-one programs and tactics.

WHAT ONE-TO-ONE MARKETING IS AND WHAT IT MEANS TO YOU

Whenever I fly, I choose United Airlines. Their service is probably no better than any other airline, but here's where they differ. You see, I am a Premier Executive member, which means I fly more than fifty thousand mile a year on United. That's a lot of miles, so they want to treat me nice; they let me board the plane before the general passengers. That means I can find a place to store my suitcase before they run out of room. I can also request an exit row seat, which has more legroom so I have a little bit more comfort. That's why I fly United.

Notice what United did. I perceived great value from these services. However, it didn't cost United a penny. After all, they had to give the seat to someone, and they had to let me board sometime anyway. Because they chose this particular way to do so, I have given my loyalty to United. That's the beauty of a loyalty program: I have flown so many miles on United that I can't begin to fly with anyone else. I am locked in.

I can't go back to being a normal passenger on another airline and fight with everyone else for that last precious cargo space!

I also belong to the Hertz Gold Club. Whenever I land at an airport, a rental car will be waiting for me, with the engine running and the paperwork completed. If I weren't a club member, I would have to stand in line for 45 minutes and fill out forms before they would give me the car. This level of convenience makes me a customer for life.

These two stories illustrate the key points in one-to-one marketing, the hottest concept in marketing today: companies shouldn't think in terms of market share, or how much of the market they own, as they have for generations; instead, they should think in terms of customer share, or how much of the customer they own. In other words, when I consider buying an airline ticket, United owns me 95 percent of the time because they might not fly everywhere I need to go. Hertz owns 100 percent of my rental car business because they are everywhere I go. You probably have similar loyalties, too. After you develop a win-win relationship that saves your time and offers convenience, you don't want to do business with anyone else—unless they can offer substantially more benefits. That's why one-to-one marketing tactics work.

Loyalty leads to profits. Amazon.com owes more than 60 percent of its sales to repeat buyers. This marketing concept is behind one of the key factors that makes the web a great place to do business: treating every customer as an individual. Companies can treat customers as individuals, as markets of one. Because they know my preferences, they can serve me better and faster—so I return to their web stores and buy from them.

Amazon.com president Jeff Bezos says that if he has 4.5 million customers, he should have 4.5 million stores—each one customized for each person who visits. When you go to Amazon.com, you'll find a personal greeting, recommendations for books based on previous books you've purchased, and one-click ordering for new books. That means you press one button, and the computer fills in all the billing and shipping information. The computer knows this because you gave the information freely when you made your first purchase. Amazon.com also asked if you wanted to store this information; it did not assume this. This is one of the keys of permission-based marketing. Now you go back to Amazon.com because you know that you don't have to fill out long purchase orders and send your credit card over the telephone line again. They've got you! And you are glad because you benefit.

In a business-to-business setting, Dell Computers has mastered one-to-one marketing on its web site. It has created individual stores for some of the largest companies, associations, and government agencies in the United States. Any person working for those organizations types in a specialized web address to enter his company's Dell store. As he shops, his choices are limited to the computers that meet the exact requirements of his company. He knows he will leave the store with a computer that has been configured to work in his company network, operate with the same version of software that is compatible with the rest of the company, and not have to fill out reams of paperwork. To its credit, Dell has tapped into the biggest fear of computer managers: incompatibility. The company dreads having to service dozens of computers made by different manufacturers and containing hundreds of different components. By standardizing on one vendor, the company knows it will get a quality product and will be able to reduce support costs and training expenses. Dell has its customers locked in for life—and they think they are getting individual attention. Because of this strategy, Dell sells more than $5 million of computers every day on its web site. What is your customer's worst fear? Solve it and you could make a fortune.

Other companies are exploring how to personalize their sites and their products. Nearly every major search engine or portal allows you to register and record your preferences, such as stock portfolios, local weather, sports teams, horoscope, and daily news. When you go to the site, you see a page that greets you by name and displays the latest headlines, scores, and stock quotes immediately. Because of this customization, people are more likely to make this page their starting page and return to it every time they go online. Excite says its members return five times as often and stay at the site twice as long as nonmembers do. The company benefits by displaying more banner ads and generating revenue.

Customization pays off. Market researcher Jupiter Communications (www.jup.com) says sites that customize report a 52 percent rise in revenue and a rapid growth of new customers. Consider these examples that show the benefits of getting to know your customers:

- A flower company sees your zip code and infers how much money you make. The next time you go back to the page, they show you bouquets priced at a range you are comfortable with. You don't waste time wishing you had more money or feel bad because you can't afford the good ones and then leave without making a purchase. You feel good because your expectations have been met.

- You enter a web site for a clothing catalog. Because you have bought there before, they know your preferences—size, colors, and sex. Now they can show you menus and ads that have been chosen to meet your needs. You don't waste time looking at clothing ads for people of the other sex.
- You are a big supporter of the arts in your community and have joined several organizations' mailing lists so you can keep up with the latest productions. A show producer realizes that ticket sales for a particular concert date are slow. They send you a targeted e-mail message letting you know about the event—and that discounts are available. You are happy to get tickets for this event and buy them. Every major airline does this e-mail marketing technique every week to sell its slow-moving seats.

HOW TO CREATE ONE-TO-ONE PROGRAMS AND TACTICS

The Internet offers great tools and opportunities for creating one-to-one relationships with customers that last a lifetime. So how do you get started? This section will explore a strategy for making these relationships a reality at your company. The next six chapters will explore in detail how to build one-to-one relationships to make customers for life using Internet marketing tactics.

Planning is the first step in all one-to-one marketing efforts. You need to:

- Create goals.
- Attract prospects.
- Give them a compelling reason to do business with you.
- Find out who they are and what they need.
- Give it to them.
- Keep in touch with them to suggest new products and upgrades.

Case Study: Seattle FilmWorks

To get a good understanding of how to build one-to-one relationships, let's look at Seattle FilmWorks (www.Filmworks.com), a company that depends on repeat business to stay in business. Seattle FilmWorks is in the business of selling photographic film to consumers and developing pictures. They have intense competition from hundreds of companies; most of its competitors are as near and convenient to their customers as the local drug store or supermarket. Yet Seattle FilmWorks get lots of people to do business with them online. Let's see how.

Its goal is to increase the size of its database of happy customers so it can sell them additional products over their lifetimes. So how do you attract people to your web site, when the local supermarket can do the same service — and is on their list of weekly activities?

Seattle FilmWorks entices people to its web site by offering them two free rolls of film. That's an offer most people would jump at. However, now comes the interesting part. How do you get possession of the two free rolls of film? You have to tell the company where to send them! You have to provide your name and address. Now Seattle FilmWorks knows who you are and where you live. It has accomplished part one of its marketing plan: identifying customers and adding them to the database.

Now that customers have the film, what prevents them from taking it to their local supermarket and having it developed there? Seattle FilmWorks uses proprietary film. It is the only company that can process the film. You might try a proprietary way of doing business as well. In both cases, once the customer has the product, she is locked in to your way of doing business. So she sends the film back to Seattle FilmWorks, but It makes a compelling, value-added proposition: Would you like to get your pictures scanned and stored on a computer disk as well as printed on paper? With a computerized version of your pictures, you can print them on your company newsletters or insert them into your family's holiday newsletters. This is something the local supermarket could not do. When Seattle FilmWorks first made this offer, it was a compelling, competitive advantage. Today, many local photo shops can put pictures on disk as well. But at the time it first made the offer, Seattle FilmWorks had this market all to itself.

As she places her order, the web site asks her if she'd like to turn those digital pictures into a screensaver on her computer—for free. If so, she can download the software to her computer with the click of a mouse button. Now she is getting extra value from those digital pictures! Instead of seeing pictures of flying toasters or Microsoft logos, she can see pictures of her cats and kids.

Now it is a month later, and she's talking on the phone when her screensaver kicks in. A group of colleagues passes her desk and notices the pictures of her cats and kids. They ask her how this happened, and she replies, "I got two free rolls of film from Seattle FilmWorks and they gave me the screensaver software for free—and you can get it for free, too, if you go to their web site."

Seattle Filmworks now has leveraged their relationship with her, as she recommends the site to her friends. All it cost the company was a free piece of software that didn't cost anything to ship.

Let's zoom ahead 30 days. Those pictures of her cats and kids that looked so good last month are now starting to look old and stale. Does she throw out the pictures and the screensaver? No, of course not. She orders two more rolls of film from Seattle FilmWorks and starts the process all over again. She is now a customer for life.

This company also builds relationships by offering free information to make people better photographers, contests to reward them for taking good pictures, and a sense of community by getting to see other people's pictures.

Now let's look at other techniques that you can use to sell your products and services.

Building Relationships with E-mail and Private Mailing Lists

E-mail is the true killer application on the Internet. Americans sent seven times as many pieces of e-mail than regular first-class "snail mail" in 1998, according to web research firm eMarketer, Inc. (www.emarketer.com): It estimated 766.5 billion piece of e-mails sent in 1998 compared with 107 billion first-class items delivered. eMarketer said that 81 million Americans regularly use e-mail, each of whom receives on average 26.4 pieces of e-mail daily.

In this chapter, you will learn.

- The benefits of using e-mail in the marketing mix.
- How to create one-to-one relationships with prospects and customers with e-mail.
- Strategies for writing effective messages.
- Formatting issues for e-mail.

BENEFITS OF USING E-MAIL IN THE MARKETING MIX

E-mail is a terrific way for online marketers to interact with consumers and is the common denominator for reaching people in a cost-effective manner. After all, it is the one tool that everyone has, and it's easy to use. There aren't any confusing commands to learn or navigation routes to negotiate. E-mail doesn't even care whether you use a PC or a Mac or a

UNIX computer system. E-mail, comprised of text, photos, or even audio messages, can be sent to people on different online systems; thus it is the way many companies communicate with consumers to create relationships. E-mail helps companies by permitting the free flow of information without the barriers of time and space. People can send and receive e-mail at any time of the day or night. The recipients can answer at their leisure.

The benefits of using e-mail to converse with consumers include:

- Sales:
  - Educating prospects by sending information about new products and services, company background, help files, and any other material you can create to foster a relationship.
  - Converting prospects to customers by providing them with requested information, such as company overviews, product backgrounders, press releases, reports, surveys, and media reviews.
    - Notifying customers of sales and special promotions.
- Public Relations: Alerting customers, stockholders, employees, and vendors of important news.
- Branding: Developing brand loyalty by informing consumers of new products or services, sales, discounts, seminars, events, and the like.

In an integrated marketing environment, e-mail can be used as a direct communications link with prospects. Let's look at the steps involved in an integrated marketing campaign.

HOW TO CREATE ONE-TO-ONE RELATIONSHIPS WITH PROSPECTS AND CUSTOMERS

1. E-mail is the starting point in this building process. At its simplest, people who have questions about your product send you an e-mail. They might have seen the address on your letterhead, advertisement, product package, billboard, or business card or in your signature file attached to a message you posted on a discussion area.

Responding to each message individually helps develop one-to-one relationships with consumers.

After a while, you might notice that many people ask the same questions most of the time. Instead of writing an individual letter, you can access a library of texts written to account for most situations. As you receive a message about the product warranty, for example, you cut and paste the prewritten answer that explains the warranty. What used to take you five minutes to write now takes you five seconds.

2. The next step up this ladder is automating the process. You have a library of prewritten answers to the most common questions. Customers can receive those answers when they send e-mail to a specific e-mailbox. For example, if they send a message to warranty@mycompany.com, they will receive the answer in seconds. This is possible due to an auto-responder, a software program that automatically sends e-mail that has been requested. Your ISP can provide you with this service, as can many third-party companies that you can find through Yahoo! (search under "autoresponder"). You might think of this service as an online cousin to the fax response systems in which you dial a company's fax machine, type in your fax number, and the numerical code that requests a prewritten communication to be faxed back to you in seconds.

This process can save you time and money. If people read the prewritten response and still have questions, they can send a new request to a company representative who can answer the difficult ones. Thus, your staff spends its time dealing with the more difficult questions, while the routine questions are handled by the autoresponder.

Any kind of file can be sent via e-mail, whether it be text, photo, or sound. E-mail can thus provide more information than a customer support representative talking on a telephone. You can also provide answers to customers just at the moment they are most interested in developing a relationship with your company—even if that happens to be 2 A.M. Sunday when your customer support staff is at home and asleep.

3. All this time, your computer is recording the e-mail addresses of all persons who send a request. You are building a database of valuable information about where people can be contacted and what their key interests are. (You know this because they have sent e-mail to a specific e-mailbox. You would therefore know that a certain person was interested in the seminars you offer but not the books or that they are interested in the seminar in Chicago, not the one in New York.)

The tactic of using a separate e-mailbox for information replies can also be used to track the number of responses from a particular source. For example, if you have two ads written about your company and you list a different mailbox address in each ad, you'll be able to see which ad drew more responses. You can do this with articles, fliers, brochures, and any other marketing material.

4. As your database grows, you might want to establish closer lines of communication with each person by contacting them directly via e-mail. You might send them coupons for your products that entice them to order directly from you or lead them into one of your distributor's stores. You might build a relationship with them by sending a newsletter every month or quarter that suggests interesting new ways to use your products and services. You could even let them know that you've updated your web site with information that will enhance their personal or professional lives. You could encourage them to participate in surveys so you can determine where the market is heading and what new features and benefits are being sought. You could also use this material to track who actually buys your products to see if a marketing effort is successful or if your pitches need to change.

5. Use these mailing list newsletters after the sale to reinforce the buying decision, educate the customer on additional features and uses of the product, and sell additional products upgrades.

Striking while the iron is hot is a key point in sales. The Internet has great tools to make this happen by giving people information when they need it.

HOW TO EFFECTIVELY USE PRIVATE MAILING LISTS TO BUILD RELATIONSHIPS

Companies can create private mailing lists to keep in touch with their communities. Here are several tactics that you should consider using.

Create a One-Way Mailing List of Your Community Members

Benefit: Maintain close relationships with customers, retailers, editors, and other VIPs by engaging them in dialogues.

Discussion: A mailing list is an electronic tool that allows you to interact with your communities and lets each community member talk to the others. You can send press releases and product information, answer questions, let people know what's new on your web site, and even let customers talk among themselves to help solve problems.

As a mailing list owner, you are a publisher who can freely distribute marketing materials without fear of reprisals or flames. After all, people want to be on your list because they want to receive information in the first place.

To create a mailing list, you must use a software program that handles all subscriptions and manages the mailing process. Unity Mail from Revnet (www.revnet.com) provides these functions along with needed management and security features.

You will also need to create an information/welcoming message to new members that tells new and prospective subscribers what the list covers and who should join. This will help you and them make the best use of their time and resources so they don't join a list that doesn't meet their needs or yours. The message also should contain information on how to unsubscribe and FAQs about the mailing list itself. This message should also be set up as an information piece that is sent automatically to anyone who sends mail to, for example, information@mycompany.com.

The next step is to get members. You'll have to publicize the mailing list to attract subscribers. Consider these strategies:

- Posting notices in relevant newsgroups and mailing lists. Be sure to point out that this is a free service so you don't run afoul of netiquette.
- Including information in your signature file.
- Letting your customers know about the mailing list through press releases, letters, newsletters, ads, and other communications both on the Internet and in your printed materials.
- Posting information and sign-up forms on your web site.

These strategies will help to create word of mouth, which is one of the best marketing methods, as satisfied subscribers will tell their colleagues.

Be sure to include directions for subscribing and unsubscribing. For example:

To subscribe to CHAT LINES, send e-mail to lists@mycompany.com with a blank subject line and a message body of "subscribe chatlines."
To unsubscribe, send e-mail to lists@mycompany.com with a blank subject line and a message body of "unsubscribe chatlines."

Create a Two-Way Mailing List of Your Community Members

Discussion: The benefits and actions are the same as described previously for one-way mailing lists. The added benefit of a two-way mailing list is that customers can talk to one another. They can help solve each other's problems and discuss your company's strengths and weaknesses. It is a tool that can help you gauge customer interest and sentiment. You can also influence opinions by offering advice, news, and contacts with product managers or other company officials.

Create Information Packages Available via E-mail and Downloading

Benefit: Prospects get needed information when they want it without delay.

Discussion: The interactivity of consumer dialogues means that people will ask you for information about your company and its products or services. You can respond via regular mail or e-mail. Your company might already have a kit ready to be sent by mail or courier service to hot prospects but will also need one for the online consumer. You can let the customer access this information by creating files and storing them in forums or on your web site. An alternative is to let customers send you e-mail with a note in the subject line saying, for example, "send info pack one." You can create an automatic response system in which your autoresponder sends the appropriate file to the customer as soon as it receives the query. If you prefer to use a commercial online service, there won't be any automatic mail system. However, you can have an operator check messages and respond as soon as feasible. In either case, prospects will get the information they need in a timely manner—when they are hot to buy.

You must consider what kind of information should be included in this message. Each business will have a different set of considerations. Here are ideas:

- Press releases.
- Data sheets.
- Sales sheets.
- Dealer sheets.

- Company financial information.
- Reviews from newspapers and magazines.
- Tables of contents (for books).
- Catalogs.
- Brochures.
- Photos.
- Testimonial letters.
- Independent reports.
- Newsletters.
- Annual reports.
- Message from the president.

Action: Create info packages that reinforce the integrated marketing message.

Create Signature Files to Add Positioning Statements to Your Messages

Benefit: A signature file tells people who you are and what you do.

Discussion: Although every online system lets you put your name and e-mail address in the mail header, that information is next to useless to the reader. That's because there is no context for, say, joe@yourcompany.com. Is he the chief cook or bottle washer? And just what does his company do, anyway?

Fortunately, netiquette does allow mail senders to include a signature, but don't confuse this with your John Hancock. An *online signature*, or *tagline*, is a four-line message printed at the bottom of your message area in which you can present information of any kind. Business people use it commonly to tell others who they are and what they do. A suitable use for online marketers is to print your positioning statement and contact information. The benefit of this signature is that you can subtly let people know who you are and what you do without being a pest. There are no downside risks because netiquette holds this to be an acceptable practice. Here is an example:

Daniel Janal * Janal Communications * 510-459-7814

Author, Speaker, Marketing Consultant Specializing on the Internet

_ Dan Janal's Guide to Marketing on the Internet_

_Risky Business: Protect Your Business from Being Stalked,
Conned, or Blackmailed on the Web_

http://www.janal.com dan@janal.com

Signature files can also be used at the end of each message you send
to a mailing list or newsgroup.

Action: Create a signature file. If you use Netscape Navigator or
Microsoft Internet Explorer, create the signature file with your word
processor. Save it as a text file, not as a word processing file perse. Use
the browser's e-mail preferences options to select that file as the signature file. It will be appended to all your messages. America Online does
not support signature files. However, if you created a signature file in
your word processor, you can copy it and paste it into your e-mails.

Please note that when you add your web site address, include
http://www so people can click on the link to reach your site. If you
leave it off and put only, for example, janal.com or www.janal.com, the
link won't work.

Reply to Questions Quickly

Discussion: The online world expects and demands a fast response to
questions—about 24 hours seems to be the norm for new content in response to a personal question (as distinct from canned responses sent
via an autoresponder). If you don't respond quickly, you could lose credibility and frustrate customers. A middle ground is to send a quick response via an autoresponder saying "We have received your message and
will respond within 24 hours."

Action: Commit to answering messages quickly. Make this mandate
known to all employees who deal with the public.

Ask Questions and Ask for Feedback

Discussion: When someone sends you a note, reply as soon as you can
with the information and then ask a question to keep the conversation
alive. Even a simple "What do you do?" or "What do you think?" will encourage the person to reply. If you don't ask these kinds of questions, the

conversation will die. If you ask them, you will learn more about prospects so you can fill their needs.

Track Responses with E-mail

Benefit: Accurate tracking of leads from various sources.

Discussion: The harshest criticism of public relations is that it is difficult to measure. You can begin to measure public relations by creating several e-mail accounts and using them in tandem with each message you use.

Example: Let's say you want to test the price of a product and place ads in printed publications or in legitimately posted messages on online systems. You have three ads; they are the same except for the three different prices and the three different e-mail addresses. People who are interested see only one ad and send an e-mail note to the corresponding account. By tallying the number of messages in each mailbox, you can determine which test worked best. This method also works for testing leads or inquiries from articles published about your company or product or articles you have written and placed in online libraries. You can also then track the respondent's actions after he receives your marketing materials to determine which source of leads works best.

Action: Contact your service provider to create additional accounts.

Don't Buy Bulk E-Mail Lists and Don't Send Spam

Discussion: A number of direct mailers have compiled massive lists of e-mail addresses based on people who have posted messages in mailing lists and newsgroups. They sell these lists to advertisers claiming these people are all interested in a given topic. This is a bad strategy for marketers as most online citizens don't like their e-mailboxes filled with advertisements. Any advertiser who uses this tactic risks offending people. Such spamming should be avoided because the online community hates this tactic, partly because most spams are sent by adult entertainment businesses and get-rich-quick schemes. People also don't like wasting their time receiving and deleting the messages.

STRATEGIES FOR CREATING EFFECTIVE MESSAGES

E-mail marketing can be a success tool—if you write great copy. Here are several pointers to improve your response rates:

- The first thing people see in their e-mail box is the subject line. Limit your subject line to 42 characters because e-mail programs might cut it off if it is longer. Write an action-oriented, benefit-oriented headline to capture interest. Use your company name in the subject line so people won't confuse the message as being a spam.
- In the body copy, start with a benefit-oriented headline. If you use the word *free* in the headline and body copy, make it the first word to grab attention: "Free Review of Your Web Site," not "Review Your Web Site for Free."
- Put the most important information at the top. People might not read beyond the first few words, so you have to grab them quickly. Stress that they are eligible for your special offer because they are registered users. Exclusivity is a powerful appeal, says Ivan Levison.
- Next, give your URL. Some people will go right to your web site if you do. Don't make them scroll down to the bottom of the message. And don't try to make a complete sale in an e-mail message. "The medium simply isn't appropriate for conducting the sales process. E-mail is perfect for urging people to visit your web site where they'll find valuable information, a downloadable demo, etc. Don't just hype your offer. Let them know what exciting stuff is waiting for them at your site. THAT's the place where the real selling should take place," suggests Levison. "Include a unique (and hot-linked) URL for them to click on. On that custom-designed web page, you can thank them for responding to your e-mail, etc. You don't want to send them to your general-purpose home page and force them to hunt for your e-mail offer."
- Bullet the benefits. It's easier to read bullet items than lumpy body copy.
- If you are writing to your installed base, thank them for their business and let them know that they're appreciated.
- Give an incentive to buy.
- Provide multiple ways to order: via e-mail, a toll-free number, a fax-back form, or a form that can be printed and mailed. Make it easy for customers to place an order.

- "Prune your words. In general, shorter is better. This is different from sales letters, where the more you tell, the more you sell. E-mail readers are usually sorting through a bunch of messages and aren't disposed to stick with you for a long time," says Levison.
- Test alternative endings. Use a formal ending and test it against an informal, friendly ending. Test prices and headlines to see which works better. Test a long letter against a short letter.
- In general, shorter is better. This is not the case in sales letters where as a general principle, the more you tell, the more you sell. E-mail is a unique environment. Readers are quickly sorting through a bunch of messages and aren't disposed to stick with you for a long time.

With these proven techniques, your marketing messages have a better chance of being read and acted on.

FORMATTING ISSUES FOR E-MAIL

Here are strategies you can use to integrate e-mail in your marketing program:

Format the Message Properly

Benefit: Your message will be legible. Illegible messages are confusing and could be unreadable.

Discussion: Set the line width for 4.5 inches to avoid bad line wraps.

Send E-mail to Yourself to See How It Looks

Benefit: The message will look attractive.

Discussion: Before you send e-mail to customers or reporters, send it to yourself to make sure the material is formatted properly and displays properly on the screen. It is all too easy to hit the wrong key on your word processor and send 500 lines of computer characters instead of a press release or have your lines wrap badly or have paragraph markers disappear (See Figure 15.1).

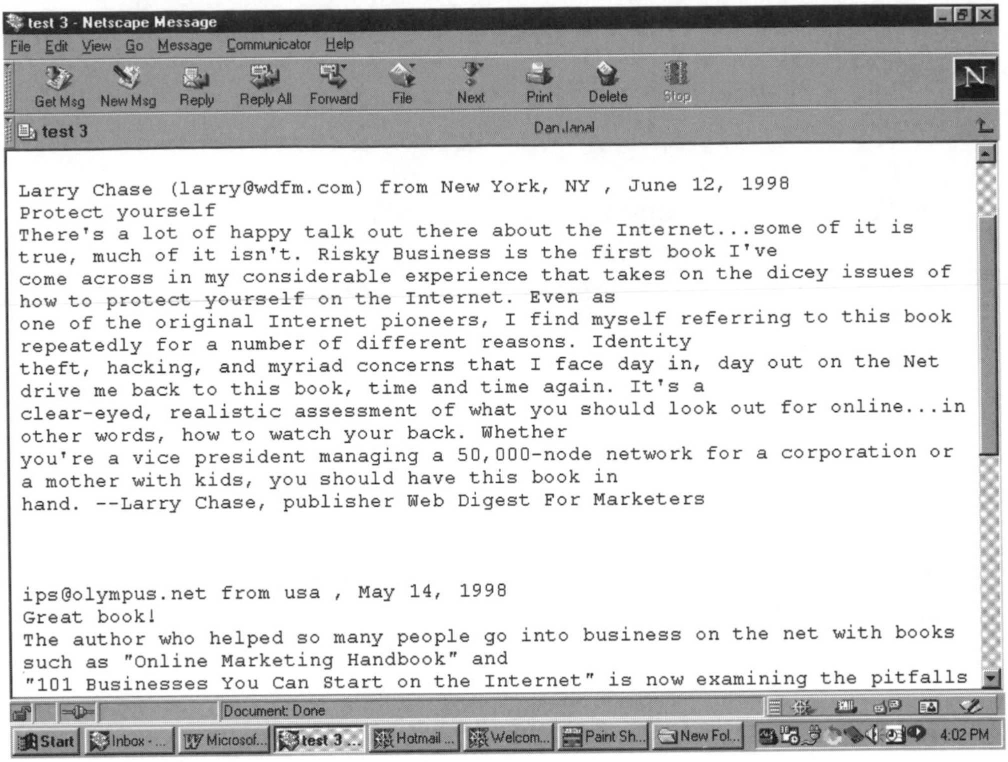

Figure 15.1 Always send e-mail newsletters to yourself before sending it to the group to make sure they are formatted properly and all the links work. This example shows bad line breaks that make reading difficult.

Make Each E-mail Look Individual

Benefit: Creates a feeling of intimacy.

Discussion: If you send e-mail to a list of 100 people, each person will see the name of every other person on the list and know this is not a personal correspondence, which lowers the intimacy factor. Also, they will see the names of the 100 people before they see your message, which means they will have to scroll past 100 lines before they can read your important message. This will increase the tick-off factor tremendously. Off-the-shelf e-mail programs don't do a very good job of explaining how to turn off the bcc (blind carbon copy) function, so test this activity thoroughly before sending messages.

Action: Send your message to a list of dummy names at your company first to make sure the blind carbon copy has turned off the name of each other recipient.

Use ASCII Text for All Documents

Benefit: Ensure data is transmitted properly.

Discussion: With so many computer systems and word processors in the world, it is fairly easy to send a file that the recipient can't read. Although some people love pages designed with high-end design programs, most people don't have the software to read them. Your best choice is to send everything in the lowest common denominator format, which is ASCII. Don't compress files in Zip format unless you are sure the recipient has the Zip uncompress utility that makes the file readable. Also, don't send files as attachments; people don't like opening them for fear of contracting a virus. If they don't have a program that can read the file, it will look like garbage, and your chance for making a good impression will be lost.

Action: Save all files to ASCII (or text) before sending.

Use HTML-Formatted Files

Benefit: Messages look better and create a more positive impression than ASCII messages.

Discussion: E-mail messages can look like web pages, with different-sized type, colors, pictures, and graphs as well as links to web sites and e-mail addresses. Use your HTML editor or Microsoft Word to create the files (use the "save as HTML" command to save your work) and send it to your lists. HTML-formatted files will take longer to load than ASCII-formatted messages. This might annoy your readers, so be careful about using this strategy. However, an advantage of using HTML e-mails is that you can include attractive ads, so you can make money.

Action: Create and distribute the files with HTML formatting.

BUILDING RELATIONSHIPS WITH NEWSLETTERS

If e-mail is the universal application, then newsletters sent by e-mail might be the universal marketing tool. In a newsletter, you have the ultimate tool to reach your customers, vendors, employees, investors, dealers, prospects, and anyone else interested in your company. You can put your name in front of them on a regular basis. Best of all, they have given you permission to do so. We're not talking about spam here; we are talking about people saying, "Send me your news, your offers, your press releases, your insights. We value this information." Marketing might not get any easier than this.

Newsletters are a cost-effective means of sales and promotion on the Internet. Unlike paper newsletters that cost money to print and send, electronic newsletters can be sent for free or a small fee. You have to pay a price to write the newsletter. But if you have a print edition, you might be able to take all or several articles and use them in the electronic version. Then you'll get more use from that material.

E-mail newsletters come in two formats: text or HTML. The text newsletter looks like any other piece of e-mail you receive (Figure 15.2). There are no pictures or colors. HTML newsletters look like web pages. They can be colorful, containing pictures and even banner ads. Both types of newsletters can contain hyperlinks to take people back to your web site. In fact, one strategy is to post only headlines or teasers in the newsletters and let people click on the link to read the full story. This strategy gets people back to your web site. However, if they are not online, they can't read anything!

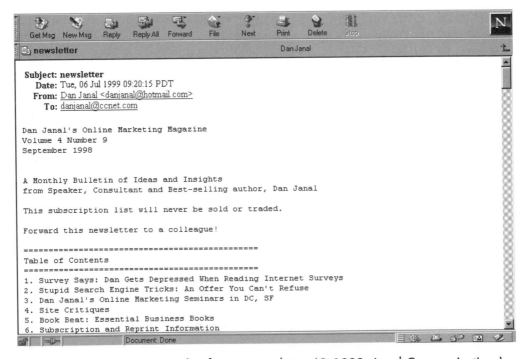

Figure 15.2 This is a sample of a text newsletter. (© 1999, Janal Communications)

Each format has advantages and disadvantages. Text newsletters load fast. HTML newsletters might load slowly because they contain graphics. HTML newsletters can print banner advertisements as any web page can. Text newsletters can run ads, but they must appear as text, which means they won't stand out very well when surrounded by other text items.

Here are the essential steps in creating an e-mail newsletter:

1. **Gather e-mail addresses of your target audience.** You can do this by posting a notice on your web site, sending e-mails to people in your database, and placing advertising notices in traditional media (as part of your current ads or stand-alone offers) and in your current print newsletter.

One ski resort marketing director wanted to use e-mail newsletters to replace her print versions for several reasons. She had 40,000 subscribers, so the cost of creating the newsletter and sending it out exceeded $40,000 an issue. Second, she wanted to let her customers know about ski conditions and special events on the weekends. It was important to get this information to customers in a timely manner. Relying on the mail would take days; relying on e-mail takes seconds. This is important when your key ingredient melts. To let people know about the new e-mail newsletter, she told them about it in the print edition.

2. **Make them an offer they can't refuse.** Show them why they should subscribe to your newsletter. Explain the features and benefits. You might say that they will get your latest insights, news, and articles as well as information on sales, closeouts, and specials and exclusive information on new products. Finally, assure them that you will guard their privacy and not send them junk mail or sell their names to companies that send spam.

3. **Write the publication.** You can use your existing content from the print edition or create new copy. Be sure to write in a style that works for the web. Compose short articles. Write in newspaper style and put the news on top. Use lists and bullets to make copy more readable. Engage the reader with feedback options (e.g., "What do you think? Send me a note with your best tip!")

4. **Distribute the newsletter by e-mail.** If you have a small group, you might be able to handle the mailing tasks manually. This could work for

employees or vendors at a small company. However, if you plan to have a large list, you will want to use a software program or service that will handle all the subscription chores by computer. Programs such as Unity Mail from Revnet (www.revnet.com) will handle all subscriptions, unsubscriptions, reports, and mailings. The New York Yankees and many other large companies and small businesses use this product.

5. The secret ingredient: Encourage people to pass the newsletter to friends and subscribe! If 5 people send your newsletter to 5 people who they in turn send it to 5 people each, you will have reached 125 people. Best yet, these new prospects will have learned about your company from a trusted source: their friends or colleagues. They will look at your newsletter as a valuable piece of literature, not an unsolicited message. And it didn't cost anyone a penny to send it.

6. Secret ingredient number 2: Encourage people to reprint your articles on their sites or in their newsletters as long as they give credit to you! This is a great way to build visibility for your and your company.

If you follow these strategies, you'll have more interaction with your customers, build a database of prospects, build credibility, and do it all at a low cost.

If you'd like to learn about more strategies, please subscribe to my free e-mail newsletter, Dan Janal's Online Marketing Newsletter. To subscribe, read a sample issue, or browse the article archives, simply go to my web site and follow the links.

If you don't have the staff or stamina to write a full newsletter, consider writing a Tip of the Day. This is like a newsletter and follows all the same steps as a newsletter, with one major difference—it is shorter! You can send a line or two or even a paragraph. This should take very little time to write. You'll reap all the benefits of a newsletter, with a lot less work. I get several of these a day and read them in seconds. I might stock my newsletters in a file and read them when I have a chance, but I always read the short tips.

SUMMARY

Effective, ethical e-mail marketing campaigns can help you build relationships and sales. However, be sure to obtain permission from your customers to e-mail them with news about your company and its products and sales; otherwise, you could receive their anger instead of their cooperation.

Building Relationships with Newsgroups

Communities of like-minded people form on the Internet just as naturally as cliques form in high school. In the online world, these people join discussion groups where they read and write messages to one another. Marketers can use these areas to prospect for new customers, study market trends, and contribute information to the community. However, selling or conducting commerce is not allowed in most of these areas. Do not violate this cardinal rule of netiquette.

In this chapter, you will learn:

- The Benefits of marketing with newsgroups.
- How to find the markets.
- How to respond correctly to messages.
- Marketing strategies that conform to netiquette.

BENEFITS OF MARKETING WITH NEWSGROUPS

Newsgroups are online bulletin boards where people can post messages to one another and discuss topics of their mutual concern. There are more than fifty thousand of these groups, and their number grows daily. There is a microcommunity for virtually every hobby, political issue, lifestyle, race, and age that marketers would be interested in reaching.

Marketers can find potential prospects for their products. Each letter that members write is called a message, an article, or a post, depending on the service.

Online marketers consider newsgroups virtual gold mines on the digital frontier. They can benefit from reading messages in these highly focused forums in the following ways:

- **Prospecting and retaining customers.** Marketers can reach hundreds and thousands of current customers and potential consumers with one message.
- **Market research.** By reading messages you can find out what is hot, what people are talking about, and what their feelings are. Although most messages are placed by members interested in finding answers to problems, you can also raise your own questions to find out what people are thinking about a topic of interest to you.
- **Crisis control and prevention.** By monitoring conversations, you can find out what people are saying about your company and its products. If the word is bad, you can attempt to control the crisis by providing information and trying to solve the problem.
- **Building relationships.** By answering customers' questions, you can help solve problems. By providing them with information, you can enrich their experiences or empower them.
- **Publicity.** You can lead people to your related forum, web site, or commercial site, provided that you do so in an informative, nonintrusive manner.
- **Becoming a recognized expert or leader in an industry.** This is a good strategy for consultants, as they can become known to hundreds or thousands of people or to a select number of people in their specialized area of interest.

HOW TO FIND TARGET GROUPS ONLINE

Finding people online with special interests can be relatively easy to do as they participate in forums catering to their needs. The online world is full of niches of people in different age groups, such as senior citizens and high school students; professions, such as doctors and farmers; hobbyists, such as mountain climbers and wine aficionados. People have congregated into niche markets that online marketers can harvest if they follow the right steps.

You can find newsgroups by going to Deja.com (www.deja.com). Another site, Liszt (www.liszt.com), also provides an index for newsgroups and mailing lists.

HOW TO RESPOND CORRECTLY TO MESSAGES

The arcane technology of posting messages can be confusing. Here are two tips for avoiding mistakes:

1. Some responses should go to the entire list; others should be sent to the poster's private e-mailbox. Be careful to do what you intend to do!
   Example: If the original post says, "I've got this brilliant brochure I'd be happy to send to the people on this list. Send me e-mail if you'd like a copy," send your reply to the brilliant brochure maker, not the entire list!.
2. When commenting on a post, quote only as much as absolutely necessary to make your points. Usually a line or two will do the trick.

NETIQUETTE IN A NUTSHELL

The golden rule of netiquette can be summed up in five words: Don't advertise in inappropriate areas. That seems pretty simple, but to drive the point home, here are a few definitions and examples of inappropriate advertising that should be avoided:

- **Blatant promotion of products.**
  Hi. I sell seashells by the seashore and online. Does anyone want to buy seashells? I can make you a good offer. Please send me e-mail and I'll respond quickly, or call this number: 800-555-5555.
- **Blatant self-promotion of consultants.**
  Hi, I prepare taxes for small businesses. If you are a small business, I'll do your taxes.
- **Messages inappropriate to the group.**
  I know this group is for people who play bagpipes, but you must be concerned with health. I sell a power drink that increases stamina while you play bagpipes.

- **Get-rich-quick schemes.**
  You can make a fortune selling my product. Call me and I'll tell you how.

Those messages would probably be killed by the system administrators on the commercial networks before they reached the public, so if you tried to send them, you would be wasting your time. If you sent those messages to newsgroups, they would be posted and read by people who have an inherent distaste for advertising. You probably would incur the wrath of hundreds of members who would flame you with hate mail filled with profanity.

The effective online marketer respects the rules of the commercial online services and the netiquette of the Internet. Like karate masters, they learn to use the power of the force instead of fighting it. Three considerations should be added for online marketers: message length, appropriateness of topic, and spamming.

1. **Message length.** Because e-mail is the main form of communication among parties on an online system, members get many pieces of mail each day. Message length becomes an issue. Messages should be short, not longer than 24 lines, which is about the size of a computer monitor. This works out to about 240 words, almost the same as a full double-spaced sheet of regular typing paper. Messages should provide the gist of the material to be covered and ask readers if they want more information. Once permission is given, the follow-up message can be as long as needed to tell the story properly. If you follow this procedure, you will not be a victim of the kill file.

2. **Appropriateness of topic.** When you visit a discussion group, you will see a subject line indicating the topic at hand. It could be anything from "need advice" to "looking for a job" to "new and need help." What these messages have in common is that people are looking for answers to specific questions. It is considered rude to jump into a conversation with a topic that doesn't match the one in the subject line. If you want to discuss something, send a private note or start a new message with a new subject.

3. **Spamming.** Posting your messages to many discussion groups is considered spamming. You might think that multiple messages are a good way of blanketing your target audience. However, if

you do this, you will kindle much ire. People don't want to spend their time reading the same message over and over or to waste time and money killing duplicate messages. The rule is: Send your message once. If you forget this rule, some members will remind you—and not so nicely.

Here are rules to help you post well-mannered messages:

- **Be commercial in the right places.** Advertising is not allowed on most message boards. If you have a commercial announcement, place it only in message areas designed for that purpose, such as a newsgroup devoted to listing classified advertisements of computers for sale. It is possible to announce products or services in the few forums and newsgroups that specifically allow classified advertising. If in doubt, check first. Read the FAQs and then lurk (read messages) for a few days or weeks before posting an article.
- **Be focused.** Stay on the subject topic. If the topic is coffee, don't reply with a message about your favorite restaurant. Save that for a new topic.
- **Be redundant.** If you are responding to a message, summarize part of the message to which you are replying. Because people get so much mail, this will help remind the sender of the information and bring other people up to speed. However, don't include the entire message, just a relevant excerpt or a paraphrase. Use arrows to indicate that this is text from an earlier message. For example:

> > On March 15, Dan Janal wrote:
> > Where's the best place to get a cappuccino in Danville?
The best place is Susan's Kitchen Cafe.

Many new versions of software automatically insert the previous message and arrows if you select the forward or reply options.

- **Be a giver.** Contribute to the community. Answer people's questions and calls for help. If you do, you will become a welcome member of the group and build credibility in the group, which can help you promote your own business in a noninvasive manner.

- **Be singular.** Don't post the same message twice on the same forum. There are personal and technical reasons for this. People don't like wading through repetitive messages, especially when they are paying for each minute they are online or paying for each message received. The technical reason is that message boards have limited space. Once the queue is filled, older messages roll off the board and are replaced by new ones. If you waste space, you knock off messages that might actually help people.

- **Be quiet.** If you answer "Thanks" and "I agree" to every message, you will inadvertently force other people's responses off the board. When appropriate, send private mail or use the abbreviation TIA for "Thanks in advance." The same is true for online conferences. Don't announce your comings and goings and don't respond with "Hi" and "Bye." If there are a dozen people in the conference and all of them send greetings, the conversation grinds to a halt. Don't spam or send copies of letters to several forums or newsgroups. People get upset if they see the same note posted; additionally, the act of posting takes away from system resources and mailbox space that could be put to better use.

- **Be legal.** Obey the forum's rules on advertising, self-promotion, and etiquette. Scams, pyramid schemes, and stock fraud are as illegal online as they are in other media.

- **Be informed.** Read messages for a while to get a feel for the discussion before jumping in. Read the help files or FAQs to learn how the system operates and what is allowed.

- **Be polite.** E-mail almost always sounds harsher than it's meant. Your comments can appear caustic, and jokes might be read as criticism because the reader can't see your facial expressions or vocal intonations. Therefore, be exceedingly polite. Err on the side of good taste. Assume that anything that could be seen as negative will be taken as such.

- **Be grammatically accurate.** Nothing looks worse than a typo. Check your spelling and grammar.

- **Be case-sensitive.** DON'T TYPE IN UPPERCASE. It looks like you are shouting.

- **Be specific.** Headlines will attract readers to your message or drive them away. "Need Help with Creating Ads" is better than "Help Wanted."

- **Be yourself.** Use your real name, not a CB handle or nickname. People deserve to know to whom they are talking. That means using your real name, business, and gender. It is difficult to conduct a serious conversation with someone named Hot Pants. A member of a commercial online service might be known as John73141 so that people won't know who he is. If you want to be respected, use your real name.
- **Be informative.** People like to read information, not ads, online.

Using proper netiquette shows that you are a member of the community who understands and respects its traditions.

MARKETING STRATEGIES THAT CONFORM TO NETIQUETTE

Lurk

Benefit: Avoid being flamed.

Discussion: To make sure you don't violate the netiquette, lurk (read without responding or otherwise announcing your presence) around the newsgroup for a few days to understand what the group discusses. You'll also avoid the faux pas of beginning a conversation about a topic that has been beaten to death.

Action: Go to your A-list of message boards; read messages, library files, FAQs, and other background files.

Answer Messages on Forums, Even If You Can't Promote Your Product

Benefit: Introduces you to the community as a model citizen. You raise your credibility when you answer questions that don't benefit you.

Discussion: Be a helpful neighbor. The best way to build credibility is to offer information. You might not actually be promoting your business or service, but you will be promoting yourself and building credibility. That will come in handy when people ask you what you do. They will be more apt to believe you because you are a member of the community.

Example:

> I need to find a sales trainer who can teach my sales staff how to prospect without wasting time.
> Does anyone know someone who can do this?

Your answer:

> Gordy Allen of Leads Plus conducts great sales seminars and has written great workbooks for the sales staff and for the sales manager. You can reach him at 800-548-4571.

You also get exposure by displaying your signature file.

Action: Read newsgroups and answer questions that other members raise.

Answer Questions from Members That Lead Them to Your Product or Service

Benefit: Prospecting and increased exposure.

Action: Look for messages that you can answer with authority and that allow you to promote your product or service. When I mention this strategy at my seminars, someone always comes up to me afterwards and tells me how they used newsgroups to find information on buying tires or planning trips to Europe or the like. For example:

Question:

> I have to write a business plan, and I've never done one. Can someone suggest a software program that will do this?

Answer:

> Yes, try Biz Plan Builder from JIAN Software for Tools.

Answer:

> I write business plans for a living. My clients have included many start-ups and medium sized companies. Please send a note if you would like more information.

Scan Message Areas for Mentions of Your Company

Benefit: Increased exposure.

Discussion: By looking for messages in which you can participate and to which you can contribute, you will help promote your company and product. It is not a violation of netiquette to join in a discussion about your company or product.

Action: Check DejaNews daily to check messages that might affect your company. Create a list of forums on each commercial online service that reaches your audience. Assign the task of monitoring these areas to an employee trained to deal with sensitive issues and irate customers.

Create a Member Profile

Benefit: Prospecting. Inbound prospecting. People will get to know you better and faster.

Discussion: Most people online might seem to be merely names and numbers. They can be more than that. Forums allow you to create a member profile, which includes your interests, from professional to personal. Member profiles can be searched so people can find others who have similar interests. If you fill one out on yourself, other people can find you. The policy on this varies from forum to forum and system to system. Professional forums frequently allow you to post a description of yourself, which can include descriptions of your product or service. Check with the forums that feature topic headings like "Resumes," "Introductions," or "I'm new and here's what I do." If you use these options, you'll find prospects, and they'll find you.

Action: Find forums that would attract your target audience. Follow the rules for creating a profile for yourself. Follow instructions for finding other members. Send them polite e-mail that strikes up a conversation. For example, let's say that you sell sailboats and supplies. You might send this message: "I see that you like to sail. I do too. I have a model x-200 and sail in San Francisco. Where do you sail?" If you get a response, you can begin to develop a relationship. As this relationship matures, you can then mention what you do and propose ways to help your new friend.

Ask for Additional Resources

Benefit: Prospecting.

Discussion: By posting questions that ask for additional sources on other forums, you might find more opportunities to interact with even more prospects. The answers might lead you to other areas on that system, to other online services, or to bulletin boards operated by enthusiasts or vendors.

Example: Let's say you sell mountain climbing equipment. You could search for sports, hiking, outdoors, exercise, vacations, and travel. Send a message:

> Does anyone know of a mailing list that covers mountain climbing?

Action: Post questions on those message boards asking if members know of other message boards for that audience.

SUMMARY

To take advantage of the vast resource of targeted communities on newsgroups, forums, and the like, you must become a contributing member. If you provide people with answers to their questions, they will be quite receptive to learning more about your company and its services. If you provide information, not persuasion, you will be accepted.

CHAPTER 17

Building a Community

Every marketer worth his or her MBA wants to know the demographics of the Internet. And many research firms are happy to oblige. But that kind of marketing misses the point. Is there any person out there who introduces himself by saying "I'm a white male, between the ages of 35 and 45, with a higher-than-average income and a higher-than-average education." Of course not. Talk to people at a cocktail party and they will tell you they are a marathon runner or a movie fanatic, that they are researching their family tree or blessed with a green thumb. That's because people are not demographics—they are people! If you focus on people's hobbies and professions, you'll find they will congregate at your site and buy your products and services. By creating communities of interest, companies can create raving fans for life who buy their products and services—and recommend those items to others.

This chapter will show:

- The impact of communities.
- What a community is.
- Examples of communities on the Internet.
- Factors you should consider in creating your community.

THE IMPACT OF COMMUNITIES, OR 26 LESSONS I LEARNED ABOUT INTERNET MARKETING BY GOING TO BROADWAY

I never really bought into the hullabaloo about online communities and chats and virtual communities. I mean, do you really want to go online and talk about how much you love your Pirelli tires? I'm not saying that virtual communities don't exist or can't be used to spread the corporate gospel or build product loyalty. There are many such success stories. I'm just saying that it wasn't for *me* . . . I thought.

The purpose of this section is to show you how I was converted into believing in virtual communities and now think they are wonderful places to conduct a variety of marketing functions.

You have to understand my perspective here. I am not a joiner. I am not a fan of chats, avatars, interactive conversations, or CB radio. Every time I've joined one of those chats, I found inane conversations (mostly "Hi Dan, Hi Dan, Hi Dan" followed by "Hi Joe, Hi Joe, Hi Joe" and the inevitable, "Bye Dan, Bye Dan, Bye Dan"). Even in professional forums, I found a lot of off-topic conversations on the message boards. In other words, a subject box might have included a topic I was interested in, such as speech writing, but when I read a message, it would invariably start like this: "Can anyone help me find a resource for speech writing?" and it would be signed by someone at a well-known company or geographic location. Without fail, the next message would be something like, "Gee, I really don't know the answer, but my Aunt Shirley works for your company [or lives in your town]; do you know her?" The next 20 messages would be about Shirley, *not* about speech writing.

And I say this as someone who served as a host on the PR forum on CompuServe for 10 years! Sometimes the conversation was good, but mostly it was useless. Nevertheless, I did get to know a few people, and it did seem as though we were old friends when we talked online or met in person at trade shows and conferences. And many more people saw my messages and felt they knew me, even though we never sent messages to each other.

So as you can see, I was not a big fan of this kind of service until I became a believer. Here's how.

Last Thanksgiving, I was watching the Macy's Thanksgiving Day Parade on TV. In between the floats, they showed dance numbers of Broadway musicals. While half-watching the TV, one number really caught my eye. Two Cleopatras sang while a chorus of Pharaohs did a wicked impression of Steve Martin's famous "King Tut" dance number. It was a hoot! I never laughed so hard in my life. I had to see that show. Unfortunately, NBC anchors Katie Couric and Willard Scott didn't mention the name of the show but went to a commercial instead.

I was possessed. I had to find out the name of the show, so I checked the obvious places. *The New York Times*'s Broadway listings didn't reveal a clue. There was no show called "Walk Like an Egyptian" or "We Share Everything," a phrase that the singers seemed to repeat several times.

Being an online maven, I decided to see if there were any clues on the Net. I saw a few Broadway web sites while scouring Yahoo!, but again, nothing looked close. Then I found Playbill On-line (www .playbill.com), the web site of the magazine that is distributed to all theatergoers. The site was really well done. It offered current news of Broadway, interviews with stars, listings of shows in New York and around the country, and—best of all—it had an ASK PLAYBILL button.

Lesson #1 learned: *If customers want to find out about your company, they will go online to find it.*

Using e-mail to ask questions is a great device. Can you imagine how unlikely it would have been for me to pick up a telephone, find the number of *Playbill,* find the right person, and then say on the phone, "Hi, I'm trying to find the name of a Broadway show that features two women who seem to be joined at the hip who sing a song that has the lyrics 'We share everything' and has a chorus of dancing Pharaohs?" But online, all fears are dismissed. I asked my question, and a few hours later the Ask Playbill sage e-mailed me that that name of the show was *Side Show.*

Lesson #2 learned: *E-mail is a very fast and efficient way for customers to find information. It also eliminates the cost of a phone call and reduces the fear that people have of identifying themselves or asking potentially embarrassing questions (are you listening, pharmaceutical manufacturers?).*

I read a review online at the *New York Magazine* site. They liked it. The show was about the lives of the Hilton Sisters, a pair of Siamese twins from the 1920s who were a rave on the vaudeville circuit. When I went to Internet World in New York a few weeks later, I saw the show. Although I expected to laugh my head off during the Egyptian number, I was totally captivated by the story and music. It was one of the best shows I had ever seen on Broadway. No one laughed during the Egyptian number, and everyone cried at the end of the performance.

Lesson #3 learned: *The Internet should be part of your integrated marketing campaign.*

Lesson #4 learned: *Even if you are not on the web, other web sites could contain information about your company or product. What are* *they saying? Can you influence their expressions? These are important points!*

That night I scoured the search engines looking for reference to the show and the real Siamese twins on whom the show was based. I found a lot of biographical information and pictures, and I learned they had starred in two movies. One site featured posters from the movies, another site had the script, and a third site had film clips!

Lesson #5 learned: *When people like your product, they* really *like your product and will want to know everything there is to know about it. You'll be amazed at what you can find on the web!*

I can't remember why I went back to Playbill On-Line, but I did. When I found the chat message boards, I investigated further and found a message board for *Side Show.* It was immediately interesting to see that while very popular shows had a few dozen messages from admirers, *Side Show* had several hundred.

Lesson #6 learned: *People, not companies, created this community and contributed to its content. Communities will exist regardless of whether the company wants them to exist. However, a good company will contribute information and value-added services to community members.*

I went to the board and read people's reviews.

Lesson #7 learned: *Every community creates its own rules* (**Corollary #1:** *This is a* fan *site. If you trash the show, we'll trash you!*).

Readers fought with people who disagreed with anyone who didn't think the show was wonderful. It was actually very interesting considering I liked the show and wanted to see what other people thought. People wanted to know more about the cast and the show.

Lesson #8 learned: *The fans want to have a close relationship with the company. In this case, the producers never interacted directly with the community. This was a mistake, as you'll soon see.*

The mother and brother of one of the stars even joined the discussion and gave insiders information about her.

Lesson #9 learned: *The most amazing people can join a community!*

The board had taken on a feeling of a village square where people came, talked, left, and returned. Board members gave themselves a new name, an identity: They now called themselves "Freaks," a loving reference to the freak show, a circus Midway act that was an instrumental part of the opening scenes, and the opening song, "Come Look at the Freaks."

Lesson #10 learned: *When you give something a name, it is no longer an inanimate object but a living, breathing entity.*

I posted a message asking if anyone had taped the number from the Macy's Parade. Two people volunteered to make copies for me.

Lesson #11 learned: *People in the community give freely to one another. No one asked for money! When the person who volunteered to make a duplicate of the tape for me realized he didn't have the equipment, he sent me his only copy! Think of it: Would you lend your only copy of anything to a complete stranger? They do online!*

Now things get interesting. It turns out that not everyone in the real world wanted to see *Side Show,* and rumors flew that the producers were thinking about closing the show. Horrors! The people on the board urged everyone to send letters and faxes to the producers before they made their final decision about the show. People in New York took to the streets and stalked the TKTS booth, which sells discount tickets to Broadway shows and talked up the show. They were joined by dedicated members of the cast.

Lesson #12 learned: *Online communities can become militant and organized in a heartbeat!*

One woman who sent e-mail by the name of "Violet Hilton," the stage name of one of the lead actresses' characters, turned out to be a TV reporter in Pennsylvania and volunteered to write a press release about the show or do whatever she could on the air to promote the show. A radio reporter volunteered to do the same.

Lesson #13 learned: *The media can join communities and become active as well!*

Several board members created their own "Save *Side Show*" web sites and posted them on free services like GeoCities!

Lesson #14 learned: *People will take time away from their already busy lives and create messages for the world to see on the web. Imagine what would happen if people didn't like your product! Just go to Yahoo!*

and type in the word suck *to see hundreds of web sites from people who hate products and companies!*

The *Side Show* community was now firmly entrenched online. Here's an interchange posted to the board by members:

> As I've mentioned on this board, I've e-mailed, written, etc. to the producers also—hopefully, this avalanche of interest will spur them to make the decision to re-open. As another point of interest, I also want this show to succeed for another reason—I LOVE THIS MESSAGE BOARD!!! I cannot believe the emotions and love of the people who post on this board. I feel as if this is a huge gathering of friends who share one thing in common— I've enjoyed reading each and every inspirational message. I hope the show continues forever,—it has a great audience!!! Annette

> I agree Annette. I enjoyed the SS 1-3 matinee greatly and was curious as to the fate of the show. I stumbled onto this board and have become addicted to its content because of the emotion of the freaks who so closely identify with the message of this brilliant show. I guess I'm a freak too as we all are unique!!! I hope SS can be saved … what a coup for this board to benefit all theater goers. [Unattributed]

The guerilla campaign seemed to be working. Ticket sales rose from 50 to 85 percent sellouts. People on the message board continued to urge people to send faxes to the producers, who were rumored to be making their decision to kill or keep the show right around Christmas.

Lesson #15 learned: *Community action can be effective. Consider that tickets, even at half price, cost about $40!*

Unfortunately, despite the best efforts of dozens of board members, the producers killed the show, which ended on January 5. However, the Freaks made plans to get together to see the final performance, meet for dinner, and plan strategies for keeping the show alive.

Lesson #16 learned: *Online communities can migrate to real-world communities and relationships.*

After the show closed, the Freaks posted reviews of the show and the audience. Others commented. Even *Playbill* noted the activity on Broadway and in the message forum. Even several weeks after the show had closed, people were still posting and reading messages on the board!

Lesson #17 learned: *The community had taken on a life of its own and was willing to exist even after the product (show) had died.*

Lesson #18 learned: *The media realized that online communities existed and took action.*

Now it gets even more interesting. A rumor flew that the producers were thinking of reviving the show in April to take advantage of the Tony Award nominations and avoid the slow winter season on Broadway. It was only a rumor, but the Freaks were alive again! They stepped up the effort to fax and mail the producers. A member of the cast, Barry, fed us whatever information he had. One day it looked good. One day it looked bad. One day they were expecting to get calls to report for work in early April, and the next day nothing happened. Every day, the Freaks came back to the message board to see what was happening.

Lesson #19 learned: *Where were the producers? Why weren't they online to dispense information instead of letting rumors fly? If you don't control the flow of information, such rumors could kill you.*

People continued to create web sites. One gentleman who goes by the name "Man in Black" created a wonderful web site that featured his idea of a new logo for the show, one that stressed its humanity and the love story in it. He also included a focus group form that asked people to state their views on the show; how it should be marketed, who would be the target market, and other relevant questions.

Lesson #20 learned: *The web can be used as a focus group to gather information. If a fan could do it, just imagine what information could have been gleaned if the producers had an official web site for the show!*

Lesson #21 learned: *Fans contributed ideas and information—without costing the producers a penny. If people are interested in your product or company, they'll do the same!*

Just when it seemed like the show was coming back to life, a reporter for the *N.Y. Daily News* wrote a cheap piece of sensationalism trashing *Side Show* and the efforts to revive it and quoted "unnamed sources." Here's an excerpt from that newspaper's January 21, 1998, edition:

> People familiar with their [the producers] thinking say they have been swayed by the *Side Show* cult, essentially musical theater fans who've

gone gaga for the show. The cultists are all over the Internet, raving about the musical and bemoaning its fate. Sources say Krieger and bookwriter Bill Russell have tapped into the cult and are convinced that, given another chance, *Side Show* will find its audience.

Lesson #22 learned: *The major media does pay attention to online happenings. In this case, the reporter continued his negative story, but he affirmed that the Net played a major part in giving the show a chance for a new life.*

The Freaks went berserk! By now, there was an e-mail list of people who contributed messages to the board, so news was being broadcast via e-mail from the leaders to the minions. Someone even typed the entire article into e-mail and broadcast it so people like me in California could see it.

Lesson #23 learned: *When people are committed, they will do extraordinary things. Would you type a newspaper article into e-mail and send it to 50 people to win a cause? One person did. Remember the awesome power of one!*

The mailing list posted the phone and fax number of the writer, and several people called and wrote to express their opinions. The Freaks sent notes and phoned the reporter. To his credit, the reporter printed some of the message, which bore a more civilized tone than did his article.

Lesson #24 learned: *The major media does, indeed, pay attention to online ramblings. If people love or hate your products, you can bet the media will find out about it online!*

Nevertheless, the next day the director decided to pull out of the show. It seemed like the producers could do nothing but kill the show. I had given up hope at this point. I would have to be content to listen to the CD of the show, which I'd memorized by now. Then, to my surprise, over the weekend I received a new mailing from the Freaks saying that the producers had decided to revive the show and that actors had been told to report to work in April! And a California production was planned for later this year!

Lesson #25 learned: *The community leaders can use the cheap and effective tools of e-mail to spread the word.*

Hopefully, this is not just another rumor and the show will indeed reopen. If it does, I urge you to see if it you're going to be in New York. You'll see the show that was saved by the Internet.

A final footnote: Not a single message from the producers or their PR firm was ever posted to the board. We don't know if they read a single article, learned from the comments and advice of the Freaks, or incorporated the Freaks' comments into their plans for a new ad campaign.

Lesson #26 learned: *The community exists. You must deal with it. In this case, the community helped the show. However, I've heard of many cases in which fan sites have been hassled by copyright attorneys who threaten legal action. In many cases, these fans are teenagers who are in love with* Star Trek *or* Barbie! *Can you imagine a faster way to create enemies for life for your company?*

WHAT IS A COMMUNITY?

At this point it is important to define *community*. Let's use this definition: **A Community is a group of like-minded people who band together for frequent interaction because it is mutually beneficial and provides a sense of safety and a sense of identity.**

Online Chatting Fosters Communities

The Internet has the ability to attract people interested in meeting and chatting with others who have the same interests and, hence, create a sense of community. Chatting is the number one reason given by online denizens for subscribing to America Online. That message is borne out by the amount of connect time devoted to community building areas such as chats, e-mail, and places where people can exchange information and opinions. These interactions can be done in real time, where members type messages to one another and get responses as soon as the recipient has time to think and type. Meetings can also be done in store-and-forward mode, in which one person leaves a message for another person who might not be online at that moment. The message is stored on the computer system and forwarded to the recipient, who reads and responds when he uses the online service. If messages are posted to the entire list, then anyone can read and respond to the discussion.

Users Created Their Own Communities

People have banded together to create communities since the beginning of the online revolution. From the earliest days, online denizens used their own initiative to create communities of like-minded people to discuss topics of mutual concern. Groups ranged from computer programmers, devotees of *Beverly Hills 90210,* parents of children with dyslexia, people with eating disorders, and lawyers, public relations professionals, or other professionals to people who identified themselves by their hobbies, such as gardening, cooking, flying model airplanes, or photography. The Internet has more than fifty thousand such communities in the form of newsgroups as well as countless mailing lists. It is important to note that people created the community on the Internet—the Internet did not create the community. The Internet merely contains the tools that allowed these communities to form. These groups coalesced without advertising or publicity, and members told their friends and colleagues, who in turn decided to join. Now is it quite common for companies to create their own communities, filled with customers. Other businesses have been created for the sole purpose of creating communities, including Parent Soup (www.parentsoup.com) and Stork Site (www.more .women.com/storksite) for parents, ThirdAge (www.thirdage.com) for senior citizens, and many, many others. In fact, some of the hottest companies on the Internet, as seen by stock prices, involve companies that create community sites, like Village.

Community Members Benefit from Participation

These community members gave freely of their time and expertise because they felt the interaction was mutually beneficial. If they answered a question for a stranger today, then someone would answer a question they had tomorrow. For some people, the mere thought of helping people was reward in itself. Others knew that if they answered a question, people would see them as experts and might hire them. CompuServe's professional forums are rife with anecdotes of consultants who have gained clients or sold products in this manner—all done with the intent of helping people, never with a blatant sales pitch that violates the netiquette of the online world.

People ask personal questions or list the problems of their companies in a public forum because the sense of community gives them feelings of safety. On the Internet, it is easy to hide behind a mask so that no one knows your name or where you live or work. This sense of anonymity also contributes to the feeling of community: Online, no one knows if you are old or young, able or disabled, white or black. They only know you by the content of your character. In this manner, people become fast friends, feel they knew one another, or are able to open up to each other. The online world has hundreds of stories of people who met and fell in love online, as documented in many newspapers across the country.

It should be noted that the members of the community are not necessarily limited by geography or proximity, like communities in the real world. People who are interested in gardening can be from all over the world; be of any age, sex, or race; and get along marvelously. These communities are based on interest, not merely on geography or demographics. People who are interested in fishing can talk with one another, even though they might not look at one another in the real world. Communities based on geography can exist as well, as people in one town go online and discover each other, just as in the real world. However, an advantage of online communities is having the ability to meet people who you might not normally run across in your geographic community.

From this mutual caring and concern arises a feeling of identity. People who contribute a great deal become well known. These online VIPs have been courted by advertisers who seek their opinions, their feedback on new products, and their endorsements. They became opinion leaders in their niche market. Other members of the community come to trust their opinions and seek their advice. IBM noticed a number of computer consultants giving free advice to people in their forum. The company decided to support these people by giving them advance information on products and provided them with advanced training not normally available to the general public. These VIPs, in turn, were able to offer high levels of support to the online community. Why did these consultants offer their time for free? That's a question for sociologists exploring this brave new online world.

EXAMPLES OF COMMUNITIES ON THE INTERNET

Smart companies are taking this common bond of community and making it their own. Although the first wave of online members created its own community and content, the new breed of marketer is creating community and content in an attempt to establish relationships with people and make them customers for life.

Examples of companies or associations sponsoring communities include Toyota, the Arthritis Foundation, and Molson Beer. Other communities are being created by companies, professional organizations, or by the people and professionals themselves who are interested in such topics as sports, politics, religion, parenting, health, and sexuality.

Let's look at a few examples of companies that have created online communities:

- Absolut Vodka, which is known for its inventive ads showing its bottle in various designs, uses its web page to show artists creating the ads. People can see the artists at work (using video clips) and ask them questions. In this way, people who come from a variety of backgrounds and interests can interact with one another based on their common interest in art, creative design, and advertising.
- Molson's beer has created a pub atmosphere to attract a community of twentysomethings who have a need to meet others and chat about music and sports.

In each of these examples, the advertiser presents content that draws people together to discuss issues of common concern. The advertiser is not blatantly selling a product as on television. Instead, the advertiser seeks to create an environment or an experience for the target audience. These examples show that advertisers can create a sense of community without violating the Net's ban on intrusive advertising.

Case Study: Reebok

Reebok's online mission is to create a community of people united in their common interest in sports fitness. To create the site, Reebok had to first identify its community and marketing mission. "Preparation is the link between fitness and sports, and every athlete is driven by his own personal motivation as he prepares to compete at his personal best," says Dave Ropes, senior vice president of integrated marketing for Reebok. "The message Reebok is delivering is that everyone who participates in sports or fitness can attain a feeling of confidence, of being in control through the proper preparation."

Reebok's web master, Marvin Chow, was able to create a feeling of community at the Reebok web site (www.reebok.com). In setting up the site, Chow studied the attitudes and perceptions of his target audience and found they had a great many things in common.

"The generation growing up today is accustomed to heavy advertising and sponsorships. All athletes are owned by companies. They are walking billboards," he observes. He decided to take that feeling of manipulation by the athletes and large companies and turn it into Reebok's advantage. "You have to take that connection and utilize it. We bring athletes to them in a live chat. We've sponsored chats with Emmett Smith and Frank Thomas." He notes, "We will target people with similar interests, feed them information, and give them a way to discuss data."

This creation of content fits in well with the Net's philosophy of providing free information. "You have to give them something back, such as information or physical stuff. They say 'What are we getting out of it?' Information is the answer," Chow says.

Reebok was among the first advertisers to create an online community and content. "Because kids are bombarded by ads, the web site has to create an entire content area. For Reebok, that area is sports fitness. We are doing more than sponsoring it. We are creating the content. We have turned from a sponsor into a content creator. We can offer them so much more," Chow says. "In every other medium we are a sponsor. On the Internet, we are a content provider. We can't show our expertise on TV. We can show it on the Net."

Reebok has been most successful in appealing to women. The web site has a wealth of information on the growing field of versatraining, a combination of aerobics, gymnastics, stepping in place, t'ai chi, and other forms of exercise that many women participate in several times a week at their local fitness centers. Such women search for information about their sport of choice. As their daily newspapers cover only professional sports, these women have no other source of information. Reebok has wisely chosen to fill this void. The web site contains articles, interviews with leading coaches and trainers, and schedules of upcoming events and meets—information that newspapers do not provide, thus giving greater value.

The company also wisely chose women as one of its key audiences. As women control 80 percent of the consumer dollar in the United States, advertisers who want to be successful must create content and community that appeals to women's interests. For many companies, thoughts about women's interests seem to be limited to cooking and recipes. Reebok shows that they can appeal to more diverse pursuits.

By adopting the "Planet Reebok" theme on its web site and its television advertising, Reebok makes use of the web as a worldwide medium. It offers chats with soccer and track stars in countries where they are heroes.

Chow says the web site is a success: "We get tons of comments. It is truly the best grassroots communication there is. We have gotten tremendously good feedback from this." Companies should also note that not all the comments are positive. In Reebok's case, viewers have debated the company's morals and actions.

This points out a situation that marketers who venture on to the Net must deal with, whether they host a community or not: They no longer control the message in this two-way medium; consumers can create messages as well. Marketers must learn to recognize and deal with this new reality of the online world.

Case Study: Parent Soup

Parent Soup (www.parentsoup.com) is one of the finest examples of an online community. The site is devoted to the needs of parents—no matter how you define *parent*. A parent can be a 14-year-old high school student or a 70-year-old grandparent who is raising children and everyone in between. The site makes money by selling advertising space to companies that are trying to reach an audience of parents.

Members contribute most of the site's editorial matter. Parents write reviews of movies and products for kids. Would you rather read a movie review for *Aladdin* by older men such as Robert Ebert who write most of the reviews in newspapers or by the mother of two preteens? Now you understand why people will read the comments of their peers.

The site offers dozens of chats for parents on such topics as breast feeding, picking a day care center, and how to be a better single parent. These chats are offered virtually every hour of the day to attract the right audience at its convenience. As we said before, the chats are designed to appeal to every possible type of parent, from teenager to senior, from traditional families to blended families, and everything in between.

Another way to get people to come back is by offering a poll, which Parent Soup conducts every day on such topics as getting along with in-laws to what the appropriate discipline should be in various situations. The results are announced as soon as each new person votes. About 1,000 people vote each day.

The site does a wonderful job of creating a warm, inviting community, as witnessed by its members' willingness to post pictures of their kids and families online. Considering the paranoia many people have about invasions of privacy, this is truly remarkable.

As a result of this intense community building, Parent Soup has attracted advertising from such companies as Pampers and Ford (for its Winstar van, aimed at families).

ACTION PLAN FOR CREATING AN ONLINE COMMUNITY

What is the reason your customers are your customers? Whatever the answer is, the answer beyond the answer is that they have adopted your core values or you have figured out what their core values are and have delivered them. This core value is what you must infuse in your community if it is to be a success. If you do, you will create customers for life and be known as the key authority on your subject on the Internet.

In the previous cases, the core values are easy to spot if you look hard enough. For Reebok, the core values for women was sports fitness. They wanted to feel better and have healthier bodies. They weren't interested in learning about team sports or hobnobbing with the athletes, which was the core value of the teenage boys. For Parent Soup, the core value is being a more informed parent so as to make children healthier, happier, and smarter. Notice that this core value transcends all ages and genders. Parent Soup doesn't care if the parent is one of a traditional two-family couple, a 14-year girl, or a 60-year old grandmother whose daughter drops the child off on her doorstep— and leaves forever!

The first step in your action plan is to determine what your company really does and to whom you want to appeal. For example, it would have been too easy (and ineffective) for Reebok to say it was in the business of making and selling sneakers and to post a site that told all about the history and manufacturing procedures of its products. As ludicrous as this sounds, many companies on the web do exactly that—as if anyone really cares about the arcane history of a humdrum, everyday item. Instead, Reebok focused on the benefits of its product and the common interests of people who buy it. The company thought of its market as people who use sneakers for participating in weight control, sports, fitness, and fun; then it created content for these areas, writing objective articles, creating interviews between members and famous athletes, and sponsoring chats among the community.

Action Steps

1. Decide what business you are really in and how that translates to an online community.
2. Brainstorm on the kinds of content (articles, information, graphics) that will entice people to your web site and enhance their personal or professional lives.
3. Add interactive elements, such as chats and conferences that will make people feel a part of the community.
4. Consider other activities outside of the web site that will add value to people's lives, such as an e-mail newsletter, discounts and coupons on your products, user group meetings in person, and the like.

The answers could be different for each company and still be effective.

ISSUES FOR MOLDERS OF ONLINE COMMUNITIES

The challenge for marketers is that they need to think outside the box to create an online community, which is a new venture for many of them. Also, they will be forced to create content that will expand their current duties. Some companies will be able to use the same materials they produce in paper format (such as newsletters, magazines, and case studies) and retrofit them for the web or e-mail. Companies must begin to budget the personnel, time, and materials for this marketing task.

As more companies realize that the Net is about content and community, there will be more competition to create web sites that realize these goals. Your company might be able to stake out the pioneer's position as the first on the web in its area, but competitors will be on your heels. Just as Molson set up its web site—the ultimate metaphor for a community where everybody knows your name—other breweries opened their virtual bars as well. Marketers must be on the prowl for competitors.

Keeping the site fresh is another key concern. If your mission is to maintain long-term relationships with customers, you must add new articles and activities. However, no one knows how often this update must be done. Should it be once a day, as in a newspaper; once a week, as in a news magazine or trade publication; or once a month, as in a magazine? Some might argue that the site must be updated every minute or hour, as in radio or TV news. Others might wonder if consumers are getting too much information and are drowning in frequent updates. As the Net evolves, the right schedule for each industry will become apparent.

"As with any product and service, web sites will do well if the focus starts and remains with the market. Constant market research (no matter how qualitative) and visitor interaction is the only route to continuous improvements on the Internet," says Marcia Olmstead, director of internal development and communications for Southam New Media.

"Keep your users coming back. Always offer the user something new—you must find a way to constantly update your site without straying from your master plan, or changing the site so much that the user becomes frustrated and never returns," says Kim Silk-Copeland, communications resource coordinator for the Discovery Channel. "Original content, prizes, free downloads, and updated services are a few great ways to attract attention. Always leave them wanting more—always keep them thinking they might miss out on an opportunity if they don't return often."

Marketers will also be placed in the unfamiliar position of managing opinion. What will happen if community members violate netiquette? How will the content provider deal with errant community members without alienating them from the fold? Companies will need to establish policies on acceptable online behavior as well as stake out the action steps for dealing with violators.

SUMMARY

The most powerful paradigm shift in online advertising is that the advertiser is adopting the role of the magazine publisher and becoming responsible for creating content. Because the hard sell and overt advertising tend to put off an audience burned out from commercials, advertisers can gain influence by creating a sense of community and an experience for their target audiences.

Public Relations Strategies for Your Communities

Public relations will enter a golden age thanks to the widespread use of the Internet and commercial online services. PR practitioners will not only be able to create strong relationships with reporters through the instant communication and information-on-demand capabilities of the online medium but will also be able to reach their communities directly—without the intervention of the editor and reporter who act as both gatekeepers and censors of information.

The Internet provides a tool for companies to talk directly to their communities. As communications professionals, we can only hope that reporters will print our press releases. But the truth is that but a small percentage of informative press releases is ever printed in newspapers or magazines.

This chapter will help you connect with your community (investors, dealers, distributors, consumers, employees and other people in your target market) by providing strategies for building relationships, prospecting for new customers, building product and brand awareness, distributing product information, and building sales.

THE FAILING OF THE MASS MEDIA

When the media act as gatekeepers, they can do a disservice to the public. Let's look at what can happen when you send a press release to a reporter. She can:

1. Throw it out—which happens more times than PR pros care to admit.
2. Print it in full—a dream that rarely occurs in real life.
3. Print parts of it, without additional comments.
4. Print parts of it, with comments by competitors who downplay your story.
5. Print parts of it, with comments by analysts who change your perspective.
6. Print parts of it in a roundup with competitors, thus diluting your message.
7. Delete the key messages that support your main point.
8. Introduce typos and errors.

So there you have eight actions, seven of which are negative or potentially negative. Those should be enough reasons for you to want to speak to directly to your audience.

Does the reader get a fair assessment of the company's side of the story? Hardly. Does the investment community understand more or less because of the editing by the gatekeepers? Obviously less. What's a PR practitioner to do? Plenty. The following sections offer some suggestions for you.

Distribute Your Press Release on a Newswire

Benefit: Avoid the media; speak directly to your audience.

Discussion: Your audience can access all press releases sent over PR Newswire (www.prnewswire.com) and Business Wire (www.businesswire.com) via the Internet. They can search on keywords, find information on search engines, or read the releases on business and financial sites.

Case Study: Intellisystems

Intellisystems, a leading provider of expert-based help systems for high technology companies, issued a press release on PR Newswire. It was printed on PointCast (www.pointcast.com), a news service that prints all press releases offered by PR Newswire.

Executives with buying authority at a major commercial online service read the press release on PointCast. They called the company and asked the president, Michael Beare, to fly to their offices for a meeting. Beare said he had been trying to get an appointment with that company for years but couldn't get in. Because of the newswire service, he got the appointment.

Post Press Releases on Your Web Site

Benefit: Your community can read the press release.

Discussion: Your readers can access press releases you post in your web site. Many, many, many high tech companies do this today. If you aren't following this tactic, you are giving your competitors an advantage.

Post Press Releases on Newsgroups That Cover Your Topic

Benefit: Your community can read the press release.

Discussion: To reach your customers directly, post the press release in message boards or newsgroups and mailing lists that appeal to them. To do this, you must first find message boards that attract your target audience and make sure the sysop allows press releases. To gain permission, send a private note to the group moderator.

Create a One-Way Mailing List of Your Community Members

Benefit: Maintain close relationships with customers, retailers, editors, and other VIPs by notifying them of news.

Discussion: A mailing list is an electronic tool that allows you to broadcast your press releases to customers' e-mailboxes. When you post a new press release or have other interesting news, you can send a message to your list. The message can contain the entire content of the press release or instruct the recipients to visit a specific page of your web site.

Companies must be committed to maintaining this dialogue for the relationship-building process to work.

Warning: Make sure you get permission from each customer. Online consumers hate junk mail. Netiquette holds that information that is *un-*

solicited is *un*appreciated. Follow this rule as if your life depended on it because if people get upset, they can and will tell 30,000 of their closest online friends with the click of a few keystrokes.

Create Information Files

Benefit: Increases exposure and credibility; possible source of leads.

Discussion: Good members of the online community give back to the community. Marketers can do well by doing good. Companies can create information-packed articles and reports that help consumers solve problems. These articles don't sell the company or product directly; instead, they sell the concept that empowers the company.

Action: Write a file that helps people solve a problem or provides them with useful, original information. These files can be stored.

Example: Let's say you are a tour guide who gives walking tours of San Francisco. You could write 500-word articles that describe sample tours with each stop explained. Another idea would be to list areas to avoid because of crime, congestion, or image. As most forums are happy to accept relevant material, send a polite query letter stating your topic and asking if the forum wants to review it for the library. If the answer is yes, send it along with a 50-word description of the article. Consultants should include their positioning statement as well. This descriptive information will be posted to the library file so that readers can see a description of the material before deciding to read it. For example:

> Jane Green conducts walking tours of San Francisco for her company, Green Ways, 800-555-1212.

Create a "10 Commandments" Article

Benefit: Prospecting. Increases exposure and positions you as an expert.

Discussion: This kind of article is a fact-based informational piece that explains a topic of interest, such as "10 Ways to Cut Your Taxes" for a tax accountant; "10 Commandments for Reducing Stress" for a psychologist, masseuse, physical therapist, or sports trainer; or "10 Keys to Financial

Freedom" for a certified financial planner or investment adviser. People love these articles because they contain good information and are easy to read quickly. You'll love them, too, because they are easy to write. The format calls for you to write an opening paragraph that presents a problem. Next, write 10 ways to solve the problem. Other good headline words are secrets, tips, hints, rules, and laws.

Action: Propose article; write the article, description, and keywords.

Example: Here is an example of a "10 Commandments" article written by a stress management consultant for an audience of accountants and tax professionals:

> As April 15 rolls around, accountants are under a great deal of stress. With the impending deadline of tax filing season, they work 20-hour days, seven days a week, and must deal with clients who are disorganized and frenzied. Tax accountants must cope with this tension. Here are 10 ways to cut agitation:
>
> 1. Exercise.
>
> 2. Eat healthy foods.
>
> 3. Avoid caffeine, sugar, and other stimulants and depressants.
>
> 4. Breath deeply.
>
> 5. Take short breaks.
>
> 6. Think pleasant thoughts.
>
> 7. Focus on how well you will feel on April 16.
>
> 8. Think of how you are helping people solve their problems.
>
> 9. Think of how you will enjoy the money you are earning.
>
> 10. Think of how you'll appreciate free time when you are done!
>
> This article was written by John Peterson of Peterson and Associates (www.ourcompany.com), a stress management firm based in San Francisco. He can be reached at joe@mycompany.com or 800-555-1212.

Notice that the tips can be as short as one or two words. If you like, this information can be expanded to paragraphs containing several sentences. There is no negative effect in writing a longer article. However, 250 to 500 words will ensure that your readers won't lose interest.

Here's a sample e-mail pitch letter for the sysop:

As April 15 rolls around, accountants will be under a great deal of stress.
I can help your readers with a 250-word article called "The 10 Rules of Reducing Stress." Can I send a copy to you to post in the library? I am qualified to write this article because I have experience as [FILL IN].

Thanks.
Your Name

Signature file

Encourage Republication of Your Files

Benefit: Increases exposure and can be a source of leads.

Discussion: If one article in one web site is good, then one article in many web sites must be better! Encourage readers to post your articles in other areas of interest, such as:

- Mailing lists and newsgroups (If they post the article, then members will regard it as noncommercial. If you post it, it might be viewed with suspicion.).
- Local bulletin boards.
- Special-interest bulletin boards.
- Newsletters published by nonprofit groups, associations, and businesses.
- Relevant publications.

You won't get paid for this editorial service, but you aren't in the business of making money from your writing. You are in business to sell your products or services. That's where the long-term benefit will come. To let people know they can reprint the work, include this line at the end of the article:

This article can be reprinted provided it is not edited in any manner and if proper credit is given. This includes listing my name as the author and my contact information.

If you like, you could instead ask people who want to reprint the article to call you and request permission individually. This way, you will know when and where the article will appear.

To protect your work, place a copyright notice at the beginning of the piece so that people can see it clearly and unmistakably. A sample copyright notice would look like this:

© 2000, Your Company
All Rights Reserved.
Published in the United States of America.

Action: Attach the preceding copyright information paragraph to your article.

Case Study: Warren Reid, Management Consultant

Warren Reid of Encino, California, a management consultant specializing in information technology (consult@primenet.com), spoke on the legal aspects of the year 2000 to a computer conference. His speech was so well received that he was asked to turn it into a 2,000-word article that was published as the lead piece in the Year 2000 Web site (www.year2000 .com). That article led to requests for reprint rights by KMPG/Canada, EDS, and Unisys, among others, who then printed it on their web sites and in their internal newsletters on the Intranet.

Since that time, he has been catapulted to fame, interviewed by *The Wall Street Journal,* and asked to write a book and lead a series of seminars for companies and conferences.

"I've moved from being the keynoter on the second day to the keynoter, period. It was the Net that did it," Reid says.

Write Articles for Online Magazines

Benefit: Increased exposure.

Discussion: Online publications welcome content that is objective and useful to their readers. By publishing articles in other venues, you can increase your exposure to audiences of prospects and raise your credibility. For example, a financial planner could write an article about how to save money on taxes and submit the article to the Smart Business Supersite (www.smartbiz.com).

Action: Find appropriate publishing venues, select a topic, and query the editor. Based on your conversation with the editor, write the article.

ONLINE CONFERENCES

The Internet and commercial online services can hold conferences with their customers using a variety of tools. Companies that have their own forums can use those resources as well as the chat areas of the commercial online services. Using this tool, a company's support personnel could, for example, send FAQs that explain how to correct a problem and show a screen shot depicting what the finished product would look like. Salespeople can conduct real-time chats with prospects by showing them pictures of products and sending audio clips of testimonials from consumers.

To hold a successful conference, companies should take a great deal of care to let consumers know what will be discussed, when the conference will take place, and how to use the tools. This information can be placed in a FAQ file that consumers can read at their convenience.

Hold Press Conferences and Annual Meetings Online

Benefit: Your community will hear the whole story.

Discussion: By holding a meeting online, your community will have access to every word and chart available to people in the audience. Most of this information would have been distilled by the media, so this is a terrific opportunity for your company to tell its story directly to the people who really care.

Example: Bell & Howell hosted the first online annual meeting. Shareholders listened to the meeting with free software offered by the company and e-mailed questions to board members stationed in Ann Arbor, Michigan. "This is the way of the future," says William White, CEO of Bell & Howell. Many major newspapers reported that B&H hosted the online meeting, thus creating good exposure for the company.

Be a Guest at Online Conferences and Educational Seminars

Benefit: Prospecting and increased exposure.

Discussion: Many forums hold online conferences to help members learn about topics of special interest. They have a lot of time and space to fill. If you submit an appropriate idea, you may be rewarded by getting increased exposure to your audience. Forum operators benefit as well since your session will generate traffic.

Action: Send a query note to the sysop with a conference topic, sample questions, and a list of what users will learn. Propose several dates. Here's an example:

> As companies lay off workers in today's difficult economy, those displaced workers need to know how to get new jobs. My company helps people find new jobs by teaching them to write resumes that get responses. I would like to host an online conference for your members that will teach them what works and doesn't work in resumes, which buzzwords are old and tired and which ones are new and exciting, and how to stand out from the crowd. I've noticed you hold forums on Thursday evenings. Would Oct. 18 or 25 work?

You will want to schedule the conference well enough in advance for the sysop to publicize the meeting to members. This could take about a month. To promote the conference, you might send a file to the library that describes your company and its services or provides tips on your area of expertise.

SUMMARY

Although the press acts as a necessary filter to edit the news and provide objectivity, companies have a vested interest in telling the rest of the story. The Internet provides a great many tools, from e-mail and mailing lists to chats, that allow their stories to be told—and found by online communities.

All these steps allow you to create long, lasting relationships with your publics. They will come to rely on you as a source of information they can't get from the daily newspapers and trade publications. Further, you'll save money by using these tools because you won't have to budget the expense of printing and mailing hundreds or thousands of press releases via snail mail.

Market Research and Online Focus Groups

The interactive nature of the Internet and e-mail gives marketers an economical and easy way to gather information from prospects and customers. Once you know who your customers are and what they want, you will be well on your way to creating customers for life.

In this chapter, you will learn:

- How to log files to find out what customers are thinking.
- How to conduct market research on your web site.
- You've got mail! Now read it! How to conduct market research with e-mail.
- How to find out the names of people visiting your site.
- Other methods of conducting focus group research.

USING LOG FILES TO FIND OUT WHAT CUSTOMERS ARE THINKING

Every time a visitor comes to your web site, she leaves a mark that can help you sell more products and services. Each visit is recorded in a log file that is kept on your ISP's records. You can find out where she found out about your site, which page she saw first, which pages she clicked on, and which page was the last she saw before going to another site. You can find how much time she spent on each page, which state or country she came from, and what time of day she started her visit. You can even find out which browser and version she used.

This information can help any web site manager. At first I thought a lot of this information was useless. After all, did it really matter what time of day a person came to visit? All I cared about was sales! However, after talking to several web marketers who studied and analyzed web logs, I realized you can extrapolate a lot of great information by studying your logs.

For example, web marketer Philippa Gamse of CyberSpeaker (www.cyberspeaker.com) tells of a client who sold pet supplies on the web. By studying the user logs, she realized that people used certain keywords on search engines to find her client's site. By rewriting the page, keywords, and title to reflect these keywords, the web site rose in the rankings on search engines!

In helping analyze lawyer Rita Risser's web site (www.fairmeasures .com), Gamse pointed out that many people were looking on a certain page. Previously, Risser hadn't thought the information on that page was anything out of the ordinary. Because she saw there was so much interest in this category, Risser decided to create a product that met the needs of these people.

These examples show that log files can yield a gold mine of information—if you know how to sift through the mounds of data.

Log files record many important facets of a person's visit to your web site:

- **Number of visitors.** This is a general indication of how popular your site is. However, don't make the classic mistake of confusing the term *visitors* with *hits,* which refers to the number of files that are downloaded from your page. A file can be a text file or a picture file. So if your home page has one text file, a picture of you, another picture of your product, and a company logo, then four hits could be registered from only one visitor. So please disregard any marketer who promises to get more hits for your site. This is an irrelevant number. Hits, as my colleague Katharine D. Paine, of Delahaye Medialink, points out, stands for "How Idiots Track Success." When looking at log files, look to see visits, not hits.

- **Which country or state their ISP is located in,** which should not be confused with where they live! If a person who lives in Kentucky uses America Online, which is based in Virginia, the log will show that the visitor is from Virginia, not Kentucky! These systems are not perfect, but they are getting better. Knowing the country or state of origin can be valuable if you are targeting customers in a certain area. You might find that you have a big following in a certain country and it might benefit everyone to translate the page into their native language. If you were selling clothing with sports logos, you would want to show a picture of the Yankees to a visitor from New York and a picture of the Broncos to a visitor from Denver.

- **The visitor's domain name.** You might get good clues as to the kinds of visitors you attract if you pay attention to domain names. For example, you might want the domain names of famous companies. However, you won't find the address or name of the user, unfortunately. You also might see a great number of visitors coming from America Online. This will alert you to design the interface to take advantage of AOL's limitations. I noticed several visitors from a prospect's web site in my logs. I knew they were checking me out!

- **The visitor's extension.** We're all familiar with the *.com* extension, which denotes a business or general user. But there are several extensions, such as *.edu* for education and *.mil* for military. Knowing this information can be important if you want to reach those marketplaces or send special messages to people in those markets. For example, if you are selling teaching supplies for the corporate and college markets, you might wish to present different messages clearly targeted for .com or .edu users. One company that offered scholarships to students presented one home page for readers who had .edu extensions and another for those with .com extensions.

- **What time of day the person visited.** The time of day can be important to you if you advertise on radio or television and want to see if the visits rise after an ad is broadcast. Did the number of visitors go up after your ad was aired? If not, maybe your ad offer isn't effective or is timed poorly. For example, if you advertise right before the business report on news radio in prime-time drive time, you might not get a bump in web traffic because people are in their cars and can't access the Internet! You'll need to move your ads to a time when people are at home. Or you might find that you get a surge in traffic 20 minutes after the ad ran, because people are now in their offices and can reach your site.

- **Which page they entered first.** This tells you where visitors started their journey. Once you have this information, you can begin to test your marketing programs, especially if this page is linked to an ad you have placed.

- **The last page they read before they left.** This can be useful in determining if people liked your message and bought your product—or didn't get excited and left. Did they leave on a page that included a form? Could that mean that the form was too complicated to fill out? Or could it mean other things? Web analysis won't show you *why* people bailed out, only that they did. You have to figure out the why.

- **The most requested pages.** This information will show you what your customers want.

- **The least requested pages.** Why do these pages not work? "Do they contain key information? Maybe you aren't making them enticing enough," says Gamse.

- **The percentage of your traffic that views your home page as a single-access page, that is, that doesn't go beyond the home page.** "If this [percentage] is high, your home page is not doing its job," says Gamse. People should delve deeper into your site to find out more information about your products and services. If the front page turns them off, they won't learn about the great things you can do for them!

- **How much time they spent on each page and each visit.** This information can show you if people are reading your pages. However, this figure could be deceptive, because the log file can't determine if the reason people stayed on the page for a long time was because they were truly interested and read every word or because the graphics were so large that the page took a long time to load or because the customer's boss decided to chat with that person for a few minutes while your page timer ticked away! Still, this could be good information. If you find people spend less than 10 seconds on the page, you might assume the graphics load so slowly that people won't wait for the page to load. You can fix the problem by removing, replacing, or resizing the graphic. Once this is done, you will probably see more people spending more time on that page.

"If you have a content-rich site, and this time is low, something is wrong," says Gamse. Why aren't people reading your material? Is it because they can't find it, the page is too slow to load, or some other reason?

- **How people found out about your site.** This is called "referrer" information, which is vital for showing you which ads are working, which linking campaigns are paying off, and which search engines are building traffic for you. "Do you recognize all the referring URLs? If not, check out the links, and if appropriate, thank the web site owner—you never know what it might lead to," says Gamse.
- **Which search engine they used to find your site and which keywords they used.** This can be very important in determining what your customers think of you or want from your company. The data can also be used to improve your ranking in search engines (see Figure 19.1).
- **Which search terms are being used in search engines.** "Are there search terms that are working well in some search engines, but not others? Could be a good idea to work out why, tweak the pages, and resubmit," suggests Gamse.

| Bookmarks | Location: | http://www.fairmeasures.com/webtrends/march99/ | What's Related |

Top Search Phrases

General Statistics
General Statistics
Resources Accessed
Most Requested Pages
Top Entry Pages
Top Exit Pages
Top Paths Through Site
Most Submitted Forms
Visitors & Demograph
Top Users
Most Active Organizations
Organization Breakdown
Activity Statistics
Summary of Activity by Ti
Activity Level by Day of W
Activity Level by Hour
Technical Statistics
Technical Statistics
Forms Submitted By Users
Client Errors
Page Not Found Errors
Referrers & Keywords
Top Referring Sites
Top Referring URLs
Top Search Engines
Top Search Phrases

The first table identifies Phrases which led the most visitors to the site (regardless of the search engine). The second table identifies, for each phrase, which search engines led visitors to the site.

	Top Search Phrases		
	Phrases	**Phrases found**	**% of Total**
1	down blouse	113	5.19%
2	lawsuits	64	2.94%
3	wrongful termination	42	1.93%
4	sexual harassment	31	1.42%
5	legal advice	31	1.42%
6	insubordination	20	0.91%
7	nepotism	18	0.82%
8	americans with disabilites act	18	0.82%
9	employee lawsuits	18	0.82%
10	fair measures	16	0.73%
11	exempt employee	16	0.73%
13	employee law	12	0.55%
14	ask lawyer	11	0.5%
15	www.fairmeasures.com	10	0.45%

Document: Done

Figure 19.1 This table show the search engines and phrases used to reach lawyer Rita Risser's site, Fair Measures.com. (© 1999, Fair Measures, Inc.)

HOW CAN I ACCESS THE LOG FILE?

Log files are kept on the server from your ISP. A good ISP will let you access the file with its own software utilities that create reports in chart and numerical forms. Sometimes a chart can show you a trend much more accurately and prominently than numbers can! However, not all ISPs offer the software or even keep track of the visits. Be sure to check with your ISP to see what information it offers. "If they don't record this information, find a new ISP," Gamse says. "The information is that important."

The log file data is stored in your access area. If you looked at it with a text reader, you would see each visitor's experience. This information is hard to read. You will need a software program to decipher the visits and present the information in a report that gives you a snapshot of the information—not the individual brush strokes of each visit. One of the best programs for analyzing this data is called WebTrends (www .webtrends.com). It provides you with dozens of reports in both numerical and graphical formats (in color!). You can easily see what users are doing on your web site. You can also tailor the reports to include factoids that are relevant to you and exclude the rest. For example, you might not care what time people visit your site. With this program, you won't waste time reading irrelevant data.

For a quick overview of your activity, check out Hitomoter (www.hitometer.com), which provides total number of visits, referring pages, search engine keywords, domains, and browsers.

At the high end of the spectrum, large companies with significant traffic should consider Accrue Insight, (www.accrue.com), which provides very detailed reports and can combine activity from multiple locations, normally a daunting task.

Other programs are on the market as well, so please read their literature and reviews to find the one that best meets your needs.

Case Study: Profiting from Perversity: Using Log File Analysis to Increase Marketing Effectiveness

Can the Net's obsession with porn actually help lead traffic to your business web site? At first glance, no way. But a careful analysis of one lawyer's web site showed that there are ways to profit from perversity.

Lawyer Rita Risser (www.fairmeasures.com) and her web marketing consultant Philippa Gamse (www.cyberspeaker.com) studied user logs, which are the statistics that show how many people visited a site, which pages they viewed, and how they found about the site, among other things. They discovered that one of the top phrases used to find Risser's site of legal information was "down blouse," a term that refers to Net voyeur sites that point cameras down women's blouses.

You might be wondering why Risser's site would pop up with this odd keyword. It turns out that Risser is the Net's legal equivalent of "Dear Abby." She answers people's questions about workplace issues. As it happens, she answered a question from a reader who asked if a man could be fired for looking down a woman's blouse. So when the search engine indexed her massive site (more than four hundred pages of content), it found the words *down blouse* and listed that page along with porn sites. Not surprisingly, that page was listed as one of the most popular on her site, as voyeurs clicked there and clicked away.

Here comes the fun part. You can say, "Oh well, who needs these perverts?" or you can do as Risser and Gamse did and realize that nobody needs a book on sexual harassment issues in the workplace more than people who were using the Internet to look down women's blouses. To capitalize on this traffic, they put a link to Amazon.com and a book on sexual harassment in the workplace. Risser makes 15 percent commission from the Amazon Associates program and her new readers!

Here's the message for you. No, don't add dirty words to your META tags. Rather, analyze your user logs to find the keywords and topics your readers want. In fact, Risser found many readers wanted information on a certain topic, which led her to create a new product to meet their needs! That's smart thinking!

If you look at the keywords used to reach your site and the most frequently read pages, you just might find that your readers are telling you exactly what they want from you—which might be radically different from what you thought they wanted. Now it is up to you to create more products and services that meet these readers' needs. If you do, you'll become even more valuable to your clients and make more sales.

CONDUCTING MARKET RESEARCH ON YOUR WEB SITE

You can find out a great deal about your customers by using your web site. You might even gain more information from an online focus group than a traditional group because respondents aren't influenced by other people's comments, they are completely anonymous online, text is recorded and thus an accurate transcript is maintained, and individual lines of in-depth questioning are now possible.

The following sections present several nonintrusive techniques for conducting market research on your web site and tactics to increase the response rate.

Ask for Feedback

Customers know what features they want in a new product and where your product falls short. They will be glad to tell you—if you ask them. Give them a chance to voice their opinions by filling out a survey or sending you e-mail. You might encourage them by selecting winners and posting their entries.

Break Up the Survey

People don't like to spend a lot of time filling out survey forms. Remember, they are doing you a favor. They aren't getting as much out of this process as you are. To make the form more palatable, break it up into several screens. At the end of each screen, offer a verbal incentive for them to continue like "Thanks for helping us. Only two more screens to go" or "Your responses will help make better products." You could also break the survey into several parts and present each part when they return to the web site or send them an additional survey by e-mail.

Tell People How Long the Survey Will Take

You will get more responses if people know how long the survey will take. If you don't give an estimate, people might get upset at what will seem like a long time and bail out of the survey. By providing an estimate, you will control expectations and get more completed responses.

Show the Results

On a product page, ask people if they think the product is useful, priced right, or whatever you want. Then show the results. People will get instant gratification and be more likely to fill out other quick surveys on your site.

Sound Friendly

Use friendly sentences to improve response. Don't use cold, impersonal survey-speak. Use interesting sounding questions and offbeat choices. Ask for responses by saying "We can't decide which features to highlight in our ads. Could you give us some help, please?" You could try a multiple-choice format, as in "I thought this story was (1) great! (2) pretty good. (3) yawn. (4) a waste of time." Or tell your viewer, "We're stuck on a re-design—give us a hand, please." Ask them if they found what they needed, what they liked about your site, and how they would improve it.

Don't Ask Questions That Will Irritate Prospects

While respondents might not mind filling out basic mailing label information, they may very well balk at giving such personal information as net worth, salary, or—my all-time horror—mother's maiden name. While the first two could be merely off-putting, the latter is never needed by a marketer. This sensitive information could be extremely hazardous if it fell into the wrong hands, as bank accounts and credit cards can be accessed with this password! HotWired asked for this information and then rescinded; however, *The Wall Street Journal* requires a mother's maiden name to register for its site. This kind of invasion of privacy in a medium not known for security is equal to waving a red flag in the face of a prospect.

Test the Number of Questions People Will Answer before Giving Up

Be aware that people didn't come online at great expense to serve as guinea pigs. The more questions you ask, the less likely they will want to participate unless you offer a really great reward. No one has done research to find out what the magic number is and whether or not it is swayed by the weight of the offer involved. The findings might vary from industry to industry. To find out what works on your site, test various options and numbers.

Fill the Form with Required and Optional Information

As responses will fall off based on the number of questions asked, you need to limit the number. However, you might be able to get the information you want without turning people off if you make certain information required and other information optional. For example, you might require their name and e-mail address so you can correspond via e-mail but make the street address optional.

Require All Information

If you are in a business-to-business company, then you might not mind risking a drop-off by requiring additional information, based on the theory that if they can't qualify themselves properly, then you don't want to waste your resources dealing with them.

Check Submissions for Completeness with a Software Check

People might omit information either by accident or on purpose. A quick check by a software program will ascertain whether or they have filled out the form correctly. If they have not, the form will return with a prompt for the missing information. If they have, they will get a confirmation notice on the screen, perhaps by e-mail, and then gain access to the site. Be aware, however, that although the form is complete, it might not be accurate. Marketers face the same problem in other venues, such as telephone interviews and prospect forms at trade shows. If people have made errors, be sure to return the form with all the other answers typed in. Don't force people to fill in the form again from the very beginning. You'll annoy people, and they won't fill out the form.

Test Prices, Headlines, and Advertising Copy

Because revisions are so inexpensive to make on the Internet compared to print or broadcast media, you can test your message, prices, headlines, and other factors to see which elements are most effective.

Send Appropriate Messages to Targeted Audiences

If you find out where people last visited before coming to your site, you can send them pages specially geared for their needs. For example,if they came from a competitor's site, you could quickly point out the advantages your product or service offers. If they came from an advertisement in a magazine, you could send them a different set of pages than that given to a person who entered via your direct-mail campaign. In this manner you can tell parents that your car has the latest safety features for children while you tell college students that it goes from 0 to 60 mph faster than any other car.

YOU'VE GOT MAIL! NOW READ IT! CONDUCTING MARKET RESEARCH WITH E-MAIL

Dan Bricklin, the inventor of the spreadsheet, taught me a very important point about listening to your customers. I called his company one day to find out how to use one of his new programs. To my surprise, the great Dan Bricklin himself answered the phone. I was surprised and introduced myself. We had been speaking on a panel a few months before, so he remembered me. He asked why I was calling and I said I had a question for his support department.

"You can ask me," he said.

I hesitated and said, "You have better things to do than answer a question from me. I'm sure your support staff can help."

Then he said something that shocked me.

"I am the support staff."

He told me rules that have stayed with me and hopefully will inspire you.

"You see, every person who calls with a question, is telling me I didn't write the manual clearly or the interface wasn't designed perfectly. They are really showing me what needs to be improved. Then, 1 out of every 100 people will call to ask why the product doesn't do a certain action. I tell them that the product can't do that, but it is a good idea and I'll build it into the next edition. Now they have given me ideas for new features. Then for every thousandth person who calls and asks why the product doesn't do something, but is so far away from what the product should do, that I realize it is a great idea for a new product. That's where I get my ideas for new products."

Bricklin is a living example of why listening to your customers is a good thing—even if they have complaints. The complaints are really opportunities to improve your product. If you can get past your natural reaction to negative customers, you might realize they are telling you they like your product (or they would return it or throw it away instead of spending time calling the company). They are giving you valuable customer feedback, for which you would normally pay a lot of money if you had hired them for focus group studies! The message is clear: There is gold in them thar e-mails. If you mine it, you could become rich.

If you might not be able to read e-mails as part of your job, you should instruct others in your organization to read it—and take action.

Use E-mail Surveys

If you have developed an e-mail list of customers and prospects in your target market, consider querying them to find out what they like or dislike about your product, what products or services they would like to see, and other market research information. Lilly Walters, coauthor of *Speak and Grow Rich* (Prentice Hall, 1998) and a principal in the Walters International Speakers Bureau, sends her readers, professional speakers, and meeting planners a brief survey to find out about new trends in the marketplace. She reports a whopping 40 percent response rate. "We get a very high response rate if we keep the questions *very* simple and only ask one or two questions."

Case Study: Walters International Speaker's Bureau

We are taking this very quick survey from a list of 1,500 professional speakers, seminar leaders, and speakers bureaus (if that's not you, please disregard this). The results of this survey will be published in the second edition of *Speak and Grow Rich* by Lilly and Dottie Walters (Prentice Hall) and in our magazine *Sharing Ideas for Professional Speakers.*

Question: Are you a speaker or a speakers bureau?

Question: Which publication do you make time to read?

Question: Membership in which association has proved the most beneficial for education and information for you as a professional speaker?

Question: Membership in which association has proved the most beneficial as a source of bookings for your speaking?

Question: Which book has been the most helpful to you as a professional speaker?

Question: If you could ask 1,500 professional speakers a question, what would you ask?

Thank you!
Lilly Walters,
e-mail: LillyW@Walters-Intl.com
Author:
Speak and Grow Rich (Prentice Hall, 1996 and 1988)
What to Say When You're Dying on the Platform! (McGraw-Hill, 1995)
Secrets of Successful Speakers (McGraw-Hill, 1993).

Pose Questions or Surveys in Newspaper Ads or on TV and Ask for Response via E-mail

The San Francisco Chronicle's Business Section asked readers to vote on how stock information should be displayed (decimals or fractions) and then respond via e-mail, fax, or phone. Other businesses can ask questions in any medium and direct respondents to answer via e-mail or to go to the company site and receive a gift or free information reports for responding to the survey.

Host a Chat Session on Your Web Site

Many company web sites now feature software that allows people to chat. You could invite customers or employees to such a session and conduct a focus group online.

FINDING OUT WHO IS AT YOUR WEB SITE

One of the most perplexing problems of the Internet is that you don't ever really know who is visiting your site. When someone enters your cyberstore, you have no initial way of knowing if the person is young or old, male or female, rich or poor. A store manager at the mall can see the people who enter her shop, but online merchants don't have a clue. They must use clever tactics to identify these visitors. As Net culture is clearly opposed to manipulation and guards its privacy, simply asking visitors to tell something about themselves is not an easy task—especially when you consider they are paying money to be online and spending time away from other enjoyable or productive pursuits. They might not be in the best frame of mind to fill out a 20-page questionnaire about their likes and dislikes. This reaction is no different than a typical consumer response to a registration card that accompanies electronic products such as toasters and vacuum cleaners. Most people don't fill out the card, which asks dozens of questions about their income and buying patterns.

A survey by Cyber Dialogue (www.cyberdialogue.com) in 1997 showed these percentages of people would be willing to divulge the following kinds of information:

Hobbies and special interests—92 percent

Willing to participate in short surveys—77 percent

Demographic information to have web sites tailor content to their needs—73 percent

Age, education, and attitudes—90 percent

Their names—67 percent

Salaries—29 percent

Credit card numbers—4 percent

The following sections offer several strategies for gathering user name and demographic information from customers and prospects via the Internet.

Ask Readers to Tell You Their Opinions by E-mail or in a Guest Book

A prime benefit of the Internet is that it provides an interactive way to create relationships with prospects and customers. By asking for feedback, the beginnings of a relationship can be formed. The tools to make this happen are e-mail and guest books. E-mail can be set up on a web site with the HTML command mailto:, which allows the customer to click on the text and fill out a preaddressed e-mail message to the company. A guest book is a form that customers fill out and send to the company. Comments can be read by all customers if the company wishes. By using these tools, marketers can gain valuable anecdotal insight into the minds of respondents. If a statistically significant number of people respond, then other assumptions can be made.

Add mailto: forms, text input boxes, and guest books to your pages and encourage people to interact with the company. You should always acknowledge the interaction so people feel they are being heard. An autoresponder can be set up to acknowledge receipt of the letter with a simple thank-you. If the letter warrants a follow-up, then e-mail can be used.

If You Want to Ascertain Income, Simply Ask for a Zip Code

As people will reach a burnout factor and not want to answer too many questions (no one knows how many is too many), try to compress knowledge. For example, if you know a person's zip code, you also know the city and state in which they live and can make a good guess at their income. To find that information the hard way, you would have to ask three questions instead of one.

Offer a Contest or Free Product

For people to receive a prize or free product, they must tell you where to deliver the goodies! You will then know their name, street address, e-mail address, and that they are prospects for your product. This strategy also reduces the amount of inaccurate information posted by people afraid of having their privacy invaded and works well at consumer, service, and professional sites. For example, Cliff's Notes, the publisher of literary study guides, offers high school and college students a free "Hot Tips" study disk and a list of all titles and prices.

Require Registration to Access Deeper Levels of the Site Page

If you entice people with greater information and access to software, they may be more willing to tell you about themselves. Industry.net (www.industry.net), which publishes industry-specific trade publications, offers a smash of free, useful information to establish credibility and then asks prospects who want to search the site and download software to identify themselves by name, title, company, industry group, and buying authority. This strategy could work well for other business-to-business sites.

Try Bribery

Several sites that offer money or discounts to people to read ads require the consumers to fill out more than seven screens of information about their hobbies, interests, vacations, sports, and business interests. Because they dangle an enticing carrot (money), thousands of people have completed the forms. Cybergold (www.cybergold.com) is one such site.

OTHER METHODS OF CONDUCTING FOCUS GROUP RESEARCH

Use Newsgroups to Find Out What People Are Saying about Your Products

People use newsgroups to find recommendations about buying products. It is not unusual to find novice classic music fans asking for suggestions on which albums to buy to create a collection; car owners post messages to find out which tires they should buy, and computer users are always asking for tips. People also post their grievances online. By typing the name of your company or product on a search service like Deja.com (www.deja.com), you will find out what people are saying about your company. In one seminar I conducted, a woman from a well-known sneaker company found to her horror that customers were complaining that her company's products were falling apart! Another possible strategy is to post questions in appropriate newsgroups. However, this should be done only after making sure the group allows this kind of questioning. If you post questions without first ascertaining the permissibility of this venture, you might run the risk of alienating a large audience.

Hire a Company to Monitor Newsgroup Activity

Monitoring newsgroups and making sense of the discussion can take time that you don't have. If that's the case, consider hiring a company that specializes in monitoring and evaluating these discussions. Two such groups are eWatch (www.ewatch.com) and Delahaye Medialink (www.delahaye.com).

FOCUS GROUP TOOLS

One of the best ways to conduct focus groups online is with a tool called Place Ware Conference Center (Figure 19.2), which is produced

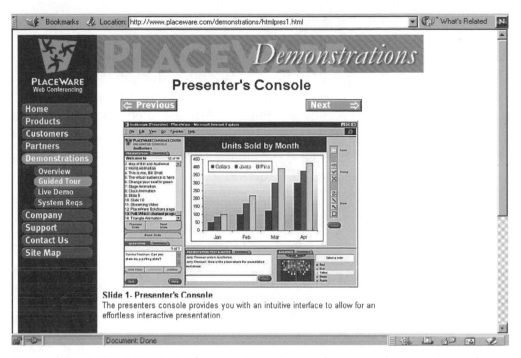

Figure 19.2 PlaceWare's Conference Center lets market researchers conduct online focus groups and obtain feedback in real time. (© 1999, PlaceWare, Inc.)

by Place Ware, Inc. (www.placeware.com), a spin-off from the highly regarded Xerox Palo Alto Research Center (PARC). The product is a highly interactive web site conference center that lets organizations conduct seminars and present sales and training materials online to a live audience and gather customer feedback in real time. Presenters give PowerPoint slide shows and answer questions from the audience. Audiences respond to the presenter and to each other, vote, and assess the product by selecting options on their keyboard or with a mouse. Presenters can ask people in the audience to vote on any number of issues, such as price or favorite colors.

Online focus groups conducted through PlaceWare can provide an extensive sampling of customer response. Audience members can ask questions, talk to each other, and even vote. In addition, participants can give spontaneous feedback, and a presenter can gauge audience response on the fly. PlaceWare has been used by PBS, Intel, and the U.S. Open Golf Association for a variety of training, presentation, service, and focus group applications.

"With the PlaceWare, customers can easily and conveniently review and evaluate product features, and marketing professionals can efficiently collect customer comments. Marketers can use a multimedia presentation to promote key features and emphasize customer benefits. And by using polling slides, marketers receive quantified voting information about an audience's preferences. Audience questions help a marketer design collateral and future products," a company representative says. "PlaceWare is seamlessly integrated with the web, so it's easy and convenient for customers to attend a product demonstration. And because PlaceWare has no physical boundaries, events can serve audiences ranging in number from tens to thousands."

SUMMARY

Your web site can yield a tremendous amount of terrific information about your customers and prospects.

Customer Service and Support Online

If you want to lose customers and create enemies for life, make sure you have lousy customer support services. If they provide outstanding customer support, however, you'll have customers singing your praises to their friends and colleagues. They will reorder products and extend service contracts. But running an expensive customer support center can be a cash drain for many companies. Fortunately, the Internet can help improve service, cut costs, and even turn this operation into a profit center!

In this chapter, you will learn:

- The benefits of online customer support systems.
- How to create an online support center.
- Strategies for creating a successful support center.

BENEFITS OF ONLINE CUSTOMER SUPPORT

The Internet and commercial online services can help your business build relationships with customers by creating online support centers to answer people's questions. Companies that respond to customers' queries quickly can build loyalty that lasts a lifetime. Also, happy customers tell potential customers—but so do unhappy customers!

By creating a customer support center online, your company can benefit from:

- **Increased loyalty from customers.** Consumers who get technical support quickly will remain happy and might see no reason to switch products.

- **Reduced returns from customers who experience problems.** Consumers who can't get support quickly can become frustrated with your product and return it for a refund.
- **Reduced bad word of mouth.** Studies have shown that happy customers tell 3 friends, while unhappy customers tell 11! One way to reduce bad word of mouth is to have good customer support that helps dissatisfied customers before they unleash a torrent of ill will.
- **Faster response to customer questions.** Some companies with small support staffs are overburdened and can't respond to customers' questions in a timely manner. By using online support centers, they can answer people's questions faster. With the use of libraries of stored text files and software patches, consumers might be able to find what they need without speaking to a support rep.
- **Lower support costs.** Customers can find information that addresses frequently asked questions. Service reps won't have to return expensive phone calls. Toll-free phone numbers won't be used as much. Questions can be answered in batches, thus making more efficient use of service reps. Questions can be delegated to people who have the right degree of skill to answer.
- **Customers helping answer other customers' questions.** This will lighten your staff's workload and build camaraderie among consumers.
- **Market research.** Customer complaints about certain features might lead to development of new products or features, thus aiding research and development. Dan Bricklin, who invented the first computer spreadsheet, VisiCalc, handled customer support calls and learned of customers' needs, which led to significant new features in other products.
- **Profit center.** If your support center generates a significant amount of traffic, your company might actually make money from the arrangement contracted with the commercial online service. Smaller companies probably won't make any money, but larger ones can do well.

"Answering support questions on the forum is far easier, quicker, and less expensive than answering letters or phone calls," says Eric Robichaud, president of Rhode Island Soft Systems (www.risoft-systems.com), a software publisher of screensavers, fonts, and games.

"You can support customers when it is convenient for you instead of having to drop everything when they call."

Another way to turn the support center into a profit center is to train the service reps to sell additional products to customers. For example, people might call about a product that has been replaced by a new model. The rep can sell the new model. Reps can also sell service contracts, additional copies of the product for friends or colleagues, other items from the product line, and complementary products from other companies.

The computer industry has embraced this concept, as most major hardware manufacturers and software publishers have online support centers, including Microsoft, Compaq, Hewlett-Packard, IBM, and Apple.

PRACTICAL CONSIDERATIONS FOR CREATING AN ONLINE SUPPORT CENTER

Although many aspects of establishing a customer support center are outside the realm of this book, online marketers should address several issues in planning one:

- **Human resources.** The support center will need to be staffed by competent professionals who not only know the ins and outs of the product but can also build rapport with people online. This is important as people who call support centers are frequently angry and frustrated because they cannot get the product to work properly. Consequently, their messages might be caustic. Support staffers must be able to deal with the situation by diffusing the anger, solving the problem, and building bridges to positive communications with the consumer. The company cannot afford to have one angry customer tell his experiences to thousands of people online!
- **Content.** Online libraries can store a great deal of technical information. Having consumers find this information by themselves can help the company save a great deal of time and expense. This can be accomplished by carefully organizing the information by the appropriate classifications. For example, a software company can have these file folders: product, installation, usage, printing, upgrade, common errors, error codes explained, how do I accomplish task x?, and many others. Material

can be cross-referenced. The material should be hyperlinked so that consumers can jump from one area to another with ease.

- **Cost.** The budget for an online support center will vary by company. While planning the budget, don't think of it as a drain on expenses. Instead, think of it as a way to save money by unburdening other forms of support—telephone, mail, and fax. Also, think of the benefit in terms of positive customer relations. Finally, create ways to turn the support center into a profit center by encouraging messages that create sales opportunities for new product versions, complementary products, and long-term support and training contracts for large companies.

Case Study: Intellisystem Knowledgebase Provides Customer Support over the Internet

Companies that need to provide customer support via the Internet, phones, and fax can use the IntelliSystem proprietary system created by IntelliSystems of Reno, Nevada (www.intellisystems.com). This knowledge-based system is used by Netscape Communications (help.netscape.com), developer of the world's most used browser.

Customers with questions can get instant worldwide access to product support information. The IntelliSystem knowledgebase contains the answers to most of the questions most frequently asked by customers. Its format was designed for distribution to end users. The information is complete and is fully tested and reviewed before it is made available to customers.

The cost to handle a customer online is a fraction of the cost of live support. More than three thousand seven hundred people visited Netscape's help center in its first day of operation and accessed more than one hundred thousand pages of information, making it the most visited area of the Netscape Support Page, company officials said. As the industry average cost for a call handled by a customer support technician is $10, Netscape saved nearly $40,000 in the first day of operation.

"The World Wide Web has emerged as a new and viable option for providing support to customers of high-technology companies. The same knowledgebase that offloads calls by phone and fax can now be leveraged further to answer the questions of customers electronically," says Michael Beare of IntelliSystems. "Customers now have access to online support without taking up support reps' time by sending e-mail back and forth. By adding the IntelliSystem knowledgebase to the options offered from a web page, support calls and questions can be offloaded before they reach the support department. This increases customer support availability and reduces costs."

To make the knowledgebase easily accessible via the Internet, IntelliSystems developed a conversion process that takes the content of the knowledgebase files and turns them into hundreds of intelligently (and automatically) linked HTML files. These files can then be simply loaded on an existing web server and a startup link provided from the index web page. Access to existing support information can be provided immediately with minimal involvement of support staff resources. The IntelliSystem knowledgebase conversion process can usually be completed in a few days.

"IntelliSystems's Smart Site is easy to set up and to maintain," says Beare. Although the expert system contains answers to thousands of questions, Netscape was able to create it in a matter of days because the company had been using the same expert database on its IntelliSystems phone system.

Netscape is able to resolve more than 10 percent of its support calls using the IntelliSystems telephone phone system, according to Bob Beaulieu, director of tech support for Netscape.

"This system takes customer support to the next higher level," Beare continues. "Not only does it leverage their investment in the phone help system, but it provides the fastest possible help for their customers."

Previously, customers who needed customer support had to search through FAQs, use search engines, or send e-mail to the company. All these solutions had problems. FAQs can be difficult to search through. Search engines found many possible answers, but the customer had to dig through a maze of possibilities to find the correct information. E-mail questions might go unanswered for a day or two (or longer).

"By our interactive system, with our Q-and-A format, we drive you to your answers quickly, unlike a database search engine, which gives you 100 possible answers. This is a very effective way of doing support," Beare says. "We wanted to make it easy for the user and make it the least frustrating experience possible."

Beare is understandably proud of this system:

IntelliSystems is the nationwide leader in providing automated customer support systems. As such, we have acquired pertinent experience in the development and implementation of this technology in support environments across several industries. During the consulting process, this experience is applied to create the first knowledgebase for the system. The first step is to look at the current caller requirements from an information standpoint: "What do our callers need to know?" This is done by a close look at current operations including call-logs, call-tracking reports, fax documents, and any established Q-and-A databases and through close cooperation with support department personnel. The process is a team effort requiring complete and honest cooperation in identifying and determining what information to place in the knowledgebase. A series of problem identification forms are filled out in the process. The next step involves the organization of the problem identification forms into a structure suitable for voice-system delivery. This provides the format of the initial menu structure presented to callers.

IntelliSystems has worked very closely over the past several years with some of the nation's largest call-processing centers to establish guidelines to make this a very quick and efficient process. A meeting with the knowledgebase engineer is then held to discuss the emerging knowledgebase's structure and design. No two knowledgebases are alike; each is heavily customized to the client's specific requirements.

The third step is for the Intellisystems's knowledge engineer to perform the original coding of the knowledgebase. This lays the foundation for future growth and establishes the first conventions for the knowledgebase. The structure is prepared for customer review several times during the process, and full explanations of the work done are given. The actual information is then added into the knowledgebase framework. The completed knowledgebase is finally delivered and explained to those responsible for its ongoing maintenance. The end product is a refined and complete knowledgebase covering some predefined knowledge domain that customers must have access to as soon as possible. A typical first knowledgebase contains from 200 to 300 troubleshooting rules, although this number may vary.

STRATEGIES TO PROVIDE CUSTOMER SUPPORT

Many tools exist to help online marketers support their customers. This section discusses popular strategies for doing so.

Use E-mail and E-mail Boxes to Help Customers

Benefit: Provide fast response to customers at a low cost to the company.

Discussion: Most people on online systems have access to e-mail and use it. Unlike other tools, such as file downloads, there is virtually no barrier to learning to use e-mail, and neither is there any hesitation in using it. Because many companies require e-mail usage, this tool is nearly universally used by online consumers.

To help support customers, companies should promote the use of e-mail as the preferred way of communicating with the company. In this model, the customer sends a note to the support department, where the support representative fields the query promptly and courteously. The company benefits from decreased support costs and the customer benefits by fast response time. E-mail addresses can be listed in manuals, fliers, and advertisements or can be spoken aloud on the telephone messaging device.

To use online services to their potential, consider this scenario. Create multiple e-mailboxes that deal with separate products (e.g., printers @mycompany.com, monitors@mycompany.com). Consumers send e-mail to the mailbox of their choice, where the expert can field the question. This removes a step in the sorting process. If every e-mail note went to support@yourcompany.com, a secretary would have to read each message and send it to the proper technician.

Create Autoresponders to Respond to Common Questions

Benefit: Reduce or eliminate personnel costs in handling certain inquiries; customers receive answers faster.

Discussion: Many consumer questions are identical. Support personnel spend a great deal of time repeating the same information. By creating e-mail files of these questions and hooking them in to an autoresponder, companies can help people find and receive information faster. For example, if a company publicized a list of topics, consumers could send e-mail to topiclist@mycompany.com and receive data almost immediately. Although the Internet can provide autoresponder, the commercial online services do not. However, operators can manually send e-mail files to consumers.

Create FAQs

Benefit: Reduce or eliminate personnel costs in handling certain inquiries; customers receive answers faster.

Discussion: The problem and benefits are similar those in the preceding discussion. Posting FAQs—files containing frequently asked questions and their answers—to your company's forum, web site, or other archiving service enables consumers to find the information they need without drawing on your company's personnel resources.

Action: Interview support personnel for information. Write the FAQ.

Keep Track of New Questions

Benefit: Creates new material for FAQs; alerts company to new problems.

Discussion: Questions that aren't answered in the files can be handled individually. The files can then be updated with new information. This makes good use of the support representative's time. Also, by learning of new problems, companies can uncover bugs in the product, flaws in the instructions, or the need for new features and products to make the existing merchandise more useful.

Use File Libraries and Archives for Software Downloads

Benefit: Solve customers' problems without incurring expensive production and shipping charges.

Discussion: Product upgrades, software patches, and bug fixes can be stored in file libraries, and consumers can download them at their convenience. As the company is not manufacturing the new version on a disk and mailing it to hundreds of thousands of customers, it can save a considerable amount of money.

Create Training Tapes

Benefit: Consumers become better educated about your company's products without burdening staffers.

Discussion: Companies can create self-running computer programs that teach people how to use their products more effectively. As they become more conversant with the program, customers will depend less on calling for technical support, thus saving money for your company.

Create a Mailing List of Customers

Benefit: Quick distribution of important announcements.

Discussion: Mailing lists can be created to send notices to registered users about program updates and bug fixes as well as special notices about sales and upcoming products. For the sake of netiquette, ask people if they want to be on the list.

Conduct Online Training Conferences

Benefit: Customers will learn how to use your product.

Discussion: Consider hosting weekly or monthly online chats or conferences that bring users and company representatives together to discuss various topics. The company can promote the conference as being devoted to a particular topic and also have a question-and-answer session. This will give structure to the meeting. Capture the transcript of the chat for future reference by new users. Add the new tips, questions, and answers to your FAQ database.

SUMMARY

Making the sale is the beginning, not the end, of a relationship with a long-term customer. To keep customers happy, every effort should be made to ensure that questions are answered quickly and courteously. An upset customer can tell an online audience of thousands about his misfortune faster than you can ever hope to repair the damage. By following the strategies in this chapter, you can help build bridges to your customers that can last forever.

PART **5**

Online Marketing Tools

CHAPTER 21

Competitive Research Online

A well-orchestrated marketing program begins with solid research. The very foundation of a business plan or marketing plan is accurate, up-to-date information about the consumer, competitors, and the marketplace. Good market research enables the company to create effective product and company positioning, marketing messages, and pricing strategies. A depth of information will guide the marketer in brainstorming and creating effective advertisements, publicity, and promotions. In fact, if the marketing research is conducted properly, selling becomes almost superfluous because the company has created a product the market needs and wants. The Internet and commercial online services provide powerful tools to let you research competitors.

In this chapter, you will learn:

- How to conduct competitive research online.
- What information is available online and where to find it.

EIGHTEEN-STEP ACTION PLAN FOR CONDUCTING COMPETITIVE MARKET RESEARCH ONLINE

You can find a great deal about your competitors and your industry by using the Internet and online services. Here is an approach to finding information in your niche:

Step 1: Use Search Engines to Begin Your Quest

Search engines are electronic indexes that can instantly find references to your competitors and your industry. These devices read, analyze, and store information contained on millions of individual web pages. Information is indexed on a series of keywords and other parameters, such as beginning and end dates. In this manner you can search for all information about a competitor that has been printed since last year or since your last visit. Information can be stored on your hard disk, inserted into reports, and printed for use (copyright restrictions apply).

There are hundreds of search engines on the Internet covering general topics, including Yahoo!, Lycos, and AltaVista, and specialized search engines that provide abstracts of information pertaining to vertical market industries, like biotech and astronomy. A list of hundreds of search engines can be found MMG (www.mmgco.com).

Let's look at how several of the most popular engines can help you find the goods on your competitors in a matter of minutes. You can search for information in several ways to find an incredible amount of information:

1. You can type the name of your competitor's company and have the search engine search all the pages of the World Wide Web. The service will show you pages on which the search term is printed. The material will be displayed as a hyperlink that allows you to see the information in full simply by clicking on the text, which appears as highlighted or underlined text depending on your computer system. The pages from the company's web site will appear on your computer screen. It is amazing what you can find at your competitors' sites. Please read the next step for what kinds of information you can see.

2. Type in the industry, product, or other search term that will help you find what you are looking for, such as mortgage brokers, insurance industry, or digital cameras. You might learn about new competitors or other sources of information.

3. On some search engines that use a directory structure, you can drill down through the menu to find out about companies or products that you didn't even know existed. For instance, you could go to the business section and drill down to products, then to software, and then to psychologists to find software of interest to that audience.

Because every search engine uses a different technique for finding and displaying information, it stands to reason that each engine will have information that the others do not—as well as a lot of the same information. Therefore, it is to your benefit to search several engines to find the widest possible sources of information. However, you will find a lot of the same information on several search engines. You could also waste a lot of time dealing with duplicate listings. You can eliminate this duplication by using one of several web sites that search several search engines at the same time and present the findings to you without the duplication. These sites include Dogpile (www.dogpile.com) and Metasearch (www.metasearch.com). Copernic (www.copernic.com) is a free software program that performs this task but also allows you to print the results and perform more sophisticated searches. Searching this way will save you time and money.

Step 2: Search Your Competitor's Web Site

You can go to your competitor's web site and read a great deal of information. You might find all the information made available to the public, such as annual reports, quarterly statements, biographies of executives, product information, press releases, and job openings. By analyzing this information, you might be able to see strengths, weaknesses, and areas for your company to exploit.

It is amazing how much information you can find on a company's web site. You can read about competing products, read press releases, product sales sheets, and pricing information. In fact, you probably will find more information online than you would read in the industry newsletters and magazines because editors cut information to fit space. But online, there is no limitation for space, so companies can post all the material they want.

If you are clever, you might be able to deduce certain things about your competitors. If they are hiring lots of sales people, they might be enjoying massive growth.

Some companies post information about where customers can buy their products. Now you know where your salespeople can find potential new markets for your products!

Just in case you are wondering—yes, your competitors will look at your web site as well. You have to wonder how much information to post. If you post lots of information, you are tipping your hand to your competitors. But if you don't post the information, your prospects won't know your whole story. This is a difficult position to be in. The rule of thumb for deciding what information to print is: Print only information you are comfortable with. This is the same rule you would use at a trade show in which your competitors can—and do—hear your presentations, read your literature, and talk to your salespeople and engineers.

Step 3: Use an Automated Software Program to Notify You of Changes to the Site

Once you've found the sites you want to monitor, consider using a software program that downloads updated pages (including text and images) to your hard disk according to a schedule that you create. These programs can save you a great deal of time searching for new information manually. Several products that do this task are:

- Web Whacker (www.bluesquirrel.com).
- Microsoft Internet Explorer (www.microsoft.com).
- CatchtheWeb (www.catchtheweb.com).

Step 4: Hunt for Trade Associations

Trade associations could post a treasure chest of unbiased information and statistics that may give you an advantage over competitors. They might have information about trends and interesting articles written by industry leaders. These sites also usually have lists of member companies who could become customers for your products or services. Use the search engines to look for addresses of trade associations and nonprofit groups in your industry.

Step 5: Search for Personal Pages

Personal pages are web sites created by individuals who have a deep interest in a given topic. When I wanted to by a digital audio tape player, I found a personal page that contained links to hundreds of reports about that product, for example. You might be pleasantly surprised to find that a personal page contains information and links about your subject. You might be enthralled that this individual actually commands the respect and attention of a large audience that matches your interests as well. You also might find a site created by a disgruntled customer or former employee that provides a great deal of information about the inner workings of the company.

You should search for personal web sites of people in your target group to find news, gossip, and other interesting facts. You'll find personal home pages by using the search engines. Enter the name of the company, industry, or product to find the results.

While conducting research for a psychologist and author of books on eating disorders who wanted to post a new site on eating disorders, I found several sites operated by ordinary people and other psychologists. These sites contained a great deal of useful information for my client. They also generously provided a link to my client's web site, which aided in her marketing.

Step 6: Ask Your Target Market

Your target market possesses a great deal of information about their likes and dislikes. Send queries to online VIPs at web sites, personal pages, newsgroups, and mailing lists. Also, post questions and surveys on your web site. Many people will fill the forms out if they think you will actually use the information to make better products. Other consumers will be enticed to answer questions only if you provide an incentive, such as a chance to win a prize.

You can collect a great deal of information by investing nothing more than your time. In the real world, it could cost thousands of dollars to gather the same kind of material. You can get the same data with a minimum of effort by using the Internet.

Step 7: Search Newsgroups and Post Queries

Newsgroups are online bulletin boards for people interested in specific topics, such as baseball, computer programming, and parenting. More than fifty thousand newsgroups operate via the Internet. These groups very well could discuss your industry, company, or competitors.

To find out what people are saying on the newsgroups, use Deja.com (www.deja.com). This free service will scour each newsgroup for the terms you specify. For example, you can ask it to look for references to Ford, Chrysler, General Motors, Toyota, Honda, and the car industry to find out what is going on. These tools are invaluable for finding and tracing rumors and trends. In fact, reporters use this service to find possible news stories and sources for their articles.

When you do a search, you will see headlines of each message that meets your search criteria. You also will see the e-mail address of the person who wrote the message, the name of the newsgroup in which the message was posted, and the date the message was posted.

Because the searching mechanism isn't perfect, you'll also find a lot of garbage that is off topic. For example, you might search for Tide detergent but find references to the ocean's tides. You will need to scan each message heading to see if the posting relates to your needs. Also check the name of the newsgroup to see if it sounds like it could worth-while. For example, if you found Tide in the alt.sciencefiction newsgroup, you might assume the posting had nothing to do with your topic. If, on the other hand, the newsgroup was alt.environment, you might find a question from someone wondering if the detergent was environmentally friendly.

The only way you'll know what's in the message is by clicking on the headline. You'll also be able to read all the other messages that preceded this one, so you can read the entire conversation.

By reading the articles, you will find out what is hot in the industry. You can also post questions to newsgroup members. A great many people might join the discussion and provide you with invaluable information. However, be sure not to make the message a commercial, because people don't appreciate that form of marketing.

You can also find the e-mail address of the person who wrote the message. You might find it useful to contact the person if she is a big fan or a mortal enemy. In either case, you could ask those persons if they would like to try the new product and provide their opinions.

"Simply reading newsgroups and forums can be the most effective market research around. Monitor the comments of your target market to learn what features matter and what causes folks to love or hate a product," says Christina O'Connell, an online marketing consultant.

Step 8: Read Mailing Lists and Post Queries

Mailing lists are like newsgroups in that they are a community of people who send messages to the group on issues germane to their interests. Unlike newsgroups, each day's messages are sent to your mailbox and cannot be searched by Deja.com.

You can find a list of mailing lists at Liszt (www.liszt.com). You might also find some mailing lists while scouring web sites or search engines.

Just as with newsgroups, you can post queries for information, as long as those messages don't violate the netiquette of the list.

Step 9: Read Online Financial Information

If you are researching a public company, you'll find lots of financial information online. Here are resources on the Internet:

DailyStocks.com (www.dailystocks.com) should be your starting point for all information about publicly traded companies. It contains links to dozens of web sites that contain almost everything you would want to find out about a company, including:

- Zacks Investment Research, www.zacks.com, which shows how many analysts are recommending stocks and whether that number is increasing or decreasing.
- Thomson Tipsheet, which shows whether company officials are selling or buying the company stock.
- Securities and Exchange Commission filings and reports.
- Discussion groups from Silicon Investor Forum and Motley Fool Message Board.
- News from CNN, Reuters, Dow Jones, *Fortune, Forbes, The L.A. Times,* the *Washington Post,* and *The New York Times.*
- Public Register's Annual Report Service has 3,000 annual reports available online for free (www.prars.com).
- Silicon Investor (www.techstocks.com) contains stock charts and chats for technology issues. Check the messages for comments about your company.

Another great site of financial news and research is Yahoo! Finance (quote.yahoo.com; note there isn't any *www* in this address.), which has links to publicly traded companies and press releases from PR Newswire and Business Wire as well as new reports and stock charts.

Step 10: Read Online Competitive Information

Hoover's Online (www.hoovers.com) profiles more than one thousand one hundred of the largest, most influential, and fastest-growing public and private companies in the United States and the world. Directory listings are searchable by company name, industry, location, and sales figures.

Step 11: Study Demographic Reports

Demographics can tell you where your customers live and which markets are emerging. The U.S. Census Bureau (www.census.gov) lets you find information using maps or zip codes. You can find how many people in a geographic area earn a certain income or belong to a specific race. This information can help you pinpoint your marketing efforts by zeroing in on the geographic area in which you want to sell your products or services. Information can be printed as a web page or an ASCII file for a spreadsheet. Easy Analytic Software, Inc. (www.easidemographics .com) creates fast demographic reports that include household income, race, and age.

Step 12: Set Up a Personalized News Service

You can create your own personal newspaper that searches various news sources and presents the findings to you whenever you go online or have the headlines sent to your pager so you can find out about new developments quickly and make informed decisions. Here is a summary of some of the more powerful or popular tools that can help provide you with a daily source of targeted, up-to-date information for decision making:

- Lexis-Nexis Traeker (www.lexis-nexis.com) provides a personalized daily briefing service that sends you relevant articles gathered from more than seven thousand one hundred sources of news and business information, including *The New York Times, The Washington Post, Fortune,* and *Business Week.* More than one hundred thousand new articles are added each day from worldwide newspapers, magazines, newswires, and trade journals.
- Nearly every major search engine offers a free daily news service. To create your personal newspaper, simply go to the search engine, find the link to the free service, register, and select the keywords and topics you want. Each day you can return to the site, type in your password, and read your customized newspaper. Go to Yahoo! (www.yahoo.com) or Excite (www.excite .com) for starters.

- NewsBot (www.wired.com/newsbot) will monitor your company, products, and competitors from a variety of newspapers, industry magazines, and newswires.

Step 13: Review Original Source Material

Newspapers are a good place to find the news, but to find the rest of the story, you need to read the original source material, such as press releases and financial reports. That's because newspapers have a limited amount of space to print their news. They must cut facts and information that, in their opinion, are less important. However, you need to know all the facts to make an informed decision. You can find the original source material from publicly traded companies for free on Business Wire (www.businesswire.com) or PR Newswire (www.prnewswire.com). In fact, you might find press releases posted on those sites before they are printed on their own companies' sites!

Step 14: Monitor Special Interest Publications and Other Media

Although the personalized news services are great tools for online researchers, they are only a beginning. That's because numerous newspapers, TV and radio stations, and trade publications are not part of the databases of these monitoring services. You need to determine which publications you need to monitor and set up a bookmark service or visit every day.

The Internet has more than one thousand daily newspapers available including *The New York Times, The Wall Street Journal,* and *USA Today.* For listings, go to Yahoo! and type the name of the paper you want to find.

Many news and business magazines for consumers and trade are now online. Not only do they offer the full text of the print edition but they also frequently include original content that didn't fit in the print edition. Electronic editions might also contain links to related stories, charts, and historical information. Furthermore, some online editions add a bulletin board where readers can post questions for reporters and engage in discussions with other readers. Some offer online conferences with editors and newsmakers; viewers can ask questions as well. Several are printed online before the print edition hits the newsstands; others are updated daily online but only once a week at the newsstand, so online readers get more information delivered faster!

Many international publications offer online editions. You can read these publications to find out news about companies based in other lands written by local reporters. These periodicals can also contain weather reports; if you are in an industry related to agricultural production, overseas weather could have an impact on your products.

Step 15: Research the Encyclopedia

The granddaddy of all encyclopedias, the *Encyclopedia Britannica,* is available at www.eb.com. It isn't free, but you'll probably find the background you need for your report.

Step 16: Search for Statistics

The web has a lot of statistics you can use in your reports and decision making if you know where to look. For Internet statistics, go to Nua (www.nua.com). Also, look for research groups in your industry. Many will post press releases or sample reports that provide many useful statistics. If you like what you see, they'll be delighted to sell you the complete report.

Step 17: Hire a Professional Researcher

A professional online researcher might be able to find information faster and more economically than you or your staff can. For referrals and references, contact Mary Ellen Bates, past president of the Association of Independent Information Professionals (mbates@batesinfo.com). Professional researchers also have experience with private databases, which are difficult to use and expensive.

Step 18: Learn More about Conducting Online Research

These books can help online researchers craft fast, efficient searches on the Internet, commercial online services, and private databases:

- Mary Ellen Bates, *The Online Deskbook:* Online Magazine's *Essential Desk Reference for Online and Internet Searchers,* ISBN 0-9010965-19-6, Pemberton Press, 1996.

- Reva Basch, *Researching Online for Dummies,* ISBN 0-764503-82-0, Dummies Technology Press, 1998.
- Alan M. Schlein, *Find It Online: The Complete Guide to Online Research,* ISBN 1-889150-06-1, Facts on Demand Press, 1999.

SUMMARY

Great marketing starts with great research. Online services provide virtual online libraries of up-to-date data that can help you find information quickly about your industry, competitors, and trends. In many ways, online research is better than resorting to printed materials because the information is revised more often, is distributed faster, and is easy to integrate into reports. If you conduct online research, your marketing plan will be much more solid.

CHAPTER **22**

Online Resources That Make You a More Effective Marketer

If you think you know it all, think again. There are ideas, visions, and dreams you have yet to experience—especially on the rapidly changing Internet. Fortunately for you, your online peers are ready, willing, and able to serve as mentors, advisors, colleagues, and reality testers.

In this chapter, you will learn:

- How you can learn from the online community.
- About online professional forums.
- About online professional resources.

LEARNING FROM THE ONLINE COMMUNITY

The playing field in online marketing changes dramatically from one day to the next. Yesterday's truisms might not apply to today's problems. New players enter the game, and new technologies take hold to change life as you know it. You need to keep up with the changes and to learn from others' successes and failures or you will waste a great deal of time and money.

The best places to keep in touch with changes in marketing strategies are newsgroups and mailing lists devoted to helping marketing professionals working at large companies, associations, and local businesses as well as work-at-home professionals and service providers. These areas are great places to learn about the new dimensions of online marketing by posting questions to noncompetitive and helpful peers. After all, who can teach you about the online community and its mores better than the people who actually use the systems?

The rules of netiquette apply to these forums, which means no advertising or solicitation of members. There are, however, slight variations on the rules for self-promotion in that people can describe what they do as a means of introducing themselves to the community.

NETWORKING ONLINE WITH HELPFUL PEERS

Need to network? Here are the web addresses for marketers who can answer your marketing questions—if you promise to help the next person who comes along.

The Internet hosts several mailing lists devoted to marketing and advertising. New ones are being added all the time, so be on the lookout for references to other mailing lists. To get the most current list, visit Kim Bayne's site (www.wolfBayne.com/lists/). The list is maintained by Kim Bayne, president of wolfBayne Communications, a public relations and marketing consultancy.

One of the best mailing lists for marketers is Internet-Sales (http://www.mmgco.com/isales/). This is a superb mailing list in which to find out about new strategies used by marketers and to get feedback on your problems. You can post questions, state your observations, and join a lively community of online practitioners trying to figure out how to sell products more effectively on the Internet. You can find a FAQ, information, archives, and subscription information at the web site.

Your peers might also create their own private mailing lists. For example, Speakernet is a weekly publication sent by e-mail to professional speakers. Recipients submit news postings, which are edited by two volunteers who also mail the publication. Ask your peers if a newsletter for your industry exists. If not, consider starting one yourself. People like Glenn Fleischman and John Audette have become Internet industry luminaries because they moderated mailing lists for marketers.

You might also find newsgroups that talk about your concerns. You can hunt for these groups by going to Deja.com (www.deja.com) and using its search tools to find groups listed by interests.

MARKETING RESOURCES

You can find a lot of free marketing information on the web sites of resources from consultants, electronic editions of print publications, and newsletters sent via e-mail. Here are some starting points.

Web Sites of Resources from Consultants

- Dan Janal's Online Marketing Magazine (www.janal.com) lists new articles from the author of *Dan Janal's Guide to Marketing on the Internet.* You can find out the latest trends and read new articles specifically targeted for online marketers at this site. It also contains updates to this book.
- Guerrilla Marketing Online (www.gmarketing.com) offers articles about online marketing form the authors of the popular Guerilla marketing books.
- Efuse (www.efuse.com) contains a great deal of information about marketing, designing, and writing web sites.
- Larry Chase's Web Digest for Marketers (www.wdfm.com) provides marketers with an insightful but brief critique of new marketing sites. This weekly update is not just must reading, it is fun reading.
- The National PR Network (www.usprnet.com) has compiled a listing of 2,500 web sites covering PR, marketing communications, and advertising companies on the Internet.
- Small Business Administration (www.sbaonline.sba.gov/) has useful information.
- Smart Business Supersite (www.smartbiz.com) is one of the largest how-to business resources on the Net, with more than 60 categories of free information in such categories as advertising, raising money, and managing human resources. It also provides useful articles, checklists, reports, and worksheets geared for business executives, managers, and employees.
- ClickZ Network (www.clickz.com) has many thought-provoking articles about marketing and web site creation.
- Working Solo (www.workingsolo.com) is an online searchable database of more than one thousand two hundred valuable business listings based on Terri Lonier's popular *Working Solo* (John Wiley & Sons, 1998).

Electronic Editions of Print Publications

Print publications that cover the online world publish online editions that keep you up-to-date with new marketing trends and other online intelligence. Bookmark these sites:

- Advertising Age (www.adage.com/interactive/index.html).
- Ad Week Online Interactive News (www.adweek.com/iqinteractive/index.asp).
- DM News (www.dmnews.com).
- Industry Standard (www.thestandard.com).
- Business Week (www.businessweek.com).
- Upside (www.upside.com).
- Internet Week Online (www.interactiveage.com).

E-mail Newsletters

Several e-mail newsletters keep you up to date on the Internet and marketing strategies:

- A Clue to Online Marketing (www.ppn.org/clue/), published by veteran journalist Dana Blankenhorn, is a weekly newsletter that highlights companies that are doing well on the Internet and those that are not doing so well.
- Newslinx (www.newslinx.com) is a daily news service that provides headlines of dozens of web-related articles and links to the full text. There's always a good article about online marketing and advertising as well as news about fascinating trends of online use, such as online addiction and the latest on the spam wars.

SUMMARY

By joining professional groups on the Internet, online marketers can hone their skills and learn new strategies. To get the most out of these forums, you have to do more than just join—you must participate. You can exchange war stories, stay abreast of new trends, test ideas, get advice, and impart wisdom. Chances are, the more you contribute, the more benefit you will receive.

Creating Effective Banner Ads

People can zap your ad in a heartbeat. "This sends a very clear message to marketers," says Larry Chase, president of Chase Online Marketing Strategies (www.chaseonline.com). "Your commercial message has to be as compelling as the content it sponsors, or people will fast forward past you."

In this chapter you will learn to create effective banner ads that can get more people to visit your web site.

BANNER AD BACKGROUNDER

Banner ads are advertisements that companies buy and place on other companies' advertising vehicles, such as search engines, chat rooms, online magazines, and web sites. For the sake of simplicity, we will call the companies that sell advertising space "publishers." We will call the companies that buy the ads "advertisers."

Because of their rectangular shape, these ads are called "banners." Banners can contain several colors or even a picture and can be placed at the top or bottom of the screen. Some ads are smaller and placed along the sides of pages as well.

The standard banner ad size approved by the Internet Advertising Bureau are:

468 × 60 pixels (Full Banner).

392 × 72 pixels (Full Banner with Vertical Navigation Bar).

234 × 60 pixels (Half Banner).

120 × 240 pixels (Vertical Banner).

120 × 90 pixels (Button 1).

120 × 60 pixels (Button 2).

125 × 125 pixels (Square Button).

88 × 31 pixels (Micro Button).

Software programs will help even the least artistic business owner create attractive, animated banner ads of every size, shape, and color. Try Headline Studio from Meta Creations (www.metacreations.com).

Banners can display a call to action and link to a specific web page that contains more information. Interactive banners have pulldown boxes that let people select exactly what information they want to see. For example, Garden.com lets people select the type of flowers they want to grow. When they click on the ad, they are taken to a page with information about that flower. These banners help the advertiser gather demographic information and customer information as the person interacts with the ad.

Although banner ads offer the benefit of attracting customers to your web site, there are several criticisms as well. There are so many banner ads that people filter them out mentally. They almost don't see the ads, much as they might pass a billboard on the highway without looking. They also might use filtering software that hides the ad from view. Or they might turn off the picture-loading feature on their browser so the ad doesn't even display on their screen!

WHAT'S WRONG WITH BANNERS?

The main form of advertising on the Internet is banner ads. Before we get into a discussion of what makes for a great banner ad in terms of layout, ad copy, and placement, let's take a quick, personal quiz.

Think back to a banner ad that you saw that you liked immediately and led to a compelling offer that knocked your socks off and spurred you to take action.

Take your time.

That's okay, take a little more time.

Okay, let's make this easier. Think of a banner ad you saw—*any* banner ad—and name the advertiser.

Stumped?

I think you get the point. Banner ads are *not* effective, at least not as they are being used today.

No more than 2 percent of people who see a banner ad actually click through, or press the button on the ad to learn more about the product or offer. Although 2 percent is considered a great response in the direct-mail industry, many advertisers who write the checks for these banner ads aren't exactly thrilled with the terrible twos.

CREATING EFFECTIVE BANNER ADS

At best, banner ads average a 2 percent click-through rate. Let's explore the ways you can increase the effectiveness of your banners.

Writing copy for banners is similar to writing for an envelope in direct mail—except that you have even less space. You can easily fit 5 to 7 words in the banner. If you use an animated banner, you could easily layer three screens and fit 21 words. The words you choose should rely on tested success from direct marketing. *Free* is the best word. Offer a free report, a free download, or a free subscription to your e-mail newsletter. Other good words are *win,* because contests are big on the Internet, and *save,* for obvious reasons.

The words *click here* are the strongest call to action in a banner ad. As stupid as this sounds, ads that have these words actually get more people to take action than ads that don't have those words.

Ads will be more effective if you target the right audience by purchasing ads on the correct sites. Be sure to check the demographic reports of the publisher to ensure you will reach your prospects. You'll need to study the results of each campaign to be certain that you have made the correct choice. Consider buying ads on several sites so you can test the effectiveness of each site.

Ad will be more effective if they are seen in the proper context. An ad for a business service product is best seen on a business site, for example.

While the typical click-through rate for banner ads is between 1 and 4 percent, which mirrors direct-mail response, advertisers always want to do whatever they can to improve the response to their ads. This list of tactics from DoubleClick, the advertising network, and other sources shows how to increase advertising effectiveness.

- **Target your ad.** In traditional advertising, you want your message to be seen by your target audience. You try to select the medium that attracts the audience most similar to the one you are trying to reach. But you don't know for sure exactly who is viewing your ad. The web however, offers the ultimate in accountability. By utilizing the web's ability to target, you can recognize and reach only your intended audience. You can deliver your message to specific industries, include or exclude specific geographic regions or cities, target by user interest, and even control frequency. This eliminates waste and makes your campaign more effective. Taking advantage of the web's ability to deliver information to highly targeted audiences will create the one-to-one relationship that will extend and build your brand.

- **Pose questions.** Don't just make statements or show pretty pictures. Use questions ("Looking for free software?" "Have you seen?"). They initiate an interaction with the banner by acting as a teaser. They entice people to click on your banner. More importantly, they can raise click-through by 16 percent over average.

- **Use bright colors.** Using bright colors can help attract a user's eye, contributing to higher response rates. Research has shown that blue, green, and yellow work best, while white, red, and black are less effective.

- **Use animation.** Animation can help you catch a user's eye. Strategic use of movement grabs attention more effectively than static banners by 25 percent.

- **Call to action.** As in traditional direct response, telling consumers what to do helps raise response rates. Simple phrases such as "Click Here," "Visit Now," and "Enter Here" tend to improve response rates by 15 percent. These phrases should be strategically placed in the ad, preferably on the right side. This is where the eye will be drawn.

- **Avoid banner burnout.** After what number of targeted impressions does click-through rate significantly drop off? After how many impressions do people start ignoring your banner? Double Click concluded that there indeed is a sweet spot for user response. After the fourth impression, average response rates dropped to under 1 percent. We call this *banner burnout,* the point at which a banner stops delivering a good return on investment. These findings are incredibly significant. Controlling your frequency extends your reach and maximizes your ad dollar.

Finally, ask people to support your advertisers. People who are receiving free content from your web site or e-mail newsletters have been known to click on an ad after reading a simple message from the publisher saying "Please support our advertisers so we can continue to bring you free information."

CHAPTER **24**

Buying and Selling Banner Ads

Advertising on the Internet can be a cost-effective tool to reach targeted market—or a complete waste of time if you do it wrong.

In this chapter you will learn:

- Objectives of online advertising.
- Advantages of online advertising.
- Integrating online advertising with your traditional media.
- Key terms.
- Pricing models for online ads.
- Advertising rates.
- A checklist for buying ads.
- How to advertise in e-zines and mailing lists.
- How to sell ads on your web site.
- The challenges of online advertising.

OBJECTIVES OF ONLINE ADVERTISING

Online advertising can be used to achieve four basic objectives:

- **Build brand awareness.** Many Fortune 500 companies, from Kodak to IBM, use the Internet to tell the world about their products, support their dealer channels, and educate the public about their companies or products. Even if people don't click on the ads, they still learn about your product or company (see Figures 24.1 and 24.2).

Figure 24.1 Banners are effective in creating
and reinforcing brand image and identity.
(© 1999, Janal Communications)

Figure 24.2 A banner ad can convey a great
deal of information with just a few words and
pictures. (© 1999, Janal Communications)

- **Drive traffic to the web site.** Online advertisements offer a
  proven way to steer interested buyers to your web site, where
  you can tell them more about your products and services.
- **Develop qualified leads.** While at the web site, your best copy
  writing and photographs can convince prospects they should do
  business with you. Your questions can determine how best to follow up with each qualified prospect.
- **Conduct sales.** As the prospects become warm, you can close
  the sale either online or direct them to your dealer channel if
  that is your sales strategy.

As you can see, online advertising can be used as a strategic tool in
your integrated marketing campaign to help achieve many objectives.

ADVANTAGES OF ONLINE ADVERTISING

The benefits of online advertising have been discussed at length in this
book, especially in Chapter 2. In summary, online advertising offers advantages over other media in that:

- It is interactive. Consumers can pick and choose the information, sales message, and buying modes that fit their individual
  needs.
- It offers the best of push-and-pull advertising in that merchants
  can pull in consumers based on their advertising and push out
  material to them once they have created a relationship.

- It is highly targeted. Advertisers can buy ads on web sites that reach their target audience so they are almost guaranteed that a highly qualified prospect will see the ad.
- Because users select the sites they visit from online ads, merchants are almost guaranteed a warm prospect is reading their material.
- Once the prospect identifies herself to the merchant, they can engage in a one-to-one relationship that can last a lifetime.

INTEGRATING ONLINE ADVERTISING WITH YOUR TRADITIONAL MEDIA

Major corporations as well as small businesses and home offices should consider using the Internet as part of their integrated marketing program. Because a paid advertisement on TV or radio or in a newspaper can tell only so much about the product (or rather, so little), the best it can hope to do is create interest. Traditionally, that interest would stimulate a consumer to call the company or visit a store to find out more about the product and buy it. Online marketers know that they can save time and money by using their traditional ads to steer traffic to their web sites, where consumers can read and hear about the products when it is convenient for them. If the web site is designed and written properly, it can do an admirable job of playing the role of salesperson. When the consumer is ready to buy, he can order in the manner he is most comfortable with, online, by phone, or by visiting the merchant's store.

Examples of this tight integration can be seen daily on TV and radio and in newspaper display and classified ads by nearly every type of company. Hollywood movie studios run ads on TV and always include the web address for the movie. Business-to-business companies place the URL and e-mail address in print ads in trade publications. Consumer companies do the same with their newspaper advertising. Even smaller consultants, tax preparers, and home-based businesses use their classified ads to draw people to their web sites.

KEY TERMS

Before entering a general discussion about the opportunities and risks of banner advertising, let's look at key terms you need to understand.

Ad clicks: The number of times users click on an ad.

Ad click rate: Referred to as the "click-through," this is the percentage of ad views that resulted in users clicking on a banner to see more information.

Hits: An ineffective measurement technique that counts the number of files displayed on a page. Advertisers should not be concerned with hits. They should use "visitors" or "unique visits" instead.

Page impressions, page views, and visits: A much better statistic is page impressions, page views, or visits, which all refer to one person visiting one page or many pages during one session.

CPM (cost per thousand impressions): This is the standard advertising term used in the real world. Advertising is bought and sold based on the CPM. For example, if an advertising site on the web charged 2 cents per viewer or $20 CPM and claimed 100,000 readers, the cost to advertise would be $2,000. This model is taking hold as the standard on the Internet, but it faces challenges.

Impressions: The number of times a reader sees the sponsor's banner image.

Inventory: The total number of impressions a page generates.

Per inquiry: This means that ads are paid for on the basis of how many people click through and see the web site.

Per order: This means that ads are paid for only if the person sees the ad, clicks on it, visits the site, and buys a product.

PRICING MODELS FOR BANNER ADS

The pricing system for online advertising is still in transition. Here are the most popular models:

- **CPM.** The CPM model used in traditional advertising seems to be taking hold. In this model, advertisers pay a set price for every 1,000 times the ad is shown.
- **Flat fee.** Advertisers pay a set fee for a set time period, regardless of how many people see the ads. Advertisers can buy days, weeks, or months of time. Sponsorships generally follow this model.

- **Click through.** Advertisers pay only for each time the consumer clicks on the ad, not when she sees the ad. This model assures advertisers that they are reaching more highly qualified prospects.
- **Transaction based.** Advertisers get free ads on a web site. If someone clicks through and orders a product, the publisher gets a commission. This is the model for the affiliate programs offered by many companies, including Amazon.com.

ADVERTISING RATES

The price for banners varies all over the board. Most sites that accept advertising charge from 2 to 5 cents per banner view or $20 to $50 per 1,000 viewers. However, premiums of all amounts are charged for placement and position, keyword, targeting, duration, and number of impressions. Further, ad rates can be discounted off rate cards, although no sales rep will ever admit to this in public.

There are no set rules, and everyone seems to be charging whatever they think they can get away with.

CHECKLIST FOR BUYING ADVERTISING

Here are questions you should ask to evaluate advertising opportunities:

- What is the rate?
- Is the rate negotiable?
- How does this rate compare with those of other sites that reach the same market?
- What are the demographics of the site?
- What auditing procedure is involved?
- How will the publisher report activity?
- Can the contract be canceled if the performance doesn't match the promise?
- Can the publisher create the ad?
- What are the printing dimensions of the ad?
- What are the deadlines for art copy?

- Can the art copy be replaced in midrun to test different messages or prices?
- Will additional charges be incurred for switching ads?
- What is the payment schedule?

NEGOTIATING STRATEGIES FOR GETTING BETTER AD RATES

Because the quality of web demographics is questionable, because the quantity of targeted consumers in many fields is low, and because publishers are dying to make money—any money—media buyers have a considerable amount of negotiating power when buying advertising space. The wise communication manager will strike a firm negotiating stance with web publishers. Chances are the publisher will blink first. Of all the publishers vying for web advertising dollars, only a handful have any experience in the field. The traditional publishing companies (*USA Today, The Wall Street Journal,* Hearst, Time Warner, etc.) know how to price properly and stick to their guns at the bargaining table. However, as any 16-year-old who knows HTML can open an ezine, you can negotiate quite favorably because the ezine has a different economy of scale—to make a profit or simply keep the doors open or buy a new modem. This can be a boon to a company because the 16-year-old might publish an ezine that reaches your audience more effectively than the large publishing companies! For example, if you sell boogie boards, there might be a vigorous ezine that reaches that small but essential marketplace, a marketplace that large publishers won't touch because the numbers aren't large enough to be massively profitable.

FREE ADVERTISING

You can place banner ads for free on highly targeted sites—if you agree to have ads placed on your site as well. Several companies offer this service, including MSN LinkExchange (www.linkexchange.com), Free-Banners (www.free-banners.com), and Banner Co-op.com (www.bannerco-op .com). The deal works like this: For every two ads shown on your site, you get one ad shown on another company's site. You can choose which market you want to advertise on. You can also restrict ads that appear on your site, so your competitors' ads won't display, for example.

ADVERTISING IN EZINES AND MAILING LISTS

Targeting your message is the key to effective advertising. Every marketer knows this. But it seems that when people post their web sites, they forget this important dictum. They advertise anywhere they can for a cheap price—regardless of whether it is a good fit.

That might be why the effectiveness of banner advertising on web sites aimed at unfocused markets is diminishing. Critics say consumers are treating banners like billboards along the highway—the billboards are there, but no one sees them. When people do see banners, less than 2 percent of the people click through, which pales in comparison to earlier times when click-through rates of 5 to 6 percent were common. Even worse, advertisers are saying that people who do read the ads aren't buying their products. Clearly, banner advertising on random web sites is on the way out.

Notice the operative words—*web sites.* Banners can still work. However, these banners must be placed in targeted publications that clearly reach highly focused groups of consumers and business-to-business audiences. Mailing lists and ezines are two of the best new media in which to advertise to reach your target market.

Let's define these terms. Mailing lists are periodicals that address a given subject, such as marketing or stamp collecting. The content usually includes e-mail messages from subscribers who ask and answer questions from other subscribers. One of the most popular, I-Sales, is published daily and reaches tens of thousands of people who discuss Internet marketing issues. These mailing lists are sent via e-mail to people who have asked to subscribe, usually for free. Mailing lists should not be confused with spam or lists of e-mail addresses that are sold by shady operators of get-rich schemes.

The other advertising vehicles are ezines, or magazines and newsletters sent via e-mail to voluntary subscribers. These periodicals are written by a company and contain thoughtful articles on a given topic. Unlike lists, these publications usually don't include questions and answers from subscribers. The primary focus is to learn from the masters.

Some e-mail newsletters are sent as ASCII files, which can be read by any e-mail program. These periodicals don't include art, so colorful banners filled with different sized fonts can't be printed. Instead, the advertisements appear as regular text. Other newsletters are written in HTML and contain artwork and can even include animated banners. However, older browsers and e-mail programs can't read these rich-text documents. Instead of seeing beautiful pages that look like web pages, they see the HTML coding, which is impossible to decipher at a glance. As time goes by, more and more people will upgrade their e-mail programs to include this HTML feature because it is a great way of communicating! Ads in either type of ezine or mailing list can contain hot links to your web site so interested consumers can read more about your product or service.

There are thousands, if not tens of thousands, of newsletters and ezines on such topics as Internet marketing or entertainment, health, or pets. You can find a large group of mailing lists at www.yahoo.com and type "mailing lists" or "ezines" or "newsletters." Unfortunately, there is no central directory of ezines or mailing lists that accept advertising.

There are many advantages to advertising in an ezine or mailing list, according to Larry Chase, publisher of *Web Digest for Marketers* (www.wdfm.com), one of the oldest ezines on the Net. "There is a direct cause and effect," Chase says. "You can see your sales go up or not." One key advantage is that you are reaching a targeted audience.

"The people who are reading are more than likely to be qualified leads as the list is likely to be topical and the people on the list have made a conscious decision to join," he goes on to say. "Those people know they are on the list and just didn't stumble onto a web page from AltaVista and wonder what the web site is all about. You are more apt to reach a targeted audience." Another advantage is that your production costs for creating the ad are next to nothing if you choose to advertise in an ASCII-based newsletter, which prints only normal text, not pictures.

"There are no production costs. It is all ASCII so your production costs are zero," he continues. "Your only production cost is your time." Chase also thinks that ASCII newsletters are better than HTML versions because the former are faster to download. "Why import the World Wide Wait to e-mail? You might as well put 'hate me' in the subject header." Ads in ezines can be timed for your promotions.

"If you advertise in a zine, you know when they are going to get your ad. If you advertise in a web site, you know they will see it something over the course of the month but you don't know when," he says. "With an ezine, you know your ad will appear on a certain date, so you can get a better handle on the response." Just like a print publication, people forward e-mails to their colleagues and friends, so you can reach additional numbers of people, way beyond the number printed on the rate card.

"The pass-along for an ezine is much greater than for a web page. It is easier to forward an e-mail document than a web page. How many people know how to forward a web page? Not many. Everyone knows how to forward email," he says.

Chase doesn't charge extra for the pass-along. "I sell by primary impressions. The fact they pass it along is gravy. Of course, I tell the advertiser that so they understand that advertising is a good deal and the pass-along makes it an even better deal." The cost of e-banner ads is comparable to banner ads, about $30 to $60 per CPM. (A free CPM calculator is available at http://wdfm.com/advertising.html).

According to *Forbes* magazine, most web sites have an excess number of ad spaces available, so don't accept their first offer. You can save a considerable amount of money by negotiating.

How do you decide which publications will work best for you? Chase advises clever online marketers to research the publications before they spend their limited advertising dollars: "You have to make sure they are worthy of your advertising. Read the list for a few weeks. Make sure the content is up to snuff. Would you read it?" Then ask the publisher for the number of subscribers and other demographic material they have gathered. But be warned: There aren't any third-party services that authenticate and verify these statistics, so you have to take the web publisher's figures on good faith.

"It is a trust thing," says Chase. "People take advertisements in WDFM on faith because they figure I have a brand name to protect. The figure I am going to be pretty honest about it." But circulation figures can only tell a small part of the story. The real story is how well does the ad work with that audience. Of course, the true test of a marketing campaign is not how many impressions you created, but in how much activity those impressions generated.

"People look at the back end. They look at conversions. They look at how many people took action," Chase says. "I can say I have a million people on my list, but if they run an ad and no one goes to their web site or takes them up on their offer, then it doesn't matter if I have a billion people on my list. They are not going to come back and advertise. Most advertisers are interested in final results. They are looking for direct marketing units of measure to judge the effectiveness of their money spent." To figure out the true cost of the ad, don't rely on the CPM. Look at your return on investment (ROI) instead. Chase advises looking at how much each visit cost or how much each sale cost. For example, if you spent $100 on an ad and 1,000 people visited the site, the cost for attracting each visitor would be 1 cent. If 100 people bought something, the cost of attracting buyers would be $1. With those figures in hand, you can begin to measure your return on investment.

If your marketing plans calls for spending money on advertising, do yourself a favor and choose a targeted ezine or mailing list. They are fast, cheap, and better directed than web sites.

INCREASING INCOME BY SELLING ADS ON YOUR WEB SITE

You can make money by selling banner ads on your web site to companies that want to reach your readers. The more highly targeted your audience is, the more you can charge for advertising.

To sell space, you have to convince ad space buyers that you have a market that meets their demographic objectives. To do this, you must keep a log of users and capture their demographic information. You must be able to prove to potential advertisers that your audience is composed of likely consumers of their product.

Charging for your ad space or links should be done based on the CPM model, as most advertising buyers are familiar with it and can compare it with other advertising choices. The rate will depend on how targeted your audience is and how hard they are to reach.

The process of selling the ads can be done in three ways:

1. You can hire a staff to call on customers, create an advertising sales kit, and the like. The advantage is that you will keep more of the money and have a tighter control over the process. The disadvantage is that you have to hire, train, and create sales tools from scratch.

2. You can hire a rep firm to sell ads. The advantage is it will have a staff in place, is familiar with the Internet and its advertising norms and practices, and might even have contacts at advertising agencies or potential advertisers. The disadvantage is that you have less control over the sale and take a smaller share of the income than if you had an in-house staff. Agencies charge anywhere from 30 to 50 percent commission on each ad they sell. Some firms also charge expenses for office charges, travel, and

entertainment, which can be considerable. Make sure you are aware of all possible expenses before signing a contract. Companies that offer this service include:

- ◦ DoubleClick (www.doubleclick.com).
- ◦ WebConnect (www.worlddata.com).

Here are several issues to consider when retaining an ad rep firm:

- ◦ Can the task of selling ads be done more efficiently or cost-effectively in house?
- ◦ How long has the firm been in business?
- ◦ What accounts does it handle?
- ◦ What kind of reports does it produce?
- ◦ How long is the service contract in force?
- ◦ Are commissions paid after a contract ends?

3. Ad Auctions. Companies that have excess advertising inventory are auctioning off their wares. Companies like Adauction.com (www.adauction.com) can help you.

CHALLENGES TO ONLINE ADVERTISING

Of course, online advertising faces barriers and challenges. Chief among them are:

- **Personal filters.** People might not want to see ads or act on them. Just as in other media, only a small percentage of people will ever buy your product. That's okay. The key is to target your message so that people who are interested in your product will buy it.
- **Technology filters.** Software programs like Ad Filter (www .adblocker.com) are being created to filter out advertisements such as banner ads. Your ad might never reach its target.
- **Lack of good writing and marketing techniques.** Many web sites don't use the tried-and-true methods of selling off the page. Merely presenting features and benefits is not enough to sell in the online world. You must make a compelling offer that is irresistible to your prospects.
- **Holding the Internet to a higher standard than other advertising.** What is your response rate for cold calls? For direct mail? For advertising? For walk-in traffic? Use those yardsticks as

measurements for online advertising. To expect the Internet to be the all-in-one answer is foolhardy.

SUMMARY

Many new advertising opportunities are on the World Wide Web. Because online advertising is so new, prices and paradigms have yet to evolve fully. There is much debate over the effectiveness of banner ads and how they should be measured and paid for. Meanwhile, new advertising models are percolating. Time will tell which formats prove most effective.

Online Media Relations

Interactive Media Relations

Online communications give public relations professionals and corporate communicators new tools to build relationships with reporters and communities in a timely and cost-effective manner.

This chapter will help you build relationships with reporters by providing you with information on:

- How public relations helps you.
- Advantages of online PR versus traditional PR.
- How the media uses the Internet.
- How to integrate online media communications into the marketing mix.
- How to build a world-class web site for media use.
- Measuring the effectiveness of publicity efforts.

HOW PUBLIC RELATIONS HELPS YOU

The most cost-efficient weapon in the marketer's arsenal is public relations (also called publicity and PR). For a fraction of the cost of advertising, public relations can help accomplish the following objectives:

- Build a more favorable image for the company or product.
- Expose the company or product to new audiences.
- Reinforce images and messages within an audience to create demand for products.
- Build relationships with new customers.
- Cement relationships with old customers.

You achieve these goals by implementing a public relations campaign—a targeted marketing tool—that begins with writing down your goals and ends with reporters writing articles about your company or product.

Public relations can build credibility for products and services in a way that advertising cannot. When reporters write favorable articles, they implicitly or explicitly endorse your product, company, or cause. Advertising doesn't carry that same weighty endorsement.

Public relations can't make up for a bad product. It has been said that publicity for a bad product will just let the world know that much faster to avoid that product.

ADVANTAGES OF ONLINE PR VERSUS TRADITIONAL PR

Online publicity offers distinct advantages over traditional public relations (conducted in newspapers and magazines and on television and radio). With online services, corporate communicators can take PR into their hands and influence their publics directly as well as build relationships with reporters. Online publicity puts the public back in public relations.

In the traditional media, there is a gatekeeper—an editor, reporter, producer, or host—who decides whether or not your message will see the light of day and in what context the message will be viewed. The gatekeeper can kill the story because she doesn't think the message would interest her readers, because there isn't enough room in the day's program even though readers would be interested, or she's just having a bad day and wants to take it out on a PR person (stranger things have been known to happen).

Online systems offer tremendous opportunities for companies to boost image and sales through publicity. The online world lets you broadcast your message directly to the audience without the intervention of the media. This is an important distinction. Companies can accomplish this by disseminating their messages through their web site, certain newsgroups, e-mail, and other methods that will be discussed in this section. Public relations, used correctly and in full compliance with netiquette, can be an asset to you and your customers.

In summary, with online public relations you have tools to influence reporters and your publics. You have the best of both worlds!

The New Deadline

One of the most profound changes that the Internet is having on the news media is that traditional daily or weekly deadlines are dissolving because the media can disseminate news around the clock on their web sites. Instead of once-a-day newspaper printing deadlines, online newspapers have deadlines akin to those of news radio: Publish it when the news is fresh.

This move has great benefits for PR people. No longer constrained by a lack of space and having a need to provide up-to-the-minute freshness, many mainstream publications are printing additional news stories and features online. Stories that would not fit in the newsprint are winding up online. Reporters need more news, so more opportunities for placing stories crop up. PR people can take advantage of this need for news to place their companies in the limelight.

However, PR people need to be aware that this opportunity poses a challenge as well. They used to plan press tours so that stories would break at the same time. For example, if you visited a reporter of a weekly publication on a Tuesday, you knew he couldn't print the story until the following Monday. Now you can be assured that the story could be printed on the publication's web site before you arrive at your next appointment.

This move has dramatic implications for communications professionals because they no longer control the timing of the story. They must also be more sensitive to releasing information to all reporters at the same time, or the reporters at the tail end of the tour will feel slighted at being given yesterday's news.

PUBLIC RELATIONS VERSUS ADVERTISING

Many people commonly mistake public relations and advertising as being one and the same. This is not true. Companies pay for advertisements. These ads contain the exact message the company created. Therefore, people don't always believe the message in ads. Public relations, on the other hand, tries to influence reporters to see the company's point of view. The reporters write their stories based on the public relations message and their own independent research. People read the articles by reporters and make up their own minds based on the information, which they believe to be true or at least impartial. That's why public relations people try to influence reporters—because people tend to believe reviews while they don't believe ads.

HOW THE MEDIA USE THE INTERNET

The Internet is changing the way reporters gather and disseminate news.

In the annual seminal study of reporters, Steven S. Ross and Don Middleberg (www.middleberg.com) interviewed writers, editors, and investigative reporters at daily and weekly newspapers and business magazines. Their findings and conclusions are must reading for professional communicators. Their latest study shows that 98 percent of reporters have access to the Internet. Nearly 60 percent of the publications have an online edition. And most important, reporters are going to the Internet when a crisis breaks to find sources of information. Many news organizations expect web sites to have press releases, photos, and camera-ready art they can grab and print.

Another report shows that the Internet truly is changing reporters' work styles. "The press no longer have to—and don't want to—pick up the phone to research stories," says John Tsantes, president of Tsantes & Associates (www.tsantes.com). "In the high-tech industry where new products and technologies are introduced daily, the press now depend on the web as a virtual filing cabinet of information."

The report showed that of the journalists surveyed, 80 percent consider the web a "valuable source of information." More than 60 percent of respondents scan newswires regularly online, and Technology-related Usenet newsgroups are monitored by 48 percent of the respondents.

The Internet allows people to get raw data from companies and government. The journalist's role will always be to filter the news and put it in perspective.

Reporters search the Internet for news, controversy, consumer comments, and research. The media can find the latest press releases printed on company web sites. Although many companies have a press center feature on their sites, companies can also post breaking news on their home page as well. For example, when IBM completed the purchase of Lotus on a Sunday, the story was plastered on the home page hours before the daily newspapers could print the story in their Monday editions. Reporters who went to the site found information and quotes from officials at both companies. Yet some companies don't take advantage of the Net. When the TWA flight 800 crashed on July 17, 1996, near Long Island, New York, there was no mention of it on the TWA web site. The company could have posted reams of information about the plane, the rescue mission, and flight policy to calm the public's fears and feed its appetite for information.

Editors can read original source press releases in online versions of PR Newswire, Business Wire, and Canadian Corporate NewsNet, services that are paid by companies to distribute material to reporters. With the advent of the online medium, consumers and businesspeople can also read these press releases on the Internet and commercial online services.

Reporters for trade publications search online forums and newsgroups for controversy or consumer complaints about companies or new products. If people find problems with new computer hardware or software products, they are sure to post notices in newsgroups. It is not unusual for a company that claims its new product is perfect to find a story on the front page of Info World quoting customers who point out bugs.

Reporters also post messages on newsgroups to find experts and customers who can talk about their experiences with a company or product, and they also use Amazon.com to find authors to comment on articles because they are experts.

Monitor Discussion Areas for Comments about Your Company

Benefit: Build relationships; quell rumors; correct facts.

Discussion: It is important for PR professionals to monitor newsgroups for negative comments so that they can provide answers and solutions quickly. Not only will this dispel negative news, but it will also build customer loyalty and reflect positively on the company.

It would be impossible for any PR staff to read every message in every newsgroup to search for customers with complaints. Fortunately, there is a tool called Deja.com (www.deja.com) that searches every newsgroup to find articles that mention keywords you choose. In just a few minutes you can locate every mention of your company posted in any given time frame. Reporters use this tool as well to find examples of controversy.

Action: Assign this task. Create keywords to use for the search. Respond to comments. Not all the news is bad. Reporters also look in discussion areas to find unbiased sources to comment on companies and products. They frequently post notices in newsgroups and forums asking for people who have experience or knowledge in certain areas.

Check the Editorial Calendar of Publications

Benefit: You find out what reporters want to write about so you can give them the information they need.

Discussion: To help advertisers, many publications print editorial calendars that show the kinds of stories they will be writing in the future as well as the name of the reporter writing the article. Smart reporters use the Internet to create relationships with public relations officials and other sources. They might print their editorial calendars on their own sites so PR people can contact them with relevant information. Others post their articles online so PR people can understand what they write about. It is a way of saying "Here's what I'm interested in. If you can help me, get in touch." Several reporters print their own newsletters online, including Gina Smith of *Good Morning America* and Yael Li-Ron of the *Contra Costa* (California) *Times*. The contents include what articles they are working on, industry gossip, and editorial calendars.

Action: Research the web sites of the media that covers your industry and company to see if they are planning to write an article to which you might contribute. Contact the reporter and offer your information.

In summary, the media use the Internet and online services to gather news and publish it. They enjoy greater control over the flow of information and the ability to find additional sources from online libraries, competitors, and consumers. Communications professionals must learn to be a resource to these reporters.

HOW TO INTEGRATE ONLINE MEDIA COMMUNICATIONS INTO THE MARKETING MIX

When I gave my first talk on publicity on the web many years ago, a person in the audience asked an incredible question: "How much longer after I send out a press release should I post it online?"

The answer, of course, is that the press release should be posted on your web site at the same time it is made available to every medium. Today, very few people would think of asking such a question.

Online press campaigns should be part of the general strategy for every product launch or other newsworthy story because reporters and your targeted audiences will expect to find information on your web site. All press releases should be placed in the pressroom area of your site. In addition, the release can be sent via e-mail to customers, employees, shareholders, and the like who have told you in advance they want to be notified of all new announcements.

Case Study: IntelliSystems

IntelliSystems, a leading manufacturer of customer support systems via telephone and the Internet, wanted to announce that Netscape had decided to use its system to provide Internet customer support. Here is a review of its media program, which encompassed traditional and online public relations. This format could serve as a checklist for your public relations campaign.

- Write a press release.
  - Research via the Internet.
  - Copy/paste key documents into the draft of the press release.
  - Interview key speakers via telephone.
  - Write the press release.
  - E-mail the press release to key speakers for comments and approvals.
- Send out the press release.
  - Send to the regular mailing list via U.S. mail, fax, and e-mail.
  - Send to PR Newswire via fax; then distribute via e-mail and online databases.
  - Send to appropriate newsgroups and mailing lists.

- Post press release on company site.
  - Add links to client sites.
  - Call "A-List" reporters via phone.
  - Respond to other reporters who read the release and contact you.

Notice that this strategy used the following media: online, print, mail, fax, and phone!

Case Study: Blanc & Otis

Blanc & Otis, one of the largest public relations firms in the San Francisco Bay area, conducted a media campaign for a client's product launch. Due to scheduling conflicts, all of the scheduled in-person meetings for the press/analyst tour had to be done via teleconference. Among other problems, the phone meetings would not allow for the kind of relationship-building that face-to-face meetings offer. Furthermore, the product could not be demonstrated over the phone. The latter issue seemed an especially high hurdle as none of the press had even seen the client's type of product and questioned its ability.

To combat this hurdle, Blanc & Otis provided the press with the address of the client's web site, which contained screen shots; these were discussed during the phone interview. As a result, the demos were conducted during the phone tour with 11 analysts and 8 editors.

The launch was a huge success, as the client was able to speak with more industry influencers than it had on any previous tour and received articles in such publications as *Business Week, Web Week,* and *Interactive Week.*

HOW TO BUILD A WORLD-CLASS WEB SITE FOR MEDIA USE

Thanks to the interactive nature of the Internet, communications professionals find themselves in a new role: They are content creators. In effect, they are now publishers of news and information for reporters—their *stakeholders,* a term communicators use to describe all key audiences, such as investors, employees, dealers, distributors, vendors, and the community at large.

The key tool that communicators have is the web site. Reporters are coming to realize that companies will have the latest information and background information and pictures on their web sites—even as the story breaks.

Reporters come to rely on these tools as a way to get information quickly and accurately. Several reporters have told me they wished that all company press releases were in a searchable database online. When they get an assignment to cover a product or company they are not familiar with, they are able to get a quick read from the company's perspective. They don't want to rely on other reporters' articles! Even reporters realize that errors and bias could enter stories printed in the trade magazines and daily newspapers. Yes, hard as it is to believe, some reporters actually value press releases!

The task here is to create a world-class web site that helps reporters and stakeholders so that they can tell the company's story. Be sure to add navigational links to each page so reporters can find information easily.

The site should have a link to the press center, which can be called the media center, pressroom, press release, or the like. The first press page should contain an overview of the material that can be found and links to press releases, case studies, and so on. The first page of each of those categories should contain the headlines, date of publication, and any other relevant comments. Each headline should be linked to the full press release. The story itself ought not be merely a reprinting of the paper press release but an interactive version, complete with links to supporting materials. The next chapter will show how to create the kinds of links that can make your press releases truly valuable.

An online media center should contain the following elements:

1. Contacts.
    - Names, titles, and areas of specialty of each contact person, along with desk phone number and e-mail address.
    - Bios of contacts so reporters can understand the person's background and develop rapport. (For example, if the public relations person has a degree in engineering, reporters might feel they can carry on an intelligent conversation and get informed answers to their technical questions. You might also find that a relationship can be built if the reporter has something in common with the media contact, such as being graduates of the same university or from the same hometown.) "This enhances the relationship building. Bios are personal. I have what influenced

me growing up. They can get a sense of who I am as a person and it breaks the ice," says Skye Ketonen of Microsoft's LinkExchange.

2. News press releases.
   - Title page, including headlines sorted by date, company division, and/or product line. The headlines link to full text.
   - Full text version of the press release.
   - Audio and video excerpts and sound bites.
   - Other useful information to illustrate the story, such as spreadsheets, graphs, art, and photos.

3. Products press releases.
   - New products.
   - Updates.
   - Recalls.
   - Case histories.
   - Testimonials.
   - Reviews.
   - Competitive analysis.
   - White papers.
   - Charts and graphs.
   - Audio and video clips (variety of formats).
   - Pictures (variety of formats for IBM and Apple computers).

4. Company news.
   - Hiring.
   - Promotions.
   - Layoffs.
   - Financial news.
   - Annual reports.
   - Quarterly financial statements.
   - Forecasts and updates.
   - Case histories.

5. Company background.
   - Message from the chair. (Some reporters have labeled this tactic as corny, but these messages can begin to show a company's personality.)
   - Executive bios and contact information.
   - Photos.

6. Stock price. Use an icon or text to link to a stock market service that provides the latest price.

7. Offer to join a private mailing list. This list can be used to identify your stakeholders and send them update notices of news releases and newsletters.

It is truly surprising how few companies on the Internet have used all these tools on their web sites. Many companies don't list such basic elements as press releases or names of public relations representatives. Companies that don't take advantage of these opportunities will fall behind their competitors.

MEASURING THE EFFECTIVENESS OF PUBLICITY EFFORTS

Most PR professionals sigh when their corporate managers ask them to justify and quantify the results of a public relations campaign. That's because there are very few tools available to measure campaign effectiveness. However, the online world has several tools and strategies that can be employed to measure the reach of the program.

The web site can be used to track public relations activities that appear online or in other media by using the strategies outlined in the following sections.

Create Separate Sites with Unique URLs for Each Press Release and Communications Document

Benefit: Track the effectiveness of each message and medium.

Discussion: Each press release or communications document should refer to a unique web site to contact for more information. For example, a press release sent to the trade press could ask readers to see www.mycompany.com/press1.html, while a press release sent to a consumer publication could carry the URL www.mycompany.com/press2 .html.

This information can be used to find out which publication venue or message is more effective at reaching your audience and prompting them to take action. The results could be shared with the advertising department at your company so it can target its ad dollars effectively.

Action: Create targeted web sites with a message for each targeted audience. Add a counter to track the number of visits.

Create Autoresponders with Unique Addresses for Targeted Audiences and Reporters

Benefit: Track the effectiveness of each message and medium.

Discussion: An autoresponder is an information file that is sent by e-mail to people who request it by e-mail. People might learn of the autoresponder by reading a print article or an article on your web site that says, "For more information, send e-mail to autoresponder@ourcompany.com." This tactic is similar to the one described previously, with the added benefit that the information is sent directly to a person's e-mailbox so they can get the information they requested promptly.

Similarly, inquires could be sent to autoresponders with tags such as infopackl@mycompany.com or infopack2@mycompany.com.

The autoresponders should contain information tailored to suit the prospect's interests. You will know that a certain writer is a dealer because he sent e-mail to an address that only a dealer would have access to. Therefore, you can send a response that answers his most frequently asked questions and uses keywords that appeal to dealers. Likewise, if a consumer from a woman's magazine responds, you can tailor the message appropriately.

Action: Create the text for the autoresponders. Call your ISP for help.

Create Specific Messages on Web Sites and Autoresponders for Each Audience You Target via the Previous Methods

Benefit: Your audiences will get information they need without having to wade through generic or irrelevant material.

Discussion: Let's say you issue a press release for a new product. The trade press wants to know feature and benefits, the business press wants to know how this announcement will affect the stock price, and dealers want to know about their special pricing and advertising discounts. If you put all this information in one release, you might as well write a book! You would be sending lots of paper or bits to people who couldn't care less. However, if you create separate press releases and white papers for each audience and post them to unique web sites or autoresponders, you will be able to deliver the information each stakeholder needs most. Thus, you can incorporate one-to-one marketing programs much more effectively.

Action: Create the web pages and autoresponders. Post the unique addresses on press releases. Be careful to send the correct release to the correct audience.

Measure Messages in Newsgroups and E-mail

Benefit: Find out what people are thinking about your company or product.

Discussion: People make their feelings known by posting messages in newsgroups and by sending e-mail to the company. If you monitor these messages, you will be able to count the number of positive and negative comments. Count the number every day and place the numbers on a chart. Although you'll never have 100 percent approval, by using this method, you will be able to see if your communications messages are having the desired effect by reducing the number of negative comments.

Action: Assign the task. Find newsgroups you need to monitor. Count messages. With e-mail, create a link on your web page, e-mail newsletter, or print newsletter so that messages are routed directly to the person counting the messages.

SUMMARY

Public relations strategies can be used online to build relationships with reporters, customers, and prospects. The Internet is changing the way reporters work, and therefore PR people must change the way they work with reporters.

CHAPTER 26

Writing and Distributing Interactive Publicity Materials Online

Now that you understand how online reporting operates, you are ready to begin writing online press materials and distributing them.

This chapter will help show:

- How to write interactive press releases.
- How to write effective e-mail pitch letters.
- How to put an annual report online.
- How to find reporters online.
- How to distribute news materials online.
- How to create a live event online (press conference, annual meeting, or seminar).
- New publicity opportunities online.

HOW TO WRITE INTERACTIVE PRESS RELEASES

Press releases in the real world are usually two pages long because reporters have requested that length. But that restriction is based more on the mercurial demands of reporters than the public's right to be fully informed. Thus, a lot of good information never gets disseminated because there isn't enough space in a printed publication or enough time in a television or radio broadcast. However, in the online world, no limitation on space exists, so writers can present all the information they want to tell the story completely. Because people can read only a limited amount of information on a computer screen at a given time, writers create separate pages for longer stories, with each new page containing a different topic or deeper levels of information. Each page is linked to the main press release and possibly other subpages, so reporters and stakeholders can read as much information as they want. These interactive press releases can also contain files of audio, video, spreadsheets, databases, and graphs. These elements would never fit in a traditional press release. The following sections offer several strategies for turning normal press releases into value-added press releases.

Add Contact Hyperlinks

Example: Add e-mail addresses and the mailto: commands to each press release for each contact person.

Benefit: Allows reporters to contact company representatives in a quick, efficient manner. The mailto: command is an HTML command whereby the reader sends an e-mail to the person specified. For example, the HTML script

Contact: <a href = "mailto:dan@janal.com"> Dan Janal</a>, 510-459-7814

would appear on screen as

Contact: <u>Dan Janal</u>, 510-459-7814

Action: Take all press materials and add the e-mail address and mailto commands.

Print the Contact Information at the Top and Bottom of the Press Release

Benefit: Reduces the need to scroll.

Action: Type information into HTML and e-mail versions of the press release.

Define Industry Terms with a Glossary

Benefit: Adds more information than could otherwise fit in a standard news release.

Action: Create the glossary and link keywords to it.

Link to Historical Articles and Related Issues on the Web Site

Benefit: Adds more information than could otherwise fit in a standard news release. Information could include old press releases and white papers as well as links to current stock quotes and investor ratings or reviews.

Action: Find and post the material. Create the links.

Link to Historical Articles and Related Issues on External Web Sites

Benefit: Adds more information than could otherwise fit in a standard news release.

Action: Find and post the material. Create the links.

List and Link to Art, Graphics, and Head Shots That Illustrate Your Story

Benefit: A picture tells 1,000 stories. Putting the art on a press release page will slow down the time the article appears on the screen. By having links to the artwork, reporters can view the material they need when they need it.

Action: Upload files. Create links.

Link to Audio and Video Clips, Spreadsheets, and Graphics

Benefit: Reporters can use the material directly from the web and put it into their TV and radio newscasts as well as online newscasts. Business Wire calls this a "Smart News Release": "It enhances the communications

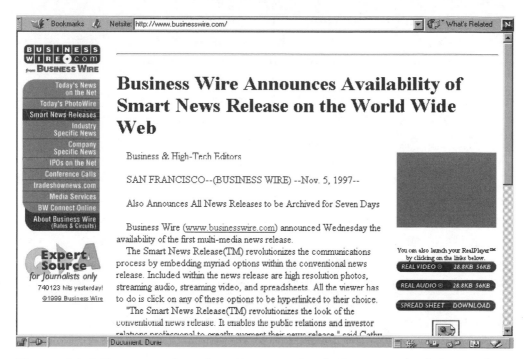

Figure 26.1 This press release from Business Wire displays icons that link to audio and video files. (© 1999, Business Wire)

process for PR and IR [investor relations] by embedding multimedia files into your written news release. The Smart News Release is an ideal way to include a downloadable spreadsheet file with your earnings release or a slide show illustrating a new product."

Action: Upload files. Create links. See Figure 26.1.

Create a Template for Press Releases

Benefit: Saves time. Whenever you need to write a new press release, simply open the template and type or copy your text from your word processor into the template. All contact information, copyright and license data, and other boilerplate items will be ready to use.

Action: Create the template.

Add a Password to Limit Access to Bona Fide Reporters

Benefit: Keeps unwanted people out of the media center.

Discussion: This is a delicate strategy. You might want to limit access to the press center to reporters only. Fuji did this with its Olympic press site so reporters could find and retrieve digital pictures quickly and easily. If the entire world had access to these pictures, the competition to download the files would be huge, and the wait time could affect reporters' deadlines. Oil companies do not permit the general public access to their press area for fear of environmental groups downloading pictures of company buildings, defacing them, and posting them online! If your press materials are not this widely demanded or sensitive, you probably would not want to add a password.

An alternative strategy is to create a site that only the media knows about. Use a simple name, like ourcompanymedia.com so reporters remember it easily. Also, use easy-to-remember passwords, such as media or news, for both the username and the password. Some companies permit immediate access, as they assume the only people who would know about the site are journalists who have been invited to join. Other companies check out the credentials of all persons who apply for access on the basis that they don't want activists to gain access to their files.

Action: Add a password screen. Contact key media people and give them passwords. Create a system to check the credentials of new reporters who apply for a password. Consider creating mirror sites or adding additional computers to handle increased demands.

Format Your Press Releases for the Web

Discussion: Printed material looks different on the web, and material must be formatted so that it can be read easily. It is very easy for the web to make material hard to read by adding line breaks and other visual distractions. You need to check everything you post to the web for formatting problems (See Figure 26.2). Additionally, certain printing conventions used in printed press releases are not needed on the web. That's because everything appears as one page on the web, whereas in print, copy spills over to several pages.

Action: Follow these steps to ensure copy looks good on the Internet:

- Don't type in all uppercase. It looks like shouting and is hard to read.

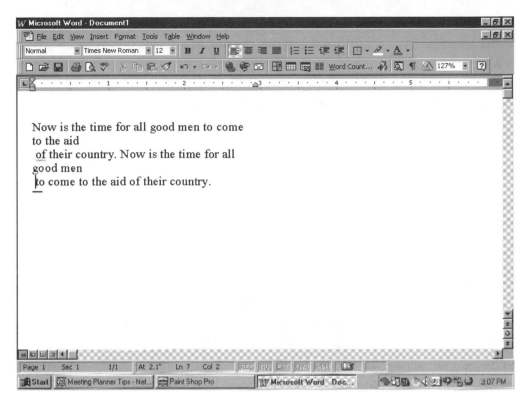

Figure 26.2 An example of badly formatted text. Notice how the lines break badly, making the release hard to read.

- Use ### at the end of the release to indicate the end.
- Don't use-*more*-between screens to indicate a new page.
- Ensure that hard line breaks have not been inserted into the material.
- Ensure that all lines flow properly.
- Format the release as you would like to see it printed, because people will print it.

Convert Existing Press Releases to HTML Format

Discussion: In the old days of the Internet, formatting a press release for your web site was an arduous task that required the help of the information technology (IT) department. With advances in software programs, every person who uses Microsoft Word can easily convert a press release into an interactive press release. Simply write your press release using Word 7.0 and save it as an HTML document. The command to do this is in the File menu under Save As. In seconds, your work is saved in a format

the web can read and print. You don't have to understand HTML to perform this task. By doing this process, you will save time and money by reducing the number of people and operations to create the document.

Action: Convert all your press releases.

HOW TO WRITE EFFECTIVE E-MAIL PITCH LETTERS

A popular public relations strategy is to send reporters a pitch letter that
describes what the news is and the action you would like them to take
(write an article, interview the chair, see a company representative at
their offices, tour a new facility, etc.). This section describes how to write
an e-mail pitch letter.

The Internet is primarily a text medium (although sound and pictures will become increasingly important). However, the standard rules
of formal business writing do not apply! Although good grammar and
spelling will always be required, the tone of online writing is less formal
and more conversational. Messages should be no longer than a screen
unless something major is happening.

Case Study: Phase Two Public Relations

"Online communications gives you the ability to develop a close relationship and be more efficient. If I had to depend on a phone call, it would fall
by the wayside by busy editors. A well-formulated e-mail gets a better response than a well-formulated voice mail. Giving good e-mail is essential.
The more depth you give, the better response you will get," says Chris
Boehlke, principal of Phase Two Public Relations in San Francisco. "It is so
much more convenient for them to reply to us. It takes them a minute to say
yes or no. With voice mail, the response is much lower. It is easier to click
on REPLY."

She likes to limit pitch letters to three paragraphs, maximum. "If they are
interested, I'll come back with more detail. I equate it to training someone to
talk on TV rather than in print. It is almost an alive medium," she says.

No one wants "It was great seeing you last week." They want "We'll
be in town next week; let's get together." It has to be much more to the
point.

Using e-mail, Boehlke is able to book 70 percent of her clients' media
tours.

Write Effective E-mail Pitch Letters to Reporters

Benefit: Gain favorable media attention and improve the chances of coverage.

Discussion: The worst way to approach reporters is the traditional method of sending voluminous press kits complete with backgrounders, white papers, and copies of previous press releases detailing the company's history. Instead, the proper approach is to send a short note explaining what is new and what you want the reporter to do. The entire note should be less than the depth of a computer screen (about 24 lines).

An effective e-mail pitch letter should go like this:

> Optical Data Corporation is introducing two computer games that teach science, social studies, and math to children ages 3 to 8 next week at the Consumer Electronics Show. If you would like to schedule an appointment, review the games, or see the complete press kit online, please send an e-mail note to me. For more information, please call me at 555-1212, email me at chris@ourcompany.com, or visit our web site, www.example .com.

This example gets to the heart of the matter quickly (new product introduction), describes the benefits of the product and the target market, and then asks for action. Best yet, it accomplishes this task in fewer than 60 words! Reporters are intrigued by brevity. When they commit to writing a story, that's when they want tons of data. When the reporter responds, you can send the appropriate information.

Another tactic is to send a brief query and asking the reporter to call or e-mail for more information. Still another variation on this theme is to send a brief query, ask the reporter to call or e-mail for more information, and then announce that the rest of the information follows, as in the following example:

> Dan,
> Q: Which company lets you check your credit on the web, enables you to shop for cars online (free) and apply for financing in-real-time on the Net, and has formed alliances with such industry powerhouses as Yahoo! and Netscape?
> A: ADP. The 3.5 billion dollar computing company has leveraged its expertise in electronic commerce applications and created a comprehensive virtual

automotive shopping mall with ADP AutoConnect (http://autoconnect.net). With more than 4,000 auto dealers online and more than 800 links to auto manufacturers and other sites, ADP AutoConnect is the largest collection of automotive information on the Internet and great example of electronic commerce on the web.

If you are interested in meeting the brains behind ADP AutoConnect, please give me a call at 312-240-2611 or email rbenecke@edelman.com. Following is more info on ADP AutoConnect:

With the growing number of consumers using computers and the Internet ... (the press release continues).

Tailor Your Message to Fit Individual Reporters' Needs

Benefit: Builds rapport with reporters; improves chances of gaining coverage.

Discussion: It is critical for you to realize that each reporter needs to develop her own story for her audience. One size story does not fit all reporters. Reporters can influence several audiences:

- The online community.
- Vertical markets.
- General consumers.
- Retailers and distributors.

For example, the retail press looks for a story about how manufacturers offer incentives to retailers to sell their products, general consumer reporters are interested in new products that their readers will find interesting, and the business reporter wants to know how the company's stock will be affected by the introduction of the new product. If you consider the reporter's target audience, you will be much more successful in dealing with reporters.

Action: Target the story.

WRITING THE SUBJECT OR HEADING

Perhaps the most important step you will undertake to get the press's attention is when you create the heading, or subject lines, that will appear in the reporter's e-mail reader program. If the heading is weak or confusing, the reporter won't read it. If the subject is misleading, you will ruin your credibility with the reporter. So you must take great care in creating the subject line.

Also, remember when creating the subject line that reporters do not have the same context for the material as you do. They might see 50 new messages every time they retrieve their mail. Some messages are press releases, others are notes from colleagues and editors, and still others are spam. Reporters must sift through the mess just like you do! They delete messages the same way you do. They don't even open many of their e-mails—just like you! So when we talk about context, you might think everyone knows about your company or product. But they don't. They have their attention split in many directions. Therefore, you must give the message a context and give the essence of the story.

Create a Compelling Subject Line

Benefit: Get attention.

Discussion: The subject line is the first piece of text that is displayed in a reporter's e-mail box. If you write an interesting subject line, reporters will read the message. If you don't, they will hit the *delete* key. A good subject line breathes life into the message. For example:

- Company CEO shows new antivirus program.
- New baseball game predicts World Series winners.

"Identify what you bring to the party," says Boehlke. "It is very much like TV or headline copy. Every word must be perfect. Messiness is not tolerated in e-mail."

Be careful not to be too cute or misleading. Nothing is worse than seeing a subject line that says "Sex" only to find a message that says, "Now that I've gotten your attention, let's talk about insurance," says Skye Ketonen, of the Microsoft LinkExchange.

Action: Write several subject lines. Test them with your colleagues. Select the best one.

Ask for Feedback

Benefit: Encourages dialogue with reporters.

Action: At the end of the press release, ask reporters for comments. This might help you begin a relationship with the reporter. Include a mailto: form to ease the process.

HOW TO PUT YOUR ANNUAL REPORT ONLINE

Case Study: Annual Reports Online: Suncor Energy, Inc.

"The Internet is here to stay, and lots of people are using it to get information, including financial information about companies. Brokers, analysts, fund managers, and other investment professionals have been wired for years and they are increasingly using the World Wide Web to conduct research," says Ron Shewchuck, manager of external communications for Suncor, Inc., a major Canadian energy company based in Calgary (www.suncor.com). His company spent $250,000 to print an annual report but needed only $6,000 to $8,000 to create an online annual report.

Each month, 300 to 400 people read the online annual report, and 25 to 40 download the financial reports in Excel file formats. These numbers are large, considering the targeted nature of the audience and the material.

Here are his tips for success:

- Integrate the creation of your online annual report into your regular annual report production schedule and publish your online report on the same day as it is filed with securities commissions and mailed to shareholders.
- Publish the whole report, not pieces of it or a summary. Investors and potential investors want all the information they can get in a form that is easy to use. Organize the online report so it is web friendly. That means structuring the information so the user can get to the information he needs, at the level of detail he needs, in the shortest number of mouse clicks possible.
- Give the user choices as to how he would like to view the material. Provide the report both as a downloadable Adobe Acrobat file and as a fully linked HTML document.
- Link but don't overlink. Provide a minimum number of links in the overview material such as the chair's message and operating highlights

because you don't want to distract people from your key messages. But make sure you link the notes to the financial statement to the appropriate parts of the statements themselves.

- Avoid bells and whistles but provide cool ways to view your information. Make key charts and tables available as downloadable Microsoft Excel files so analysts can do what they want with your numbers. The key is to make it easy for them to know your company.

FINDING REPORTERS ONLINE

Now that you have written your press release and pitch letter, you need to send it to reporters. You can find out which reporters are online by several methods:

- Check the mastheads of magazines. More and more publications are listing their reporters' e-mail addresses in the print publications.
- Ask reporters for their e-mail addresses when you meet them at trade shows, conventions, and press conferences or when you speak to them on the phone.
- Look at their business cards or at the end of their articles.

Most reporters online are those from the technology press, with a smattering of reporters at daily newspapers who cover technology. Consumer publication editors have not yet jumped online. However, this is changing almost daily. Many publications have realized they can make money by having an online presence. Once they launch the service, their reporters get online and can be contacted. America Online seems to be attracting a good number of consumer reporters.

Reporters welcome press releases and queries via e-mail because of these qualities:

- **Speediness.** They get the release faster than they would by mail.
- **Responsiveness.** Reporters can send questions by e-mail.

- **Editability.** The information can be imported into reporters' word processors where it can be edited, reformatted, or filed for later use.

Encourage Reporters to Register to Receive Your Press Release

Discussion: It is all well and good to proactively search for reporters interested in writing about your company, but some reporters are actually scouring the web looking for you! Use your web site to initiate a dialogue with them.

Action: Create a form that includes fields for the reporter's name, title, publication, address, phone, e-mail, web site, topics they cover, and best way to reach them (some reporter prefer e-mail, but others want fax, mail, or phone calls for urgent news). When a story breaks, you can search the database quickly to distribute information that the reporter has requested, such as earnings reports or new product announcements. Frequently, different reporters on the same publication will cover different topics, so this system will help ensure that your press release reach the correct person.

Send Personal Pitch Letters to Multiple Recipients

Benefit: Reach many reporters quickly.

Discussion: Another advantage of e-mail is that you can send one pitch letter to hundreds of reporters in the time it takes to send one note. First you target the reporters, find out their e-mail addresses, and follow your favorite online service's steps for sending a mailing list.

Action: Create a list, write a pitch letter, and send the letter.

Warning: Make sure that the reporter sees only the copy addressed to her. The last thing you want is to let the reporter see she is part of a 100-person routing list. Depending on the service, she might see the names of each person on a separate line before she sees your message. That means the reporter sees the first 100 lines, the equivalent of two sheets of paper or four computer screens. That is a sure turnoff.

HOW TO DISTRIBUTE PRESS MATERIALS ONLINE

Send the Press Release to a News Wire Service for Distribution

Benefit: Exposure.

Discussion: Business Wire (www.businesswire.com), PR Newswire (www.prnewswire.com), and Canadian Corporate Newsnet (www.cdn-news.net) distribute company press releases for a fee. These press releases are posted to several online services and the Internet, where reporters and the public can read them. Both U.S. services are so well established that the Securities and Exchange Commission considers transmission of business information on these services to be a primary requirement for complying with its rules to make information available to the public in a timely and equal manner. Both services send the press releases to more than two thousand media outlets, the online services, and 85 electronic database services.

There are many advantages to using such a service. You reach reporters quickly and relatively inexpensively. Many reporters read these wires to get leads for writing news stories and features. You will save a great deal of time, money, and labor by not having to print and mail press releases. All press releases are carried by a number of online news services.

Many online discussions in marketing forums center on which service is more effective, and the results are always split. So you can feel free to select either one and know that the service will be comparable. There is no need to put a release on both services as there is a great degree of duplication of media outlets.

Both services charge by the word. There is a minimum fee for the first 400 words and an additional fee for each additional 100 words. Different prices exist for selecting specialized news lists, such as those for sports, entertainment, automotive news, health, and legal markets or for those targeted to certain parts of the country. Because prices can change, please call the services for more information: Business Wire's number is 800-237-8212. PR Newswire's number is 800-832-5522.

To use either service, follow these basic steps:

1. Create an account with either service.
2. Write your press release.

3. Transmit the press release to the company via fax and modem.
4. Discuss with your account executive which lists of reporters should receive the press release and when.
5. Your account executive will call you after the release has been sent.
6. Check the online service to make sure the press release has indeed been distributed and there aren't any errors.
7. Ask the service to count how many reporters open the e-mail containing your release and to count the number of visits to the press release web page. That way you'll be able to see who really read your release.

STAGING LIVE EVENTS ONLINE

The interactive nature of the Internet allows companies to present live events to their customers, investors, and employees. For many years, companies held press conferences, meetings, and seminars by typing messages to one another. This was called "chatting." The introduction of audio and Internet telephony now allows companies to hold these events with voice and audio.

Companies can broadcast their meetings using real voices. If their customers have multimedia computers, modems, and Internet connections, they can actually hear the meeting and ask questions just as if they were talking to the company by a telephone.

Case Study: Bell & Howell's Online Annual Meetings

Bell & Howell (www.bellhowell.com) became the first company to host its annual meeting on the Internet in 1996. It went so well that it did so again in 1997. Here's the inside story on how this company did it and how your company can go online successfully.

"Bell & Howell is a high tech company. By putting our annual meeting online, we are able to act like a high tech company," said Hank D'Ambrosio, vice president of administration for Bell & Howell Company.

"If you are interested in communicating with your shareholders on a global basis, broadcasting your annual meting on the Internet may be an inexpensive way to communicate your corporate image," he says. "Corporate America's new attitude is to keep it brief, simple, and keep costs low. Our approach was to limit presentations of year-end financials and spend more time communicating vision and company culture. We also wanted to leave plenty of time for questions and answers from our shareholders. The logical solution was to utilize the Internet. This forces you to keep the message short. It is cost-effective. And you may reach investors around the globe.

"In 1997 there were 1,761 people who listened live to our annual meeting broadcast. In addition, 25 percent of our shares were voted online. In 1996, 230 people listened to the broadcast.

"The broadcast is similar to a remote radio broadcast requiring phone connections, PCs for the Internet and e-mail questions, and a mixing board for the web broadcast. The recipient needs a PC, a Real Audio Player (which can be downloaded off the web), and some form of Internet connectivity.

"The live audience and the Internet audience were able to view a slide show while listening to the annual meeting broadcast. E-mail questions could be sent from two days prior to the meeting all the way through the annual meeting. All questions were read in their entirety by our chairman and answered in the order they were received.

"While there is a considerable amount of planning involved, the event has gone very smoothly and has been very well received by shareholders, investors and the media," he adds.

The key ingredients for success were simple visual materials; planning the presentation for people who have the least effective technology; planning well in advance and installing ISDN lines, phone lines, and backups in case something went wrong; having a technical support team at the site; and rehearsing. He credits the success of the program with having a reputable broadcast partner (Audio Net) and knowledgeable project management (The Reynolds Communications Group).

The event was promoted by a colorful invitation that stood out in the annual report, along with notices on the web site and through traditional public relations.

"It is amazing the amount of publicity we got from this event," he concludes. The meeting archives are kept on the web site for several months and are then removed.

NEW PUBLICITY OPPORTUNITIES ONLINE

The Internet and commercial online services are creating new media properties that corporate communicators can use as publicity outlets.

Opportunities exist to place company representatives as guests on conferences sponsored by these publications as well as to place news and feature articles about companies and products.

Search for New Media Opportunities to Promote Your Product or Company

Benefit: Exposure to targeted audience.

Discussion: New publications are springing up every day on the Net. They welcome informed guests who can provide information that benefits their audiences.

Action: Search for these new opportunities by checking newsgroups, search engines, and PR Newswire, Business Wire, and Canadian Corporate Newsnet. Study their formats to see what kind of information they want or what type of appearance (interview) would be appropriate. Pitch the topic. Prepare the host and spokesperson with sample questions. Promote the appearance both before and after the event.

Online Versions of Traditional Print Publications

More than one thousand daily newspapers are now online, and thousands of trade publications and TV and radio stations are joining them as well.

These publications exist in the real world and post online editions on the Internet. In some cases they print the same news as in the print edition; in other cases, they add more stories and host archives of old editions. A great many publications print news online as soon as they can, so material online is much fresher than in the print edition. Several offer online discussions with experts or chats between online members.

New Media Publications

These publications exist only online. They might have large or small readerships but should be courted as readers are devoted followers and passionate about the subject.

- One group of publications is called *ezines,* which is short for electronic magazines. One of the most prominent, Slate, published by Microsoft and edited by a noted journalist, joins hundreds of ezines dedicated to diverse interests and audiences. Be on the lookout for new publications. Before pitching them, read the ezine to see if the audience is appropriate. If it is, then determine which message the publication would most likely want to write about.

- Consultants publish private newsletters on hundreds of topics. Find them through the search engines and then contact the writers. They could interview you experts or reprint information articles you have written.
- Web sites produced by trade groups, associations, and the like could also be venues for placing articles and links.

Internet Radio Shows and Stations

Audio is becoming a more prevalent feature on the Internet. As a result, online radio stations are being created that offer shows on such diverse topics as current events, technology, music, business, personal finance, and sports.

- Cyber Media Show with Kim Bayne (www.cybermedia.org) is a radio show that interviews Internet industry figures and marketing experts on public radio and the Internet.
- Several dozen radio stations simultaneously broadcast their shows on the Internet via broadcast.com (www.broadcast.com). These shows include talk radio, sports, commentary, politics, food, and music. By pitching to these live shows you will be able to reach an audience on the Net as well—especially if you promote the appearance.
- Hundreds of other radio stations have web sites, but they all seem to be advertisements and press kits for their on-air station. Look for these stations to begin broadcasting live on the Internet as technology improves.

TV Stations

- ESPN, CNN, NBC, and other broadcast outlets are online with print and/or audio editions. Look for more audio and video programming and original content online as technology improves. MSNBC is a joint venture of Microsoft and NBC News. The web site features 24-hour news and links to related stories and web sites.

- ZDTV (www.zdnet.com/zdtv) is a television show that reports on companies doing interesting things on the Internet. The show is also shown on the Internet, and old stories are archived for on-demand viewing.
- C|net is a hybrid in that the online service and TV show are developed simultaneously and intended to work off each other. Its web site (www.cnet.com) is one of the most innovative news sites on the Internet in terms of creating original content to meet the needs of its audience—those who are keenly interested in personal computing and enjoying the Internet.

Online Conferences

Forums on CompuServe and America Online are always looking for experts to serve as guests on a wide variety of topics. These guests can be promoted on the service for free on the highlights or "what's new" features. Really big guests can be promoted in *USA Today's* Cyberlistings, printed every day next to the TV schedule. Benefits include awareness from pre-event publicity, interacting with prospects at the event itself, and building relationships after the event with prospects who read the transcript of the event. Conferences can be held in two venues:

1. People meet in a designated online area at an appointed time and interact by typing questions. A moderator fields questions and keeps order.
2. One expert is available for a set period of time, say, a week, in a bulletin board area. He posts the beginning overview and questions for the discussion. People answer those questions and add their own questions, thoughts, and observations. The guest can respond to messages as often as he likes but at least once a day.

These conferences offer your company the opportunity to deliver its message, portray itself in a good light, and show its responsiveness to the community.

Best yet, whereas TV broadcasts messages to wide groups of people, online services can be used to broadcast and narrowcast messages. If your company is the kind that appeals to a broad audience, such as an entertainment organization, travel-related company, or the like, a conference can help. Small companies and consultants, speakers, and trainers can talk directly to highly targeted groups of prospects.

Online services love to feature big-name speakers and celebrities that attract large markets—and network charges. For example, Vice President Al Gore "spoke" on a moderated conference on CompuServe that drew 900 people. Jerry Seinfeld and Jay Leno participated in talks on Prodigy's entertainment area. Technology guru Esther Dyson participated in a conference on America Online. In an interesting use of integrated marketing, a Garth Brooks online conference, which drew 500 people to the NBC/McDonald's area on America Online, tied in with McDonald's promotion to sell Brooks' CDs at their restaurants.

Be a Guest on a Conference

Benefit: Exposure to targeted audience.

Discussion: Forums on the commercial online services are always looking for interesting guests.

Action: Search for these new opportunities by checking newsgroups, search engines, and PR Newswire and Business Wire. Study their formats to see what kind of information they want or what type of appearance (interview) would be appropriate. Pitch the topic. Prepare the host and spokesperson with sample questions. Promote the appearance both before and after the event.

Create Your Own Conference

Benefit: Provide newsworthy material to your audience and reporters.

Discussion: Companies can host their own conferences that feature the CEO or other newsmakers. By using any number of conference or chat software programs, you can get your message out to the world inexpensively. Charles Schwab, the discount stock brokerage, frequently hosts conferences with leading analysts and presidents of Fortune 500 companies. They promote the event by sending post cards to their clients.

Action: Identify a leader in your company who has newsworthy ideas. Find a software program to broadcast the event. Promote the event, both online and offline, to your key stakeholders and the media.

SUMMARY

Writing online press material is challenging because it must be brief. Never has a communicator's skill for transmitting messages clearly and succinctly been so put to the test—the DELETE key is so close! Fortunately, the rules for writing for rapport with editors are manageable if you are willing to choose each word with care.

Building Relationships with Reporters

Despite the aggressive, wolf-pack image you might have of the media because of TV news crews and made-for-TV movies, it isn't difficult to build rapport with reporters.

Reporters have one main goal: to present information that interests their readers. They are not in business to print your press releases. If you convince reporters that you have a story that will grab their readers' attention, then you will have a good chance of having a story written about your company.

This chapter will show you easy strategies and case studies for building rapport with reporters.

RAPPORT-BUILDING STRATEGIES

Don't Lie

Benefit: Builds credibility.

Discussion: Reporters will find out if you are lying. When they do, they won't ever speak to you again.

Action: Tell the truth.

Be a Reporter's Resource

Benefit: Build rapport; improve chances of gaining coverage.

Discussion: A great way to build rapport with reporters is to become their trusted resource. This means you:

- Return phone calls as soon as possible.
- Provide reporters with the information or products they need.
- Grant access to people at your company who have information.
- Know everything there is to know about your company and its products and if you don't, get the answer by deadline.
- Know about competitors' products and talk knowledgeably about them.
- Know about the industry and provide gossip and tips.
- Admit when you do not know the answer and promise to find it.
- Never cover up.
- Always tell the truth!

Case Study: Skye Ketonen, Microsoft LinkExchange

Skye Ketonen is one of the new breed of online public relations agents. The key to success is her ability to create rapport with reporters. Her clients are regularly featured in top-tier publications such as *Business Week* because she has developed a personal relationship with reporters.

"I build relationships with reporters as people, not as editors," she says. "I become friends with reporters. We send e-mail about things that have nothing to do about this industry."

She also approaches the relationship as an equal, not as a PR leech. "We're both passionate about this industry," she says. "I am important to you. You are important to me. Let's be friends."

The results pay off handsomely. "They get to trust me, believe me and trust me as a real person."

If you do rapport correctly, the payoff can be enormous.

Send Press Releases, Pitch Letters, and Notes via E-Mail Instead of Calling

Benefit: Build rapport with reporters.

Discussion: E-mail is a great way to build rapport with reporters. Here's why.

Reporters spend a good deal of time away from their desks covering stories, attending meetings, and—especially if they are in the trade press—at trade shows and conventions that may keep them away for as long as a week at a time. You are more likely to speak to their voice mail than to them. When they return, they are faced with dozens of messages. Naturally, reporters organize those notes into callbacks and discards. To jump ahead of the pack, you must use e-mail.

Many reporters check their e-mail several times a day, even when they are on the road. E-mail has a sense of urgency to it, so reporters read it first. Because e-mail can be answered quickly, reporters can cut through piles of it in a hurry.

Reaching reporters via e-mail is efficient because you do not have to play phone tag. Time zones do not matter; people can read and respond to messages at their leisure. Answering e-mail is faster and less expensive than calling on the phone.

E-mail can be used to pitch products, set up appointments, follow up on product reviews, answer questions, tell about seminars and dealer programs, and provide news, including earnings reports, high-level executive appointments, contracts signed, strategic partnerships, and the like.

Talk to Reporters via E-Mail

Benefit: Build rapport.

Discussion: You can create conversations with editors privately through their e-mail accounts. Although it might not be appropriate to pitch stories, you can begin to develop rapport with reporters by showing them you read their articles, are familiar with their work, and are an expert in your field.

Action: To implement this strategy, create a list of the most important editors in your universe. Find out if they have e-mail accounts or if their publications have online forums. Send them notes to engage them in dialogue. Examples include comments on recent articles and columns they have written and suggestions for stories about trends you see emerging. They will value this information as good for background or as a lead for a story idea. You don't have to plug your own company to build rapport!

Warning: Gratuitous, self-serving messages will not be appreciated. How do you know when you've crossed the line? Ask yourself: "If I were a reporter, would I value this letter, or would I toss it?" The answer is obvious. The second litmus test is the "Oh, what the heck" test, as in "I don't

know if he'll want to read this, but what the heck—it doesn't cost anything." Wrong. It can cost you your credibility, a commodity that cannot
be recovered after it has been spent.

Don't Abuse E-Mail

Benefit: Builds rapport.

Discussion: While e-mail is an easy medium to use, it is possible to
make faux pas that will land you in a reporter's dog house. Charles Pizzo,
head of P.R. PR, Inc. (www.prnet.com), in New Orleans, warns:

- Do not send e-mail to dozens of reporters at the same time, as all
  the addresses will appear on the screen. This tells each reporter
  that everyone else has the story and, therefore, that he is not
  unique. Also, seeing dozens of names before the story slows
  down the time to actually read the story. This leaves a bad impression.
- Do not send e-mail to a periodical's reader feedback e-mail address. The message probably won't be delivered to the reporter.

If you participate in newsgroups or mailing lists, identify yourself as
a company spokesperson; otherwise, reporters will think you are a consumer, which could cloud issues.

Find Out How Reporters Want to Receive Information

Benefit: Builds rapport.

Discussion: Few actions irritate reporters more than sending their press
material in the wrong channel. Some reporters like to get e-mail, while
others prefer faxes. Still others prefer a phone call. If you send e-mail to a
reporter who wants a fax, you will upset her. It may sound picky to you
and me, but that is a fact of life. You must learn to deal with it.

Business Wire and PR Newswire maintain databases on how reporters want to receive information. If you use their services, you'll be
assured of sending your release in the proper manner.

Action: Find out how reporters want to be contacted. Ask them or use a
reference source like PR Newswire or Business Wire.

Ask Reporters to Subscribe to Mailing Lists

Benefit: Increased communication; target marketing.

Discussion: Ask reporters who visit your web site to identify themselves and their interests in your company and its products. Offer them the opportunity to join your mailing list so they can receive press releases and alerts as Technopolis® does in Figure 27.1. This way, reporters who are only interested in your new products will receive that targeted information instead of company financials. Or reporters who are interested in products from Division A will not receive product announcements from Division B. You'll benefit also by knowing whom to contact and whom to follow up with. Although you might already have this information for your A-list reporters, this tactic will let second- and third-tier reporters and newsletter editors receive your materials without you having to spend additional time away from your primary media contacts. Intel (www.intel.com) has created a press release filter on its web site to ensure that reporters receive only relevant materials.

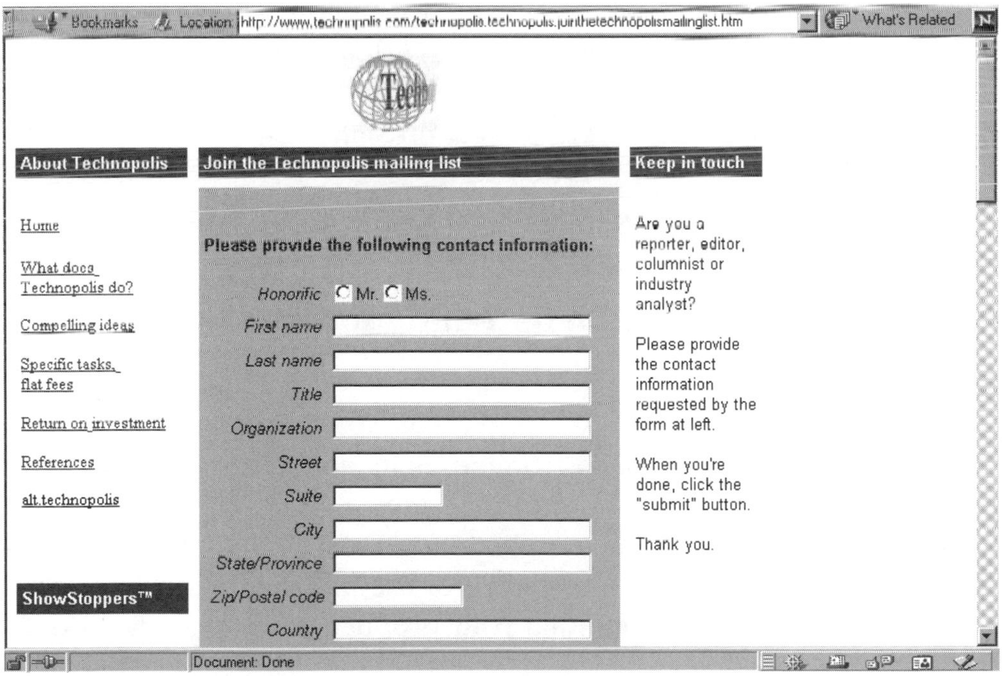

Figure 27.1 Technopolis® Communications asks reporters to register on the web site. (© 1999, by Technopolis® Communications, Inc.)

Look for Reporters' Queries in Newsgroups and Mailing Lists

Benefit: Get press coverage.

Discussion: Savvy online reporters post query notices in forums to find subjects to interview for articles.

Action: Scan your favorite message areas and answer appropriate queries.

Look for Reporters' Queries in ProfNet

Benefit: Get press coverage.

Discussion: The hardest part of getting publicity is finding the one reporter in a haystack who wants to write about your product. You could make 50 phone calls to find one reporter who won't just hang up the phone on you. ProfNet is a daily service sent by e-mail from PR Newswire. It is an indispensable aid for public relations. Reporters post queries about articles they are writing. They are looking for experts to provide information and quotes. It doesn't get any better than this. They tell you what they are writing about, their deadline, and the best way to contact them. Communicators can call reporters directly and pitch their stories. Queries have come from such high-profile daily newspapers as *The New York Times* and television networks like CNN.

Action: Subscribe to ProfNet (www.profnet.com); see Figure 27.2.

Participate in Online Chats with Editors

Benefit: Build rapport.

Discussion: Many editors host online chats and conferences at their publication's site or as guests on other sites. By participating in these conferences, you might be able to build a relationship with an editor as you impress her with your knowledge of the industry by asking intelligent questions (not by promoting your product directly, unless asked).

Action: Look for notices of conferences, think of dynamite questions, and attend.

PN 3754:Group Therapy/Bioterrorism/Face-to-Face Meetings
Copyright (c) 1999 ProfNet, Inc. All rights reserved. Any resale or redistribution of this information beyond your organization without the written consent of ProfNet, Inc. is strictly prohibited.

PROFNET SEARCH 3754
April 7, 1999
[Sent Wednesday at 2:36 p.m. EDT]

SUMMARY

DEADLINE TODAY:

1. Kosovo Conflict and Hollywood-Fox News Channel

2. Russian Political Parties-MS. Magazine

BOOSTER:

3. Origin of the Term "Ring Shout"-Encarta Africana Encyclopedia

BEHAVIOR/RELATIONSHIPS:

4. Group Therapy-Clinical Psychiatry News

BUSINESS:

5. Face-to-Face Meetings-Los Angeles Times (CA)

6. Career-Planning Books-Coverstory

7. Arizona Mining Industry-Phoenix Now Times (AZ)

8. Spin-Offs and Acquisitions-Office.com

QUERIES

DEADLINE TODAY

**1. KOSOVO CONFLICT AND HOLLYWOOD-FOX NEWS CHANNEL. I'm looking for articles or stories that discuss how the Hollywood community or actors/actresses are dealing with the Kosovo conflict. Need leads by 4 p.m. EDT today, April 7. > > > Bill Cowin Email: cowin@foxnews.com [T::4/7:3754]

**2.RUSSIAN POLITICAL PARTIES-MS. MAGAZINE. Miranda Kennedy is looking for information on The Russian Party for the Defense of Women, headed by Tatyana Roshchina. She's seen news articles in the Moscow Times; she's looking for authoritative sources who can discuss this party. Needs leads today, April 7. Email: Msmagazine@aol.com Phone: 212-509-2092, ext. 220 [T::4/7:3754]

(continued)

Figure 27.2 Reporters look for experts to comment for their articles on the ProfNet service. (© 1999, PR Newswire).

SEGMENTED QUERIES

**3. ORIGIN OF THE TERM "RING SHOUT"-ENCARTA AFRICANA ENCYCLOPEDIA.

Karen Conrad continues to seek sources who can discuss the origin of the term "ring shout." Some references claim that it comes from the Arabic term "saut", which is said to refer to counterclockwise circumambulation by devout Muslim pilgrims of Kaaba, the sacred shrine of Mecca, Saudi Arabia. Looking for sources who can confirm this definition. Is "saut" spoken as "shout" or was the word "shout" derived from the vocals that accompany the dance? Email: a-kareco@microsoft.com [T::4/7:3754]

BEHAVIOR/RELATIONSHIPS

**4. GROUP THERAPY-CLINICAL PSYCHIATRY NEWS. I am interested in speaking with psychiatrists who have opinions about whether group therapy is the most efficient way to provide psychotherapy for most psychiatric patients. Need leads by tomorrow, April 8. > > > Kathryn DeMott Email: kdemott@imng.com Phone: 301-816-8790 [T::4/7:3754]

BUSINESS

**5. FACE-TO-FACE MEETINGS-LOS ANGELES TIMES (CA). Coll Metcalfe is looking for experts who can discuss the importance of personal meetings in business, given the electronic age in which much can be accomplished without talking to anyone. Are face-to-face meetings still important? Becoming more important? Also looking for companies that facilitate these meetings between their staff and clients, and maybe any colleges that conduct seminars in face-to-face interaction. Needs leads by Friday, April 9. Phone: 805-446-4777 Email: coll.metcalfe@latimes.com [T::4/7:3754]

**6. CAREER-PLANNING BOOKS-COVERSTORY. I am doing a book round-up feature on career-planning books. I would love to receive notice of books on this subject that have been published in 1999 and are appropriate for recent graduates. I also would like to interview the authors of such books. If a publisher would like his or her author to be interviewed, I must see the book—otherwise a press release is fine. Coverstory is a weekly entertainment and lifestyle supplement published by Thomson Target Media and sent to more than 100 newspapers in the U.S. and Canada. Need leads by April 19. > > > Bev Bennett Email: Bevben@aol.com Phone: 847-491-6024 [T::4/7:3754]

**7. ARIZONA MINING INDUSTRY-PHOENIX NEW TIMES (AZ). I am looking for a business, economics or tax expert who can talk about the current state of the mining industry in Arizona. > > > Amy Silverman Email: asilverman@newtimes.com Phone: 602-229-8443 [T::4/7:3754]

Figure 27.2 *(Continued)*

Case Study: Lawrence Custis

Teamwork consultant Lawrence Custis (custisen@teleport.com) used the Internet to market his services nationwide.

"The one feature of online services that has enhanced my efforts is live chat conferences. I've used this medium to meet magazine editors and staff and have become a conference giver myself," he says. "Since then I have received calls from firms in California and have been interviewed for articles in *Entrepreneur* magazine and *Small Office Computing* magazine. Also, I have received invaluable advice on using media releases and other marketing strategies, live, from Scott DeGarmo (editor/publisher, *Success* magazine), Jay Conrad Levinson (Guerrilla Marketing), Dennis Esko (editor-in-chief, *Home Office Computing* magazine), and many others."

SUMMARY

By being a reporter's resource instead of a pest, you can build credibility with reporters and maintain a relationship that can help your company achieve its marketing goals online.

Crisis Communications

Crisis. Even the sound of the word strikes fear into the hearts of corporate communications managers. Although these managers have traditionally used the media of print, television, and radio and the tools of press releases, press conferences, and good old-fashioned phone calls to handle catastrophes and calamities, even the best crisis communications program can be improved by using Internet tools. When integrated with traditional crisis communications procedures, the Internet-savvy company has a much greater variety of choices and tactics to combat their crises.

This chapter will describe how to use the Internet to handle a crisis. We'll explore tools and tactics to:

- Prepare for crisis.
- Find the crisis.
- Deal with the crisis.
- Evaluate your activities.
- Recognize and avert online crises.

PHASE 1: PREPARE FOR CRISIS

When I teach my PR class at Berkeley, I always ask my students when the best time is to deal with a crisis. Every neophyte class has responded, "Before the crisis happens." The Internet can help you deal with crises in a timely manner—before the crisis happens.

According to the Institute for Crisis Management, the majority of business crises are not accidental or sudden; they develop well before they thrust an organization onto the evening news.

A number of crises can be anticipated, such as dismal earnings reports, accidents and deaths, shareholder suits, and strikes. During the planning phases, the Internet can help you with:

- Tactics for creating policies and messages.
- Tactics for training personnel.
- Tactics for media relations.

The follow sections present these tactics for you.

Use Video Conferences to Link Offices and Meetings

Video conferences on the Internet can link offices and workers so they can see and hear each other during strategy meetings. This has the advantage of cutting down on the expense and hassle of travel. It also has the benefit of letting you interpret what people are really saying, as you can see their facial expressions and body language. These are essential traits that you cannot pick up during phone conferences.

Create a Stealth Web Site

Many crises can be seen in advance. Every company lays off workers, raises prices, and misses earning targets. Some companies might face other crises, such as the death of a key officer, a customer injury, or a recall. When the problem develops, reporters want news fast. You can create the press releases and backgrounders for these stories in advance and post them to the web when the crisis breaks. All you have to do is fill in the blanks for the press releases. You would have set up all the design, links to further information, and contact information beforehand.

Decide If the Media Needs a Password to Access Materials

Although full access is generally a good rule of thumb to follow in responding to crises, in some situations you might want only a limited group to read certain files. For example, you might want to keep the general public from a site so that the access time to read information and download large picture or video files is not hindered. If this is the case, then use a password system that enables reporters to enjoy full access to the material only after you have made it generally available to them. You will need to create a password system with your information technology department or ISP and issue passwords to beat reporters who would need to access the information when a crisis develops. The area should be kept empty until the appropriate personnel declare the time is right for reporters to read the materials.

If you create a media distribution list in advance, you can e-mail the password to reporters. They can all have the same password to ease the registration and confirmation process.

You can also set up passwords for selected key groups such as investors, dealers, and employees. The material stored in each directory can be molded to meet their needs. By doing this, you fulfill your obligation to provide timely information to your key audiences without slowing access by the media.

Use the Internet to Train Employees

Through a computer-based training program, you can teach employees how to respond in times of crisis. Course material can be stored online. Employees can take the training and answer test questions to show they understand the materials. By using audio and video, they can see and hear how to act and respond during a crisis.

Build Relationships with Reporters before the Crisis

The best time to build relationships with reporters is before the crisis develops. As reporters have limited time to do their jobs, many rely on e-mail correspondence to find information and further their relationships. As an online professional, you must find the reporters who cover your company and industry and build relationships with them. If they have e-mail addresses, you can curry favor with them by providing useful information and insight into industry trends. When a crisis develops and the reporters turn to you as a source, you will have established a degree of credibility and rapport.

Find Reporters' E-mail Addresses

To find reporters' e-mail addresses, ask them or look at their signed columns, publication mastheads, and business cards. Keep addresses stored in an e-mail folder so you can contact reporters quickly.

Find Out How Reporters Want to Be Contacted

Ask which method of correspondence they prefer. Some reporters have distinct preferences for e-mail, fax, phone, or mail for general correspondence and perhaps a different set of priorities for crisis calls. Find out the favored method and add to your credibility.

Assign Passwords (If Applicable)

At the very least, even the most hard-bitten reporters want to know whom to contact during a crisis. You can provide them with your regular contact information as well as tell them about your online command center that will be stocked with vital information that they can access as needed. If you will require them to use a password, this would be a good time to tell them their code. All codes should be easy to remember, such as the reporter's name or the word *crisis* or *media*.

PHASE 2: FIND THE CRISIS

A communications professional's worst nightmare is to learn about a crisis by picking up a phone and hearing the bad news come directly from a reporter. The Internet provides professionals with many sources to find crises:

- Online newspapers and archives.
- Web sites operated by competitors and associations.
- Newsgroups.

Online Newspapers and Archives

The Internet is one of the largest news sources available to any public relations professional. More than one thousand daily newspapers and thousands of trade publications have online editions that are updated daily or even hourly. This vast resource library helps you find potential crises at your company and in your industry much faster than waiting for the morning paper.

By contracting with any number of news services online, you can get updates on news stories affecting your company virtually every minute of the day. If you do this, you won't be surprised by reporters who find out about a crisis before you do.

Web Sites Operated by Competitors and Associations

Web sites of competitors or special interest groups can also contain misinformation about your company or its products. Use the downloading software programs to monitor those sites and ensure that the truth is being told. Be sure to check product comparison sheets, which can hold many errors.

Web sites run by your competitors could contain inaccurate information about your company or products. Check the product feature lists to ensure that they don't claim their product is the only one to provide a benefit or was the first to do so (provided your company can back up the claim).

Reporters and the public can read this information and regard it as fact. Comparison charts also should be checked for accuracy. When I handled the PR for a computer company, a competitor printed a comparison chart in an advertisement that said its computer could display 64 colors. Under the box for my client's features, the ad merely showed the word "yes." However, my client's computer could display *millions* of colors. This simple act made the competitor's computer look more powerful when in fact it was inferior!

If competitors or special interest groups issue press releases over PR Newswire or Business Wire, you will be able to catch them by using a news filter.

Web sites operated by industry associations and trade groups can print breaking news and contain invaluable information about industry statistics and resources.

If you check you competitors' sites, you won't be blindsided.

Newsgroups

Controversies can also be found in the tens of thousands of newsgroups. People post messages stating opinions or asking questions. Their comrades respond in writing. The world can see the printed transcript of the dialogue and add their comments.

Although these dialogues are a wonderful exercise in free speech and the sharing of information, they can also become breeding grounds of controversy for companies. For example, if a dissatisfied customer posts a message saying he is not happy with your product, the whole world can see it.

A surprisingly large number of people use newsgroups to find information and opinions about products they intend to buy—from automobile tires and classical music selections to stereo equipment. Not surprisingly, a lot of inaccurate information is sent unintentionally, as are personal likes and dislikes about products. One recent search found people debating the merits of Diet Snapple. Current events also are discussed in newsgroups as people give their opinions on news stories they read about in newspapers and see on television.

It is vitally important for companies to monitor these newsgroups for libelous or inaccurate material because unchallenged statements will be quoted and regarded as truth. Consumers who read those postings could be negatively influenced about your company or product. Companies can also be the targets of special interest groups that hold opposing points of view on certain issues, such as tobacco, the environment, home schooling, abortion, and the like.

Even worse than simply affecting the millions of newsgroup subscribers, reporters from daily newspapers and trade publications frequently read newsgroup postings to find out what customers are saying about products. If they read many negative messages about your company or product, the good reporters will call you for a comment; the sloppy reporters will print the flames without calling you to set the record straight.

Companies need to respond and set the record straight because these messages can be seen by hundreds of thousands of people today and in the future; messages can be retrieved forever by using special tools and services such as Deja.com a database of all messages posted to newsgroups.

When you enter a query, Deja.com responds with the e-mail address of the person who wrote the article, the newsgroup in which it appeared, and the title of the article. Both the e-mail address and the headline are linked to additional information. By clicking on the headline, you will be able to read the entire text of the article. You can then find additional articles that commented on this one so you can see how people reacted to the posting. Did they agree or disagree, or did the subject die? You can also find every article the writer ever posted to any newsgroup by clicking on her e-mail address. This might be useful in developing a profile of the writer. You might discover that the writer works for a competitor! You might be able to ascertain whether the writer is a crank or a credible person with a legitimate complaint.

There is a strong bias against advertising and commerce in newsgroups, but no one objects to the right of companies to defend their good name or set the record straight. Care should be taken in selecting the appropriate rank of the responder.

- If the problem involves inaccurate information, a product manager or public relations person can correct the price of a product or talk about its features.
- If the situation involves a more serious matter, such as company policy, the president, chair, or division vice president should respond.
- In only the rarest of matters should an attorney respond because the title *attorney* sends a message that could be misinterpreted as a threat.

Not only is it important for the appropriate person to respond, but that person must also have his own e-mail account. Nothing looks cheesier than to have a message signed by the president of the company but have the header read "Joe Doe, public relations." Readers will think Joe wrote it and tried to pass it off as coming from the executive office. If the president of the company doesn't have an e-mail account, he won't have any credibility with his message posted on another person's account.

There is no similar service for mailing lists or forums on the commercial online services.

Another type of online crisis that communications managers must deal with comes from the new breed of Net celebrities and opinion leaders who have sizable audiences that rely on their opinion. If these opinion leaders blast your product or company, you will want to contact them to set the record straight and minimize damage.

Investor relations managers also need to monitor the Internet and commercial online services, which are breeding a new crop of investment analysts who promote stocks. Their recommendations can lead to a surprising surge in trading volume.

One company can monitor newsgroups and websites for you. eWatch (www.ewatch.com) can uncover insider trading, stock manipulation, rumors and anticorporate activism originating on the unregulated stock message boards, newsgroups, online service forums, and activist web sites.

An estimated 75 percent of large corporations actively monitor the Internet's public discussion bulletin boards, and 44 percent routinely monitor web sites. More than six hundred companies have turned to eWatch to help them accurately track what appears on the Internet each day. The intelligence uncovered by eWatch is used to safeguard shareholder value, improve customer service, protect corporate reputation and brand integrity, monitor competition, and pinpoint corporate activism. eWatch monitors more than fifty thousand public electronic bulletin boards in the Usenet groups, electronic mailing lists, America Online, Prodigy, CompuServe, and Microsoft Network. Collectively, eWatch tracks more than two hundred and fifty thousand new messages each day. Major customers include The H. J. Heinz Company, Northwest Airlines, US WEST, TIAA-CREF, Owens Corning, and IBM Global Services, among others.

Although the Internet, commercial online services, and newsgroups can be breeding grounds of rumors and inaccurate statements that could lead to controversies and crises, smart public relations professionals will use the Internet to quell rumors, set the record straight, and build positive relationships.

PHASE 3: RESPOND TO THE CRISIS

Crisis communications managers will want to respond to crises using traditional media and public relations tactics as well as online tools and respond to the media by disseminating information online. Here are the online tools and how they can augment a traditional crisis communications plan:

- E-mail and mailing lists.
- News wires.
- Web sites.
- Conferences.
- Newsgroups.

Let's look at these tools and tactics that can be developed.

E-mail and Mailing Lists

E-mail can be an effective tool to send reporters press releases, back-grounders, alerts, and contact information because information can be sent and received in a matter of seconds. Notes can be prepared in advance and sent to reporters on a moment's notice.

To save time, you could create a mailing list or a distribution list of key reporters. Write one message and broadcast it to reporters on the list.

By using e-mail, you can contact 5 or 500 reporters at the same time so that no one can complain that they weren't notified before another reporter. If you do this, be sure to remove the *cc:,* or carbon copy, that tells the reporter they are 1 of 500 reporters to get the release. Nothing makes a reporter feel more insignificant than being on a list like this.

You can also create mailing lists of key audiences such as employees, stockholders, vendors, and VIPs to keep them informed of the latest events.

News Wires

All press releases should be transmitted to PR Newswire or Business Wire because they distribute these materials on the Internet. The media and key audiences can find the releases via a keyword search or by checking their individual newspapers.

Web Sites as Crisis Communication Hotlines

The Internet allows you to turn your web site into a 24-hour crisis communications online hotline. This area can contain all your printed materials as well as updates. It can also contain picture, audio, and video files that reporters can download and either print or put on the air in a timely fashion.

In addition to helping out in crisis mode, the web site can be a resource to reporters and key audiences, if it contains such information as company news, press releases, annual reports, financial statements, product information, quotes from customers and analysts, reprints of reviews, and other tools of public relations and marketing. By making this material available and updating it appropriately, your key publics and the media will learn to go to your site first when a disaster strikes.

Newsgroups

Newsgroups should be included in your plan to distribute information if your audience is likely to read a particular newsgroup. For example, your customers probably want to hear the news of your product recall directly from your company rather than from the daily newspaper, which might print a shortened version of your announcement.

Communications professionals should monitor newsgroups for offending or misleading comments posted by outside observers. Check these areas several times a day, as people post messages frequently. Also, people from different time zones could sign on after your normal business hours and post questions. The sooner their questions are answered, the better.

Paying attention to the tone of the message is vitally important. Because emotion doesn't come through in online communications, messages can seem direct and harsh. Messages can seem friendlier if you use an informal tone and avoid business or legal jargon.

Rally Your Troops

Another useful strategy is to rally your troops of loyal customers. Identify your evangelists in advance. When crisis strikes, ask them to respond to other people's complaints about the products with their own testimonials. They will be seen as impartial observers, whereas your employees might be seen as biased.

You might give these evangelists a special commendation or prize for helping out. However, chances are that your loyal customers will want to respond without hesitation to show they made the correct choice in buying your product.

Don't Hide Identities

If your employees answer questions, they must identify themselves as employees. They should not pretend to be customers. As we have seen with Deja.com, every message can be traced, and there are some newsgroup denizens whose only purpose in life is to find examples of shady corporate manipulation. If employees pose as customers, they will be found out!

PHASE 4: EVALUATE THE RESPONSE

After the crisis has passed or when it is showing signs of abatement, you can monitor the situation by using the Internet as well as traditional sources. Check newsgroups for the quality and quantity of communication. Is the tone friendly or hostile? Have messages decreased in number, or are there still many postings?

If your company is public, you can check the stock market news services for trading volume and price direction. However, be aware that most stock services offer quotes on a 20-minute delay.

Case Studies

Although most crisis communications professionals will be able to use the Internet to aid them in the fight against real-world crises, it should be noted with extreme diligence that the Internet itself can be a breeding ground of controversy that winds up on the front pages of daily newspapers and nightly news reports. Intel and Quicken, two leading companies in the computer hardware and software arenas, respectively, found their names on the front pages of hundreds of daily newspapers because of controversies that began with online postings in newsgroups. In both cases, customers complained that the products didn't work properly. Intel chose to ignore the problem and it festered, causing the company much embarrassment and a momentary decline in the price of their stock. Quicken chose a different approach, which calmed the storm quickly—so well that few people remember the problem at all, while Intel continues to fight flames from outraged consumers. Let's look at each crisis, the steps the companies chose to use to fight the problems, and how the Internet played a part in the crises.

Case Study: Intel Pentium Chip Flaw

- Problem: A university professor claimed to have found a bug in Intel's Pentium chip. He said the mathematical functions for a complex formula were not accurate on a consistent basis. The company denied there was a problem. The professor posted a notice on a newsgroup asking others if they could duplicate the problem. They could. Word spread to the university community and then to the trade press and general press.

- Steps taken: Intel denied there was a major problem and said that the situation would affect only a few people. They refused to take responsibility or replace the affected chips.

Because Intel had spent hundreds of millions of dollars on a consumer advertising campaign promoting "Intel Inside" as a standard by which to judge computers and because they are the leading computer chip vendor, the mainstream media picked up the story and placed it prominently. *The New York Times, The Wall Street Journal,* and *USA Today* all gave the story front-page coverage. These stories stoked fires on other newsgroups as well as around office watercoolers as people wondered if their computers were tainted.

The story refused to go away, but Intel refused to replace the chips, saying it would cost a fortune (never mind the lost value of their advertising campaign or the amount of bad publicity they were receiving). The company stock dropped nearly 20 points in a few weeks. Intel, however, stuck to its story that the problem affected only a few people. The company also said that every chip had bugs and the Pentium was no different. Meanwhile, jokes mocking Intel appeared in newsgroups. No one was buying Intel's story.

Just as it appeared that the story was dying, IBM announced it would not use Intel chips in its computers. The article appeared on the front page of *The New York Times.* Within a matter of days, Intel reversed its position and agreed to replace chips at no cost to consumers. In a few weeks, Intel's stock price returned to its precrisis level and then went higher.

- Analysis: Intel mishandled the entire affair from the very beginning. First it denied the problem; then it admitted there was a problem, but a minor one. It refused to accept responsibility, saying it would be expensive to replace the chip, but suffered untold costs in terms of lost credibility and the sudden worthlessness of their multimillion-dollar advertising campaign. These are classic missteps in handling a crisis.

In terms of the ramifications for online relations, this affair shows that consumers will talk among themselves online, even if the company doesn't want to hear the story. Also, reporters will find out about the controversy and locate sources willing to talk on the record about their problems. Because of the chatter in newsgroups, the story refused to die. Also, because all newsgroup messages are saved and are searchable, people can read thousands of messages about the controversy and might decide that the existence of the bug is a reason to buy a competitor's product—or boycott the company because of its malignant attitude.

Case Study: Quicken

- Problem: A bug in Quicken's tax preparation software was discovered and publicized in forums by users who asked if other people had the same problem. Reporters saw the messages. Business sections featured the story on lead pages.
- Steps taken: Quicken took fast action to admit the problem, fixed it, sent free copies of the updated program to users, and offered to pay any penalties or interest incurred by taxpayers whose returns were affected. They issued press releases.
- Outcome: The story died in a few days.
- Analysis: Quicken showed what happens when you take responsibility for your actions: The public forgives you. By accepting all financial blame, they stemmed any negative criticism and received accolades instead. Few people remember this incident. Many people remember the Intel fiasco.

POTENTIAL ONLINE CRISES

Although the bulk of this chapter has been devoted to using online services as a tool in your overall crisis communications plan, this section will discuss potential crises that might develop as a result of your company being online. We'll look at:

- Spoofing.
- Spamming.
- Boycotts.
- Domain name stealing.
- Competitive snooping.

Spoofing

Spoofing is what happens when someone posts a web site that looks and feels like your web site. For example, Bob Dole had a site for his election efforts. An unknown party posted a site lampooning Dole. The site looked like it could have been for Bob Dole until you read the text and found out that Dole was the "ripe man for the job" and that links to "family values" took you to the Marilyn Monroe Home Page! U.S. West faced a similar problem when a disgruntled customer posted the U.S. Worst home page.

Due to freedom of speech laws in the United States, there is little you can do to stop these actions unless the pages are libelous or steal your artwork, which would violate copyright laws. However, you can protect your company by registering domain names that could be used by spoofers. For example, the stretch from U.S. West to U.S. Worst is something that any high school sophomore could have thought of. But if you own the domain www.usworst.com, then the sophomore can't use it. Register every conceivable name that would spoof your company.

Spamming

Spamming is the act of sending out mountains of unsolicited junk mail to people's e-mail boxes. This is a violation of netiquette and has been discussed at length throughout this book. If your company participates in this activity, angry recipients might very well tell their friends on newsgroups and give you a black eye. Fortunately, this action doesn't have to occur. Just don't spam.

Boycotts

If you don't heed the previous warning about not spamming, your company could be the victim of a boycott via the Net. Companies that spam are listed on a boycott page. Your company can avoid this disaster simply by practicing good netiquette.

Domain Name Stealing

On the Internet, people send e-mail to your domain name, for example, dan@janal.com, or find your web site by typing *www.janal.com*. If you are smart and fast, you can easily register your domain name with Network Solutions, formerly known as InterNIC, the official organization that assigns all domain names.

Someone could register your company name as its domain name if she is there first. There are regulations that prevent a registered trademark from being used as a domain name by any party other than the official holder. But if a company that has a similar name has registered it before you, then you are out of luck. For example, if Bob Avis wants to register avis.com he can, provided the rental car company hasn't registered it already. If Bob has registered it, then the other Avis will continue to be in second place and won't get the registration no matter how hard it tries. However, if Bob Avis tried to register hertz.com, Network Solutions would not give him the name.

Companies might steal your name without even realizing it—or it can be a deliberate act. Also register your association's initials (e.g., American Association of Associated Associations would be aaaa.com).

To protect yourself, register your company name as the domain name as soon as you can.

Competitive Snooping

When you create a web site, the entire world can see what you have written—including your competitors. There are two steps to take to minimize snooping:

1. Limit the amount of information to what you wouldn't mind revealing to a stranger at a trade show booth. You have to figure your competitors are getting all your public information anyway. Just decide what the general public needs to know and don't print anything else.
2. Limit access to your site to people who register and tell you who they are and where they work. You can decide if you want them to visit your site. This is not unlike a realtor who shows multimillion-dollar houses by appointment only. She wants to make sure buyers are qualified before investing her time and effort. This is a good strategy for a business-to-business company because you want to identify and qualify each visitor. It is a bad strategy for a general consumer site that wants to sell products and services, as you might scare off potential customers.

SUMMARY

Crises can start online or offline and continue to brew online. Companies should take great care in monitoring relevant discussion areas to deal with negative comments because bad news travels fast—even faster online. In a short time, these errors look like facts because the information—or misinformation—is repeated. Companies that don't respond quickly can face serious risks. Fortunately, a great many tools and tactics can be used to combat crises.

For more information on this topic, please read my book, *Risky Business: Protect Your Business from Being Stalked, Conned, or Blackmailed on the Web* (John Wiley & Sons, 1998).

Janal Communications Seminars, Consulting

Daniel Janal, author of *Dan Janal's Guide to Marketing on the Internet*, is one of the most sought-after speakers on the Internet training and consulting circuit. He has presented lively, interactive workshops for American Express, IBM, the U.S. Postal Service, and the National Football League. He also lectures at the University of California at Berkeley and Stanford University.

Call Daniel Janal today to find out how he can train your staff or help your company present public seminars. Send e-mail to dan@janal .com or call 510-459-7814 during normal business hours.

SPEAKING AND TRAINING SEMINARS

Here are the speaking and training programs Dan conducts. Each program lasts 45 minutes and can be combined to fill any time slot. He also creates specialized programs for companies. Check the Janal Communications web site (http://www.janal.com) for updated information, programs, and schedules.

Session 1: How to Succeed As an Online Marketer— Understanding New Marketing Paradigms

The new advertising and marketing differs tremendously from the old, especially in regard to creating image and interactivity. This session shows four key differences between the two ways of thinking as well as 10 ways to think like a new marketer and incorporate this new thinking into your online marketing program.

Overview includes business reasons to be online (sales, customer support, and distribution of marketing support materials) as well as a discussion of Internet demographics, tools, and trends. You'll learn what works and what doesn't in the emerging field of interactive advertising.

Presentation format: Lecture with overhead slides, screen shots of relevant home pages, and examples drawn from home pages of your competitors or industry, when possible. Questions and answers.

Handouts: Slide presentation with notes section.

Session 2: How to Add Value and Content to Your Home Page

Successful home pages don't just show marketing materials; they add value to the customer's experience at your site. This session will show case studies of successful home pages and present proven strategies for creating enhancement experiences for consumers who visit your home page.

You'll learn how to build customers for life with these winning strategies.

Presentation format: Lecture with overhead slides, screen shots of relevant home pages, and examples drawn from home pages of your competitors or industry, when possible. Questions and answers.

Handouts: Slide presentation with notes section.

Session 3: How to Publicize Your Home Page

If you build a better home page, will people beat a path to your door? Not unless you promote and publicize it! This session will present eight strategies for promoting your site.

You'll learn how to get people to come to your home page and how to find out who they are through registration techniques, contests, and guest books.

Presentation format: Lecture with overhead slides, screen shots of relevant home pages, and examples drawn from home pages of your competitors or industry, when possible. Questions and answers.

Handouts: Slide presentation with notes section.

Session 4: Creating Direct Relationships with Customers and Analysts

Reporters kill most press releases they receive. Here are ways to get your message to your key publics without the media's help.

You'll learn how to create customers for life by creating meaningful information exchange and dialogues.

Presentation format: Lecture with overhead slides, screen shots of relevant home pages, and examples drawn from home pages of your competitors or industry, when possible. Questions and answers.

Handouts: Slide presentation with notes section.

Session 7: Designing a Home Page from the Marketer's Perspective

Find out how to incorporate your home page strategy into the integrated marketing plan.

You'll learn the fundamental steps to creating an online marketing plan, designing the page, and flowcharting the subpages, using art to support your message and avoiding costly design mistakes.

Presentation format: Lecture with overhead slides, screen shots of relevant home pages, and examples drawn from home pages of your competitors or industry, when possible. Questions and answers.

Handouts: Slide presentation with notes section.

TWO-DAY SEMINAR

The Internet is an advertising medium that is capturing the hearts and minds of marketers around the world. This course will look at the various opportunities to promote products and services on the Internet as seen from the perspective of the online marketer.

Outline (subject to change based on class needs):

1. The Online Marketing Business Plan.
   - Eight Steps in creating an online business plan.
   - Creating a marketing mission.
     ◦ Twenty reasons to benefit from online marketing.
     ◦ Six risks and how to overcome them.
   - Determining who owns the online area.
     ◦ Marketing or MIS?
     ◦ Who sets corporate policy?
   - Creating supporting marketing materials.
   - Converting to HTML (to be covered in depth later).
     ◦ Hiring a web designer.
   - Connecting to the Internet.
     ◦ ISPs versus in house, pros and cons.
     ◦ The list of ISPs nationwide.
   - Promoting the web site (to be covered in depth later).
   - Accepting cash.
   - Budgeting.
2. Demographics.
   - Myths and realities of current surveys.
   - Synthesis of surveys and trends.
   - Psychographics.
   - Audiences identity themselves.
3. New paradigms for online marketing.
   - Differences with broadcast and consumer advertising
   - Four key differences between broadcast marketing and online marketing.
   - Six strategies for success that you already know—and how the Internet can enhance each of them!
4. Internet basics.
   - How to connect.
   - How to find information.
   - Tour of various sites.
   - E-mail.
   - Infobots.
5. How to design a page for marketing.
   - Designing a home page from a marketing perspective.

- Twenty essential elements that must be on your home page.
- Ten optional elements that will enhance your chances for sales.
- Page as ad.
- Page as info center.
- Page as community.

6. Create a storyboard—workshop.
7. Promoting the page.
   - Eleven tactics.
   - Tour of Yahoo! registration online.
   - Workshop.
8. Writing styles.
9. Advertising strategies.
   - On the web.
   - Online resources.
   - Five steps to gathering demographics from your users.
10. Buying ad space on web pages.
    - Examples.
    - Rates.
    - Click-throughs versus eyeballs.
    - Placement and positioning.
11. Selling ad space on your web page.
    - Examples.
    - Rates.
    - Resources.
12. Measuring ad effectiveness in other media via the web.
    - Measurement techniques.
    - Different doors.
    - Counters/hits/visits.
13. Using e-mail to create relationships.
    - More online users have e-mail than have web access; here's how to reach them.
    - Five ways to make e-mail and infobots work for you.
    - Five steps to working effectively and responsibly with news-groups and forums.
    - How to create your own company mailing lists or electronic newsletters.
    - Ten tips for creating content for newsletters.
    - Build in-store traffic and online sales with e-coupons.
14. Publicity strategies.
15. Future trends.

- Marketing.
- Advertising.
- Publicity.
- Technology.
- Impact on corporations.

Glossary

Baud: The speed at which modems transfer data. The speed is listed in BPS, or bits per second.

Browser: The software program that allows users to read pages on the World Wide Web.

Download: Retrieve files from a computer.

Frequently Asked Questions (FAQ): A file that contains questions and answers about specific topics.

Flame: Abusive hate mail.

File Transfer Protocol (FTP): A method for sending and retrieving files from the Internet.

Hypertext Markup Language (HTML): The standard format for documents on the World Wide Web.

Hypertext: A system where documents scattered across many sites are directly linked.

Hypermedia: A system where documents, pictures, sound, and movie and animation files scattered across many sites are directly linked.

Integrated Services Digital Network (ISDN): Technology that makes it possible to move multiple digital signals through a single, conventional phone wire.

Leased line: A permanently installed telephone line connecting a local area network (LAN) to an Internet Service Provider (ISP).

Lurking: Reading messages in a forum or newgroups without adding comments.

Modem: A device that connects a computer to a phone line and enables users to transmit data between computers.

Netiquette: The etiquette of the Internet.

Newbies: Newcomers to the Internet.

Service Provider: A company that provides connections to the Internet.

Signature or **sig:** A personalized address at the bottom of a message often containing contact information and a short commercial description.

SLIP and **PPP (Serial Line Internet Protocol** and **Point-to-Point Protocol):** Two common types of connections that allow your computer to communicate with the Internet.

Smileys and **emoticons:** Typographical versions of faces that display emotions in text messages.

Spamming: Posting or mailing unwanted material to many recipients. A flagrant violation of Netiquette.

TCP/IP (Transmission Control Protocol/Internet Protocol): The standardized sets of computer guidelines that allow different machines to talk to each other on the Internet.

Sysop (System Operator): The person who administers a forum. Same as **web master.**

Upload: To Send a file from your computer to another.

Uniform Resource Locator (URL): A type of address that points to a specific document or site on the World Wide Web.

Usenet: A collection of discussion areas (bulletin boards) known as newsgroups on the Internet.

Wide Area Information System (WAIS): A system that allows users to search by keyword through the full text contained on many databases.

World Wide Web (WWW or W3 or the web): A hypertext and hypermedia system that enables users to find information about companies.

Index